THE REPUBLICAN REVOLUTION 10 YEARS LATER

THE REPUBLICAN REVOLUTION 10 YEARS LATER

Smaller Government or Business as Usual?

EDITED BY
CHRIS EDWARDS AND JOHN SAMPLES

CATO
INSTITUTE
Washington, D.C.

Library of Congress Cataloging-in-Publication Data

The Republican revolution 10 years later: smaller government or
business as usual? /
    edited by Chris Edwards and John Samples
        p. cm.
    Includes bibliographical references and index.
    ISBN 1-930865-69-4 (alk. paper) — ISBN 1-930865-72-4 (pbk.: alk.
paper)
        1. Republican Party (U.S.: 1854-) 2. United States. Congress—
Elections, 1994. 3. United States—Politics and government—2001-
4. United States—Politics and government—1993-2001. 5. United
States—Economic policy—2001- 6. United States—Economic
policy—1993-2001. 7. United States—Social policy—1993- I. Title:
Republican revolution ten years later. II. Edwards, Chris (Chris R.)
III. Samples, John Curtis, 1956-

JK2356R356 2005
320.6'0973—dc22

                                                    2004062855

Cover design by Elise Rivera.
Printed in the United States of America.

CATO INSTITUTE
1000 Massachusetts Ave., N.W.
Washington, D.C. 20001

Contents

Introduction

Chris Edwards and John Samples

> [Washington] is like a sponge. It absorbs waves of change,
> and it slows them down, and it softens them, and then one
> morning they cease to exist.
> —Newt Gingrich, November 14, 1994.

The congressional elections of 1994 produced stunning results. For the first time in 40 years, the Republicans attained a majority in the House of Representatives. They gained 54 House seats, the largest party swing since 1948. The Republicans also grabbed control of the Senate by gaining eight seats and added a ninth when Richard Shelby of Alabama switched parties. Although the GOP had held the upper hand in presidential elections for years, the congressional sweep was a real breakthrough for the party.

Major changes in domestic and foreign policies seemed likely with the dramatic end to Democratic control of Congress. Recognizing the challenge represented by the resurgent Republicans, President Bill Clinton declared in his 1996 State of the Union address that the "era of big government is over."

The 1994 elections were unusual in other ways. House elections often turn on local issues and concerns. But in 1994 the House Republicans successfully nationalized the election by making the entrenched federal establishment a key issue. Polls showed rising dissatisfaction with the government, particularly Congress, as a result of recent scandals. Gallup found that 60 percent of the public disapproved of Congress's performance in 1994, and those numbers fell to under 40 percent by 1998.[1] Because the Democrats controlled both Congress and the White House in 1994, running against Washington was the same as running against the Democrats.

Contract with America

The Contract with America, which was signed by virtually all House Republican candidates, was a key element of the 1994 campaign. It also gave the Republicans a clear policy agenda when they assembled in Washington to start the new Congress. The Contract promised House votes in the first 100 days on 10 pieces of legislation covering everything from tax cuts to term limits. In addition, "to restore the bonds of trust between the people and their elected representatives," the Contract promised that a GOP House would pass the following eight institutional reforms on its very first day:

1. Require all laws that apply to the rest of the country also apply to Congress;
2. Select a major accounting firm to conduct an audit of Congress for waste, fraud, and abuse;
3. Cut the number of House committees and committee staff by one-third;
4. Limit the terms of all committee chairs;
5. Ban the casting of proxy votes in committee;
6. Require committee meetings to be open to the public;
7. Require a three-fifths majority vote to pass tax increases;
8. Guarantee honest budget accounting by implementing zero baseline budgeting.

The House Republicans kept those promises. The House passed the eight "good government" reforms on its first day, and it brought all 10 bills from the Contract to a vote within 100 days. Nine of the 10 bills passed the House. The exception was a bill to limit the terms of House members, which fell short of the required two-thirds approval as a constitutional amendment. This volume looks at the policies announced in the Contract and examines whether the Republicans lived up to their broader promise to "end . . . government that is too big, too intrusive, and too easy with the public's money."[2]

Overview

The Republican class of 1994 invited a public assessment of its progress. Should the Republicans fail to carry out their promises, Newt Gingrich said, the electorate should hold them responsible.[3] This volume takes up Gingrich's challenge on the broader issue of reducing the federal government. We asked 16 policy experts, principally Cato Institute scholars, to assess the record of congressional Republicans after a decade in power. Scholars looked at the GOP record in each major policy area, including education, health care, regulation, taxation, and trade. Each chapter considers whether the new majority in Congress kept the promises made in the Contract and whether the GOP restored more limited, constitutional government to Washington, which was the main theme of the class of 1994. Some chapters consider how federal policy might have been different if the Democrats had remained in power and why the Republicans succeeded or failed to live up to their initial reform goals.

The volume begins with essays by the two primary architects of the 1994 election victory and subsequent House leaders, Newt Gingrich and Richard Armey. Gingrich was elected to Congress in 1978, was the key leader who spearheaded the 1994 election win, and was Speaker of the House from 1995 to 1998. In his chapter, Gingrich looks at the political strategy that led to the landmark election victory, arguing that it was not a fluke win but resulted from "brutally hard work over a very long period of time." He describes the new conservative groups that worked outside the GOP establishment to provide the fresh ideas and organization that led to success.

Dick Armey was the primary author of the Contract with America and was House majority leader from 1995 until 2002. As a former professor of economics, he has championed many pro-market policies since being elected to Congress in 1984. Armey's essay echoes some of Gingrich's views on 1994: they were "young Turks" who overthrew not just the Democrats but also an old-fashioned GOP leadership that was too comfortable getting along in the minority. He also describes how the new, more conservative GOP leaders in 1994 capitalized on President Clinton's policy blunders and the excesses of the entrenched Democratic majority.

Cato Institute president Edward H. Crane discusses the climate of ideas that led to the dramatic 1994 election results. That climate was nurtured by the limited-government ideas at the core of American political tradition, ideas that were revived in recent decades by Cato and other think tanks and scholars. Crane argues that the events of 1994, like the political movements associated with Barry Goldwater and Ronald Reagan, were animated by a rejection of the ever-expanding federal control over American society. But Crane cautions that the interventionist agenda of neoconservatives has undermined efforts to reduce federal power. He concludes that we need a more thoroughgoing revolution to deliver to Americans the honest, limited, and constitutional federal government that they deserve.

The 1994 elections came at a low point of public trust in Congress and the federal government. The new Republican majority promised to change the policy direction of the government and restore trust. Indeed, many of the promises in the Contract concerned the political process rather than the content of policy. John Samples assesses whether the Republican majority carried through on those promises. A vote on congressional term limits was held, although it did not gain a majority even among Republicans in the House. Despite the failure of term limits, public faith in Congress rose dramatically after 1994. Nevertheless, congressional elections have become less competitive during the last decade. Fewer seats are likely to switch parties today than in 1994, which suggests that the GOP majority may become as enduring as the old Democratic majority. The Republicans have fostered good government in narrow ways while continuing the dominance of incumbency.

Chris Edwards discusses how tax cuts have provided a strong unifying goal for the diverse Republican party whose elected members include social conservatives, defense hawks, libertarians, and others. After Republicans promised income tax cuts in the Contract with America, substantial cuts were delivered in 1997, 2001, and 2003. Indeed, Edwards discusses how tax cuts were a key GOP policy objective in every session of Congress during the last decade. He then summarizes the good news and bad news from 10 years of GOP tax policy. Although income tax rates were cut and taxes on saving were reduced, the GOP has presided over an increasingly complex tax code and has not moved ahead with fundamental tax reform.

Stephen Moore looks at GOP budget policies and finds that a promising start has ended up as a "triumph of Big Government." The GOP was able to balance the federal budget in 1998 for the first time since 1969. Also, the House initially pursued spending cuts under Budget Committee Chairman John Kasich, whose first budget slated hundreds of programs for termination. However, that small-government vision had been lost by the late 1990s, and few programs were actually ended. Federal spending growth was constrained during the mid-1990s, but then outlays soared from $1.7 trillion in FY 1999 to $2.3 trillion by FY 2004, a 35 percent increase. Moore concludes that although "the Gingrich Republicans were a heroic bunch

. . . the tragedy is that many of the Republicans who led the revolution have settled into power, become too comfortable with their perks and authority, and are now mirror images of what they replaced."

Daniel Griswold concludes that the GOP largely kept its promises on international trade. Republicans expanded the commercial freedom of Americans by passing permanent normal trade relations with China, presidential trade promotion authority, and other trade-expanding legislation. Nonetheless, the Republicans betrayed free-trade principles by supporting agricultural subsidies and protection in a number of cases. Griswold notes that congressional trade policy under the Republicans has largely continued the policies of previous Democratic Congresses. Meanwhile, the Democrats' historical commitment to trade liberalization has eroded during the past decade. Given that change, congressional trade policy since 1994 has almost certainly been more oriented toward free trade than it would have been under continued Democratic control.

In coming years, Social Security may become the central issue of American politics. Michael Tanner explores the GOP's changing views on Social Security reform during the past decade. Tanner notes that Newt Gingrich was initially opposed to touching what was called the "third rail" of American politics. However, the passage of time has brought greater support among Republicans for Social Security reform, especially the establishment of personal retirement accounts. In particular, younger Republicans in Congress strongly support personal accounts. President Bush also supports personal accounts, and Tanner suggests that President Clinton might have supported such reforms had impeachment not roiled the political waters.

Ron Haskins of the Brookings Institution looks at perhaps the most dramatic legislative success of the Republican Congress—welfare reform in 1996. As a key Capitol Hill staffer during the welfare reform debate, Haskins reminds us of the intense opposition that reform faced—some opposition House members even likened reforming welfare to the policies of the Nazis. But the opposition was overcome, and Haskins argues that welfare reform was a glowing policy success—just about every relevant statistical indicator has moved in a positive direction since reform. Most dramatically, federal welfare rolls have dropped 60 percent in the last decade.

This chapter makes two points clear. First, fixing damaging federal policies can have profoundly positive effects on the lives of millions of Americans. Second, determined political leaders can enact major policy reforms that limit dependence on government despite fierce opposition from entrenched interests.

In health care policy, Michael Cannon argues that the Republican revolution lost its way. After a decade, the GOP can point to only one substantial achievement that will reduce the government's power over health care decisions: health savings accounts. Unfortunately, that policy advance was outweighed by expansions of the government's role in health care, such as passing an expensive Medicare prescription drug benefit in 2003. However, Cannon believes that, had Democrats retained Congress, the government's role would have expanded even more and reforms considered by Republicans, such as health savings accounts, would not have seen the light of day.

Between 1994 and 2000, David Salisbury argues, the Republicans constrained the growth in federal education spending while seeking to strengthen local control. By 2000, however, the policies of fiscal restraint and federalism had been jettisoned. Congress returned to a policy of business as usual in education, including a rapidly expanding Department of Education budget and greater federal control over the nation's schools.

Adam Thierer discusses the GOP's mixed policy legacy in telecommunications and high technology. The main legislation in those areas, the Telecommunications Act of 1996, turned out to be deeply flawed. Thierer notes that although the preamble to the law calls for a "pro-competitive, deregulatory national policy," it delivers nothing of the kind. The legislation's poor drafting gave the Federal Communications Commission carte blanche to micromanage the communications industry. Other GOP policy blunders included giving away high-definition television spectrum, the e-rate program, prohibitions on Internet gambling, media censorship, and a general increase in Internet regulation. A few successes included relaxation of encryption controls and a moratorium on Internet access taxes. Thierer concludes that "government at all levels—federal, state, local, and even international—are actively meddling in the telecom sector and becoming players in almost every new technology or Internet issue that has arisen. The Republican revolution has not been much of a revolution at all when it comes to telecom and high-technology policy."

Clyde Wayne Crews of the Competitive Enterprise Institute looks at the regulatory environment during the past decade. Most people assumed that the new Republican majority would reduce federal regulations and rely more on free-market policy solutions. The GOP did pass some reforms, such as legislation on state mandates, small business regulatory relief, measures to address paperwork burdens, and relaxation of some excessively costly rules. But Crews finds that the knee-jerk impulse to regulate every real and imagined ill in society is thoroughly bipartisan. During the past decade, the alphabet agencies—such as the FDA (Food and Drug Administration), FTC (Federal Trade Commission), FCC (Federal Communications Commission), and SEC (Securities and Exchange Commission)—have continued to churn out high volumes of new rules, often with the support of the GOP Congress.

One regulatory area thought to be high on the GOP reform agenda was federal environmental rules. Jerry Taylor, however, finds that the 104th and subsequent Congresses did not lessen environmental regulatory burdens. Indeed, there has been an increase in environmental regulations on businesses, property owners, and state and local governments during the past decade. On environmental policy, the GOP neither fulfilled the hopes of its supporters nor realized the fears of its opponents.

Similarly, Tim Lynch finds continuity on civil liberties and criminal justice issues between the Republican era and prior Democratic eras. Republicans had promised to reinvigorate the Tenth Amendment and return federal powers over criminal justice to the states. But the GOP now presides over a burgeoning federal law enforcement bureaucracy, and the party has abandoned efforts to reduce the scope and powers of federal law enforcement.

Chris Preble looks at how national security strategy evolved during the past decade under the GOP Congress. The GOP came into office with promises that looked back to the Cold War, including national missile defense and accession of former Warsaw Pact countries to the North Atlantic Treaty Organization. He concludes that there was a "discontinuity between the real and perceived threats in the post–Cold War world and a disregard for the best means for dealing with these threats. The result was that foreign policy, so ripe for reform after the collapse of the Soviet Union, remained largely frozen in time during the 1990s and into the early 21st century."

Revolution, Modest Reform, or Bigger Government?

Did the Republican revolution result in historic policy changes? Or was an initial wave of change slowed and stopped by the entrenched interests and customs of Washington? Compared with the prior Democratic era, when big-government solutions to nearly every real and perceived problem held sway, the Republicans certainly widened the policy debate to allow alternative policy solutions to be heard. The tough part was actually enacting policies that reflected market-oriented reform thinking.

Over decades, liberals in both parties have created expensive bureaucracies, entitlement programs, and regulatory agencies that intrude on nearly every facet of the nation's economy. In the mid-1990s, the Republicans tried to tame some of the most costly parts of the vast federal apparatus, but they generally did not succeed. On the budget, they tried to eliminate hundreds of programs but failed. On taxes, the chief GOP tax writer, Bill Archer (R-Tex.), said he wanted to "tear out the income tax by its roots,"[4] but failed. On Medicare, the GOP made an initial effort to reduce spending growth, but ended up expanding the program with an expensive drug bill. On the deficit, the GOP cajoled President Clinton into signing a balanced budget deal in 1997, but by 2004 the deficit hit an all-time high. The GOP changed the structure of welfare in 1996, but spending on welfare-related programs is still far too high.

Nevertheless, the Republicans did change the course of policy compared with the likely course of continued Democratic Congresses. It is likely that, in tandem with President Clinton, a Democratic Congress would not have cut taxes, would not have reformed welfare, would have expanded health care programs even more than the GOP, and would have been more protectionist on trade policy.

Newt Gingrich was prescient in 1994 when he said that Washington absorbs and ultimately suppresses waves of political change. Coming into office, Republican reformers were up against special interest groups that had money, organization, and decades of experience in stifling any threatening changes. When the idea of a flat tax was debated in the mid-1990s, lobbyists in support of the mortgage-interest deduction and other special tax breaks helped shoot it down. In debates over Social Security reform, powerful lobbyists for the elderly have dug in their heels and opposed any changes.

The American founders, of course, set up a Constitution designed to discourage rapid policy change. By contrast, the British parliamentary system allows sweeping changes under majority governments. The ideological cousins of the 1994 Republicans, Margaret Thatcher's conservatives, were able to make radical changes to Britain's welfare state in the 1980s. This country never swung as far to the socialist left as Britain did in the mid-20th century, but Republican reformers have made only slow progress moving back toward free markets since Ronald Reagan moved the party in that direction in the 1980s.

In the U.S. system, ambition is pitted against ambition, and movement in any particular direction is slowed. The fragmentation of political power means that policy changes may be effectively vetoed by either the executive branch, the House, the Senate, or the courts. The fragmentation of power constrained the growth of American government throughout much of the nation's history. However, occasional crises such as wars and the Great Depression have given activists the chance to dramatically ratchet upward federal power. When the federal government has grabbed new powers, the constitutional structure has slowed or stopped any reforms aimed at giving power back to the states or the people.

Another hurdle for Republican reformers in the 1990s was the talented and politically skillful President Clinton. Clinton stalled and maneuvered enough to take the reform wind out of the Republican sails by the late 1990s. For example, Republicans passed substantial tax cuts every session of Congress during the 1990s, but Clinton signed into law only the modest 1997 tax reduction bill. Because tax cuts are popular with the public, Clinton often feigned support for cuts—just not the particular cuts that the Republicans proposed. With a large budget surplus in the late 1990s, Clinton argued that Social Security should be saved before taxes were cut, but he did not put forward any plan to actually fix the retirement program.

Perhaps Republicans could have worked with Clinton and other Democrats to better effect. But legislative bargains were difficult because GOP leaders felt that they could not trust Clinton's word, and the president felt under constant attack by GOP probes into his conduct. Mike Tanner discusses his view that if the Monica Lewinsky scandal had not forced Clinton to shore up his support with liberals, he might have worked with the GOP to reform Social Security. Stephen Moore thinks one lesson of the 1990s is that there needs to be more Republican outreach to reform-minded Democrats in Congress to get things done.

In the post-Clinton era, some Republicans continue to challenge the expensive and failed structures of the welfare state. An optimist might argue that the Republican revolution is not over yet. On health care, new health savings accounts may grow to become a crucial consumer-directed part of the U.S. medical system. On Social Security, reforms to introduce personal retirement accounts are high on the Republican agenda and growing in popularity. On taxes, Republican leaders continue to promise fundamental changes to scrap our complex and inefficient income tax system. In these and other policy areas, the Republicans may still make progress on ending the "era of big government."

Notes

The epigraph to this chapter is drawn from Katherine Q. Seelye, "Republicans Plan Ambitious Agenda in Next Congress," New York Times, November 15, 1994, p. A1.

1. David Rogers, "Lawmakers Face Big Backlog," *Wall Street Journal*, September 7, 2004.

2. Ed Gillespie and Bob Schellhas, eds., *Contract with America: The Bold Plan by Rep. Newt Gingrich, Rep. Dick Armey and the House Republicans to Change the Nation* (New York: Times Books, 1994).

3. Ibid., p. 19.

4. As quoted by Dick Armey in "Caveat Emptor: The Case against the National Sales Tax," *Policy Review* no. 73, Summer 1995.

1. The GOP Revolution Holds Powerful Lessons for Changing Washington

Newt Gingrich

I see the 1994 Republican victory as part three of a long process. Part one includes Barry Goldwater's 1960 book, *Conscience of a Conservative*, and the Goldwater movement that took control of the Republican Party in 1964. Part two was Ronald Reagan's rise from the 1964 film *A Time for Choosing* through his presidency. Part three was the election of 1994.

I came to Washington in the middle of this process in 1978 and proposed the then radical idea that the Republicans could become the majority in Congress. It took the GOP 16 years. Thus, if you want to get big things done in Washington but say you only have a weekend, you will not be successful.

Hard Work over a Long Period of Time

Our victory in 1994 was a product not only of conservative theory, but also of brutally hard work over a very long period of time. The work put into the Contract with America was central to our success. The Contract focused our candidates, whose otherwise natural tendency was to attack President Bill Clinton. But we knew that if we were negative, if we were the anti-Clinton party, all the Ross Perot voters would stay home.

The Contract gave relatively untested candidates powerful issues to cling to in the last 40 days of the campaign. The phrases "I am for a balanced budget; I am for a tax cut; I am for a stronger military; I am for welfare reform" were a shield with which our candidates could surround themselves, keeping them out of trouble and on message. Some of the historic personal efforts that led to victory included Dick Armey's work to build a consensus within the party on the Contract and Bill Paxon's and Joe Gaylord's work on the training and planning side of the 1994 campaign.

1

Change on the scale of 1994 required major teamwork and organization. The most important single event in the lead-up to 1994 was a dinner where Tom DeLay, Bob Walker, Dick Armey, Bill Paxon, and I agreed to put our differences aside and work together. If that team had not existed, we would not have had the energy to win control of the House.

To understand the role of teamwork and organization for the success in 1994, you have to go back and look at the role of GOPAC (a training organization for Republican candidates), from when Pete DuPont founded it, to when Bo Callaway chaired it, through when Gay Gaines took over. You have to look at the role of the Conservative Opportunity Society, which Vin Weber, Duncan Hunter, Bob Walker, Connie Mack, and others helped create. You have to look at the role of the Key Leader Team that grew up late in the cycle, thanks to the efforts of Dick Armey.

Florence Weston's *The Presidential Election of 1828*, which was required reading for everyone in those organizations, points out that to seize power from the establishment, the Jacksonians had to organize on such a scale that they simply drowned out the old order. If you look at what we did with GOPAC, what we did with Haley Barbour at the Republican National Committee, and what we tried to do inside the House, you'll see a very similar pattern that continued for about a decade.

Working outside the Republican Establishment

Throughout a long process of hard work and intense opposition, we developed a mantra that became essential to our success: cheerful persistence. We were a minority inside a minority. All our work was done against the active, continuing opposition of the traditional party. From the time I was sworn in through winning the race to become House Whip in 1989, the GOP establishment was opposed to what we were doing. They branded us radicals because we actually thought we could become a majority, were willing to fight for that goal, and proudly used the word "conservative." So not only were we being beaten up by the Democrats and ignored by the news media, we were being pressured by senior Republicans.

While training our new members in this period of tension, we discovered two things. First, to get anything done you must be persistent. Second, if you want people to work with you, you must be cheerful. When Joe Barton arrived on the scene, the first thing he was told by the leader of the Texas delegation was never to work with the Conservative Opportunity Society. He smiled and replied, "Gee, the reason I came was to work with COS." And he did. Cheerful persistence won the day.

We also realized that in order to gain control, we had to build new coalitions and develop consensus. In addition to Weston's book, Norman H. Nie's *The Changing American Voter* was required reading for all of us who sought to gain a majority. The book argues that the way you get new majorities is to arouse a base that is not used to voting. People who dismiss our victory as a fluke do not study our base very often, but we had nine million additional votes in 1994, the largest one-party increase in American history. There is a huge pool of uncommitted voters who have no interest in politics. Thus, when campaigns are able to mobilize such groups, they win in a big way. For a more recent example, look at California—Republicans Arnold Schwarzenegger and Tom McClintock garnered 61 percent in the recall race for governor. They swept counties that people figured that Republicans could not win because people said, "I am sick and tired, I am fed up, and I want a change."

We also developed a model—"Listen, Learn, Help, Lead"— that helped us build a consensus within the Republican Party about the Contract. It was essential that the Contract be a consultative process. In America, we do not have a Tory central party office as in Britain; we do not name candidates. We had to listen to and learn from our candidates so that we could develop a document they would sign. Without Dick Armey's extraordinary leadership, along with the work done by Kerry Knott, Ed Gillespie, and the team Dick assembled, we could not have done that.

Contract with America

People undervalue the truly radical nature of the Contract with America. The Contract was much more than a platform. A platform says that we are for these things; the Contract said that we will vote on these things. The American people had seen platforms before; we wanted to give them something that felt different. We wanted to give them something so they said, "Wow, you are actually going to do this?" We had zero interest in electing a congressional majority

3

that behaved like a normal Congress; our interest was in dramatically changing Washington.

Changing Washington

We did change Washington. In 1996 we reformed welfare, which over time caused a 60 percent reduction in the welfare rolls. We passed the first tax cut in 17 years against a liberal Democratic president with the power of veto. We had the first decline in spending since 1981 and only the second decline in domestic spending since World War II.

In addition, the Contract with America set the stage for an even bigger victory—the 1996 election. House Republicans had not maintained a majority since 1928, and 1996 was the first time in history they did so against a Democratic incumbent. We ran ahead of Bob Dole and Ross Perot combined that year and it was that victory, not 1994, that spurred me to get a balanced-budget agreement—an action I viewed as key to keeping our long-term commitments.

So transformation is possible, but it is a long, hard process. Today, those who seek to transform Washington should look for guidance at how we won in 1994.

2. Reflections on the Republican Revolution

Richard Armey

Ten years ago, Republicans staged a remarkable upset and gained control of Congress during the 1994 elections. Armed with a vision of limited government and individual freedom, Republicans won a majority in the Senate for the first time since 1986 and a majority in the House for the first time since 1954. Republican power was consolidated further in 2000, with President Bush's winning the White House.

Many now view the Republican takeover as having little effect on the size and scope of the federal government. Congress continues to spend at a record pace while federal regulators are expanding the reach of government into the private sector. In light of those trends, what have the Republicans accomplished?

I believe that the Republicans have made a difference, particularly when they have relied on the principles of lower taxes, less government, and more freedom. Important achievements, such as welfare reform, have had a positive effect on the lives of millions of Americans.

Unfortunately, the principles of less government and more freedom do not always drive the political debate. For example, the budget and appropriations processes tend to bias outcomes toward more spending, and there are glaring examples of costly new federal programs, such as the new prescription drug benefit for Medicare. No one spends someone else's money as wisely as they spend their own, and to the extent that Congress focuses on spending more money, taxpayers will bear the burden—regardless of who is in office.

Just as important as the Republican revolution that took place in Washington, grass-roots activism and old-fashioned "shoe-leather politics" are vital components in the pursuit of limited government.

The Contract with America was the driving force behind the Republican rise to power because it connected Republican members with grass-roots activists. It provided a clear blueprint for the tenets of limited government, such as easing the tax burden and protecting private property rights. The message resonated with the public and generated the grass-roots support necessary to make a difference in the voting booth. Engaging and mobilizing average people is a critical component for future success at limiting government. Politics and bureaucracy can overwhelm supporters of limited government in Congress, but a dedicated base of grass-roots activists can remind politicians of why they were sent to Washington in the first place.

The Contract with America: The Revolution's Defining Document

The Contract with America was an extraordinary moment in American political history that demonstrated the importance of policy over politics. In fact, there is no better example of Armey's Axiom, "When we're like us we win; when we're like them we lose."[1] The Contract was a defining document of limited government that garnered enough support to topple Democratic rule in Congress. Before the Republican takeover, Democrats had controlled the House for 40 years. In January 1995, when Republicans were sworn in, only one member of Congress had ever seen a Republican majority: Sid Yates, a Democrat who was over 80 years old. The only Republican who had ever seen a Republican majority was a member from Missouri who had been in Washington as a page.

A major reason why it had taken so long to overcome the chronic majority status of the Democrats was that Republicans had spent much of the previous 40 years becoming more and more like the Democrats. It reached the point where one ranking Republican on a committee was described in the *Wall Street Journal* as a wholly owned subsidiary of the Democratic chairman. Even more disconcerting, nobody in the ranks of the Republican leadership was concerned or offended by the comment. Some of the young Turks (myself included) who were a constant source of embarrassment to the old guard objected, but the fact of the matter was that Republicans were content to be like Democrats and just get along in peace. That fact raises another of Armey's Axioms, "If you love peace more than freedom, you lose." Before the 1995 takeover, Republicans loved peace more than freedom, and they were losing.

Ultimately, Republicans did band together to challenge the Democratic majority, which was feasible only because of the unique circumstances of the time. When President Bill Clinton was elected in 1992 and Democrats were in charge of the whole town, they overreached drastically, with the most notable example being the Clinton health care plan. As the new administration began proposing policies more radical than the median voter was willing to accept, opportunities emerged to challenge the status quo.

A true struggle emerged in the Republican ranks. When Newt Gingrich was elected Whip, and subsequently I was elected to leadership, things grew uncomfortable for the old guard of the GOP. The most significant change was the retirement of leader Bob Michel (R-Ill.), which led to new leadership whose distinct mission was to change the direction of the Republican Party.

Those changes were embodied in the Contract with America, which gained traction because of the excesses, abuses, and corruptions of the Democratic majority. The Contract consisted of 10 issues that were widely popular with the public that Democrats would not allow to come to a vote. Had they not been so arrogant, we could not have written the Contract.

The Contract was a unique political moment and political instrument. I have never seen before or since every single Republican candidate on the same song page. Some senators were reluctant to embrace our agenda, but the momentum for change was great. Indeed, even some House members were skeptical but went along with the Contract. In the end, all but one Republican candidate for the House—incumbent or challenger—signed the Contract, largely because they all felt they had been part of the process. That was really an unusual feat.

Leadership vs. the Status Quo

On the strength and popularity of the Contract, Republicans won the majority. But it is important to understand that, even at that moment in 1995 when Republicans gained the majority for the first time in 40 years, it was not a majority of small-government conservatives; they were still a minority within the party. Setting party affiliations aside, the majority, composed of Democrats and moderate

7

Republicans, still favored bigger government. For this group, it was business as usual, handing out perks and spending on pork. In fact, government would have grown were it not for the leadership's ability to exert a message of smaller government.

In retrospect, Republicans did some remarkable things in the short period after the election. One reason they were able to do so was that many Republican members were happy to be in the new majority and were much aware of the fact that the leadership had created this opportunity. Every new Republican chairman was someone who had previously been resigned to being a member of a permanent minority. Winning the majority generated an intense sense of appreciation and loyalty, and a willingness to work with the leadership that was the source of this extraordinary opportunity. Yet, as Republicans became comfortable with being in the majority, this cohesiveness began to fade, giving way to politics as usual and expanding government.

Early on, however, we were able to make remarkable strides. We were duty bound to do exactly what the Contract said in the first 100 days. That meant for the first 100 days leadership, not committee chairmen responding to interest groups, defined the entire agenda of the House. This change was important because it provided an opportunity to challenge—at least in the short run—the influence of special interests that drive the agenda at the committee level. Committees, which deal with a limited range of issues, have a parochial view driven by policy concerns. Leadership, in contrast, has a broader view that must balance the interests of competing committees and the legislative body as a whole. The deference to leadership on the part of the chairmen provided an opportunity for change. We established a pattern of the leadership setting policy goals, which gave us the ability to hold our conservative, small-government agenda together and get members to work with it.

The first 100 days were remarkable. The House passed a wide range of reforms, including tax cuts, a balanced-budget amendment, and civil justice reforms. It became more difficult moving legislation from the House to the Senate, working to encourage the Senate to act, coordinating the Senate and the House efforts, and negotiating with the president to get legislation signed into law. As time passed reform got harder, as we learned that Congress was not a world of small-government conservatives. Committee chairmen became more adept and comfortable in their roles and no longer felt so lucky to be chairmen. In fact, some chairmen developed the attitude that the party was fortunate to have them.

In sum, the willingness to go along with the party began to erode over time. We did remarkable things in those first three or four years of a Republican majority, largely because the leadership was able to impose a standard of limited government on members who felt a debt of gratitude for the new majority status. That situation no longer exists. The Senate is a far cry from that, but the majority of House Republicans are still proponents of smaller government. However, the House as a legislative body is not. Current members no longer feel the same sense of loyalty to leadership as they did in 1995. The committee system has reasserted its dominance and made it much more difficult for leadership to control the agenda.

Next Steps

Considerable work remains to secure our vision of limited government. Change has been slow, and many are growing disenchanted with the Republican revolution, including a demoralized base of activists. Of course, the tragic events of 9/11 and the war on terrorism have fueled growth in government, and the weak economy has generated pressure for increased government intervention, such as trade protection and bailouts for specific industries.

President Bush did deliver on his promise to cut taxes, but Congress has yet to muster the needed votes to make them permanent. We now face the threat that Washington's desire for big spending will undermine the long-term viability of Bush's tax cuts. Moving forward requires solidifying the gains we have made, such as welfare reform and the tax cuts. In addition, it requires the Republican leadership to pursue bold ideas that energize support for limited government. That will not happen without external pressure, which is why I joined Citizens for a Sound Economy (now FreedomWorks) when I retired from Congress.

Reestablishing the principles of limited government is not an easy challenge, but it is possible. Wresting control from appropriators who have pushed federal spending to new heights and enforcing spending discipline are important steps in the process. Moving forward, limiting government means more than just reining in discretionary spending, which currently accounts for about 40 percent of

9

the federal budget. Congress will have to tackle failing entitlement programs, including Social Security and Medicare, which are headed toward bankruptcy. Facing these challenges is an opportunity for major reforms, but external pressure is needed to alter the bias toward higher spending.

The Biggest Problem: Fiscal Discipline

Excessive spending under the Republican Congress is one of the most pressing concerns for those who support limited government. Although the deficit is expected to fall during the next few years, that will be caused by rising revenues from a stronger economy, not a reduction in spending.

Both politics and institutional biases lead to continual increases in federal spending, and programs are rarely cut or eliminated. Excessive spending occurs in both surplus and deficit years. In 2004, the federal government collected $1.9 trillion from taxpayers to fund some $2.3 trillion in spending.[2] But spending was also too high during prior years when there were surpluses. The solution is to focus not exclusively on deficits but also on overspending.

Controlling spending has been a challenge, even for Republicans. Throughout government there are inefficiencies, redundancies, and waste. The appropriations process is more concerned with allocating additional funds to programs than with cutting programs that do not work. Between fiscal years 2000 and 2004, total federal outlays increased 28 percent.[3]

With outlays on entitlement programs consuming an ever-increasing portion of the budget, discretionary spending, as well as Social Security, Medicaid, and Medicare, must be addressed. In 2004, entitlements consumed 54 percent of the budget, and demographic trends will increase costs substantially in the future. In 2003 the General Accounting Office (now the Government Accountability Office) notes that "by mid-century, absent reform of these entitlement programs, projected federal revenues may be adequate to pay little beyond interest on the debt and Social Security benefits."[4]

Opportunities for Reform

Public-choice economists have illustrated how the incentives that face members of Congress can determine the outcome of the legislative process.[5] Like any institution, Congress has established rules to

10

govern its behavior. But information shortcomings promote unjustified spending on programs that benefit narrow groups at the expense of the broader public. Politicians respond to special interests and campaign donors to maximize their reelection chances, but that policy often generates results that are economically inefficient or harmful to most Americans. These problematic incentives apply to both Republicans and Democrats.

One solution is changing the political institutions to create more efficient outcomes. I did this with the Military Base-Closing Commissions in the 1990s, which took decisions about closing unnecessary bases out of the hands of those with a vested interest in keeping the bases open. Similar ideas are being proposed in Congress today to cut other unnecessary programs. Other measures, such as a line-item veto, can also change the institutional framework to eliminate the bias toward spending. Republicans have supported such ideas in the past but have been unable as yet to overcome Democrat opposition to implement them.

When We Act Like Us, We Win

A Republican ideology of limited government has much to offer and can make a real difference in how Washington works. If Republicans are passive and they simply respond to the incentives generated by the institutional setting in Washington, change is not likely and high spending will continue. Entrepreneurs in Congress who believe in limited government should push ahead with their plans for change.

Perhaps no better example of Republicans being Republicans is the welfare reform of 1996. Even without the White House, Republicans managed to push through the most significant change in welfare policy since the program was introduced as part of President Lyndon Johnson's War on Poverty. Not only did welfare reform alter federal policies, but it also broke the cycle of poverty fostered by a generation of expanding welfare programs.

After 30 years and $9 trillion, Johnson's War on Poverty did little to alleviate poverty. However, it did much to harm economic growth, expand taxes, and create a class of citizens dependent on the government.

As a core part of the Contract with America, Republicans launched the most successful anti-poverty initiative of the past half century.

11

Before 1996, Aid to Families with Dependent Children was the largest cash assistance program and the centerpiece of the War on Poverty. Welfare reform changed the program's name to Temporary Assistance to Needy Families, which was not just a superficial change. Rather, the 1996 reforms eliminated welfare's "entitlement" status—ending the automatic "right" to benefits. Recipients who are able-bodied and need assistance now have to get training or work to receive benefits. Since 1996, welfare is better understood as temporary assistance in tough times rather than a permanent way of life.

This critical change broke the poverty of spirit and dependency that welfare created. By emphasizing work and responsibility, the 1996 reforms moved all able-bodied Americans toward independence, self-respect, and self-sufficiency. The war on poverty may have begun in 1964, but it wasn't until 1996 that we truly began winning. According to chapter 9 in this volume, by Ron Haskins, the poverty rate fell after the 1996 reforms and many other social indicators improved.

There is much more to do because there is still too much despair and poverty in America. For that reason it is important for Congress to renew and strengthen the 1996 reforms. In addition, it should pursue pro-growth economic policies because growth is the best anti-poverty program ever devised.

When We Act Like Them, We Lose

The recent expansion in Medicare to include prescription drugs provides an example of how policies that expand government are ultimately harmful to Republicans. Many politicians began the legislative debate with good goals in mind, hoping to reform this failing entitlement program. The Bush administration's initial proposal for a drug benefit, for example, was offered as one component of a reformed, more financially stable Medicare system. But rather than overhauling the system, Congress simply added a new benefit to an unreformed program. Sadly, the decision to abandon principle in favor of expediency was made before a single hearing or committee vote was even taken. There was never an attempt to generate support for market-based reforms for this failing system.

With a slim majority in the Senate and an even smaller pro-reform plurality in Congress, the reforms pushed by President Bush and

Ways and Means Chairman Bill Thomas were systematically stripped from the final drug bill. Bipartisan support pushed through the $534 billion drug benefit, but the bill did little to address the underlying failures of Medicare. Yet with an unfunded liability in the trillions of dollars, Medicare needs fundamental reforms more than ever.

We now have a situation where the political process, not the market, will make decisions about the price and availability of prescription drugs. The free market had done a fairly good job up until this point. America led the world in the introduction of new drugs—especially in the area of life-saving miracle drugs. The overwhelming majority of seniors had prescription drug coverage. It is not a perfect record, but it is doubtful that the government program will produce a better result moving forward.

Entrepreneurial Opportunities

Those of us who want less government, lower taxes, and more freedom must remember what happens as government expands. Free individuals in the competitive marketplace make fewer decisions. More decisions are made in the political marketplace where the motivations of politicians differ from concerns of individuals in the market. As a result, fewer efficient decisions will be made.

Many Republicans in office may not understand this process, but their constituents do. The drug bill's massive cost and high government spending in general have left much of the conservative base disaffected. But, many Republicans in Congress are beginning to feel the pressure to rein in the budget. A return to more-limited government in an institutional framework that is biased toward bigger government is challenging, but not impossible. The president needs to lead by vetoing excessive spending passed by Congress.

Congressional leadership can stop the fiscal drift with a concerted effort to change the federal budget process. In 1995, the Republican leadership targeted the spending process as a way to cut government. Leadership ignored seniority in favor of individuals committed to smaller government. John Kasich, for example, was selected as Budget Committee chairman over more senior members on the basis of his past efforts to control spending. With such individuals in key positions and with the support of leadership, it is possible to restrain the big spenders in both parties.

Efforts to control spending in the 1990s did not go unchallenged. Appropriators resisted, and rank-and-file members were pressured by special interests to continue the flow of dollars for income redistribution. As majority leader, I was responsible for controlling overzealous spenders, which made me highly unpopular. Democrats were particularly opposed to spending cuts and accused the GOP of cutting programs that would leave the poor homeless and hungry. This rhetoric was the politics of greed wrapped in the language of love because most spending involves horizontal wealth transfers and not vertical redistribution from the wealthy to the poor.[6] Many members would use any argument to justify more spending on special interests.

Through our leadership, efforts to control spending were initially effective. Total federal spending slowed significantly and discretionary spending actually fell. Unfortunately, in the standoff with the Clinton administration over the 1995 government shutdown, Republicans blinked, giving the White House a publicity coup and increasing spending.

Grass-Roots Pressure

Tackling overspending and government growth through strong leadership and commitment to principle is possible. The task is made easier when constituents are energized in favor of limited government. Public-choice theory has focused on the fact that many Americans are rationally ignorant and therefore uninvolved in the political process.[7] Consequently, members of Congress hear more from special interests that have narrow and identifiable gains that can be achieved through the political process. Nonetheless, a solid core of constituents exists who are active in the political process out of a sense of civic duty and who favor more freedom from government. Mobilizing those citizens is critical for cutting the government. They can counterbalance the views of special interests and hold the Republicans to their core principles of lower taxes, less government, and more freedom.

Conclusion

The most important Armey Axiom is "Freedom Works." America will prosper and create unlimited opportunity if we have limited government and reward the hard work and initiative of citizens.

Republicans are the party with the greatest commitment to those ideas.

The institutions of Congress are conservative with a small "c." Change comes slowly and reforming a century's worth of government growth overnight is difficult. But the Republican majority, despite its flaws, has made progress. Looking ahead, legislation has been introduced to enact budget process reforms that will slow the growth of spending. Also, many GOP members are supporting Social Security reform based on personal retirement accounts. If they stick to their principles they can generate the votes needed to enact reforms, but they will need help from an energized political base.

With Republicans in power, at least the right ideas are being discussed. The debate would be entirely different with Democrats in power because they focus primarily on how to best administer and grow the government. Ideas alone do not provide members of Congress the staying power to challenge the institutions of Washington. An active political base in favor of restraint is also critical to restoring fiscal responsibility.

As a result of past excesses and coming demographic changes, the debate over fiscal discipline is taking a more prominent position. A debate over discretionary spending cuts will emerge as entitlement spending rises, and Social Security, Medicaid, and Medicare all require fundamental changes. With Republicans in office, at least the door is opened to make those changes. Now the political incentives must be provided to make them happen.

In the mid-1990s, the GOP took maximum advantage of the moment. We did as much as could be done and are proud of what we accomplished. The future could be even more challenging and more rewarding. Grass-roots activism will be required to break the status quo and place the nation on a more secure fiscal footing.

Perhaps the most effective tactic will be mobilizing nontraditional voters who have little to lose from toppling the status quo. One key bloc of nontraditional voters who face much higher tax burdens unless Congress makes fundamental reforms is young adults. Reforming Social Security and other entitlement programs can avoid those higher tax burdens and should help mobilize the young, who should be a key outreach group for the GOP. Reforms such as Social Security personal accounts are both good politics and good policy.

Notes

1. Richard Armey, *Armey's Axioms: 40 Hard-Earned Truths from Politics, Faith, and Life* (Hoboken, NJ: Wiley and Sons, 2003).

2. Congressional Budget Office, "The Budget and Economic Outlook: An Update," September 2004, www.cbo.gov.

3. Ibid.

4. General Accounting Office, "Major Management Challenges and Program Risks: A Governmentwide Perspective," January 2003, p. 6, www.gao.gov/pas/2003/d0395.pdf.

5. For a discussion, see Jane Shaw, "Public Choice Theory," in *The Concise Encyclopedia of Economics*, ed. David Henderson (Indianapolis: Liberty Fund, 2002), www.econlib.org/library/Enc/PublicChoiceTheory.html.

6. For a discussion, see Dwight Lee, "Redistribution of Income," in *The Concise Encyclopedia of Economics*, ed. David Henderson (Indianapolis: Liberty Fund, 2002), www.econlib.org/library/Enc/RedistributionofIncome.html.

7. For a discussion, see James Buchanan and Gordon Tullock, *The Calculus of Consent* (Ann Arbor: University of Michigan Press, 1962). Also see James Gwartney, Richard Stroup, and Russell Sobel, *Economics: Private and Public Choice*, 9th ed. (Orlando, FL: Dryden Press, 2000), Chapter 6.

16

3. The Republican Congress in Historical Context

Edward H. Crane

The 1994 election was one of the occasional revolts that occurs from discontent over the modern welfare state. In the 1930s, the New Deal put in place policies of high taxes, heavy regulation, and centralized government that sharply diverged from the American traditions of federalism, constitutionalism, and individual liberty. Several decades later, the political movements spurred by Barry Goldwater, Ronald Reagan, and the Republicans in 1994 were animated by a rejection of the overbearing political class in Washington and its ever-expanding control over state, local, and private activities.

The New Deal

A major blow to the Constitution came in 1937, when President Franklin D. Roosevelt threatened to pack the Supreme Court unless it capitulated to his extra-constitutional initiatives. Rexford G. Tugwell, a key architect of the New Deal, wrote, "to the extent that New Deal policies developed, they were tortured interpretations of a document intended to prevent them."[1] Roosevelt's undermining of that document—the Constitution—had huge repercussions for the expansion of the federal government in subsequent decades, making his tenure the most damaging to individual liberty in the nation's history.

Americans have always guarded their liberty jealously, but they went along with Roosevelt's schemes because the media, the academy, and Congress misunderstood the causes of the Great Depression. At the time, they thought that the Depression was caused by a failure in laissez faire capitalism. Subsequent scholarship has shown that, in fact, it was a colossal failure of government policy that caused and sustained the crisis. Federal Reserve actions that sharply cut the money supply, protectionism, policies that kept wages artificially high, regulations that prevented banks from diversifying, and other misguided interventions produced economic despair for millions of Americans. Unfortunately, the canard that free markets lead to depressions lived on for decades and was used by policymakers to justify ever-broader controls over the economy.

Barry Goldwater

In time, Americans began to question and resist the changes that Roosevelt and his ideological heirs cooked up in Washington. Large-scale failures in government programs began to occur and Americans noticed taxes creeping higher and higher.

The reaction against the New Deal channeled its energy first through Goldwater's presidential campaign in 1964. Goldwater directly attacked the expanding federal establishment. He understood the American tradition and argued for it forcefully:

> I have little interest in streamlining government or making it more efficient, for I mean to reduce its size. I do not undertake to promote welfare for I propose to extend freedom. My aim is not to pass laws but to repeal them. It is not to inaugurate new programs, but to cancel old ones that do violence to the Constitution or that have failed in their purpose or impose on the people an unwanted financial burden. And if I should later be attacked for neglecting my constituents' interest, I shall reply that I was informed that their main interest is liberty and in that cause, I am doing the very best that I can.[2]

Wouldn't it be nice to hear politicians say that today? Unfortunately, Goldwater ran for office in the wake of the assassination of President John F. Kennedy, and the public was not about to endorse, in effect, an assassination by changing parties. Nevertheless, Goldwater's campaign crystallized the energy against the New Deal, and it transferred that energy to Ronald Reagan, who gave a memorable speech for Goldwater in 1964. Reagan was elected governor of California in 1966 and president in 1980.

The Short-Lived 1994 Revolution

The Goldwater and Reagan energy manifested itself again with the 1994 GOP election victory. That energy was based on the deeply ingrained American culture of wanting to be left alone by government, as well as a rejection of imperious bureaucrats and politicians with grand designs for controlling their lives. When given half a chance, and channeled by leaders with a strong and consistent message, individualism and limited government policies can win at the ballot box.

That American spirit expressed itself in the election of 1994 when clear policy choices were presented in the Contract with America:

> This year's election offers a chance, after four decades of one party control, to bring to the House a new majority that will transform the way Congress works. That historic change would be the end of government that is too big, too intrusive, and too easy with the public's money.[3]

Unfortunately, the Republicans did not live up to this promise, and by 2004 the Contract sounded almost as nostalgic as Barry Goldwater's statement.

In recent years, we have had a Republican House, Senate, and president preside over the fastest-growing federal government in decades. The Republicans have perpetuated or grown all the federal programs that the Democrats launched during their four decades of congressional control. The Republicans also enacted a new Medicare prescription drug benefit, which is the largest entitlement expansion since the 1960s.

How has this happened just 10 years after the Republican revolution began? Well, the head of the Republican National Committee, Ed Gillespie, a former lobbyist who helped push through steel tariffs, told the *Manchester Union Leader* that the Reaganite-Republican railings against the expansion of the federal government are over. He told the *Union Leader* that if the people want expanded entitlement programs and a federal government that attends to their every desire, then the Republican Party is for it. Gillespie's comments reveal a key problem for Americans seeking to reestablish limited government: there are too many opponents of liberty within the Republican Party.

Three Big Mistakes

Three big mistakes have cut short any sustained downsizing of the federal government in recent years. The first mistake was Ronald

19

Reagan's 1984 campaign. Reagan was enormously popular and presided over a growing economy. He had a great opportunity to seriously cut government, but his handlers decided to run a "Morning in America" campaign with lots of shots of pretty beaches, forests, and people having fun, but with no substance. He carried 49 states but had no mandate for further reforms. It would have been better if he had carried 40 states and had a mandate for cutting the government. After all, he ran in 1980 on the platform of abolishing the Department of Energy and the Department of Education.

The second mistake made by Reagan and the Republican Party was the nomination of George H. W. Bush for president. Reagan had lunch with Bush once a week for eight years. He should have been able to tell that Bush did not share any of his limited-government principles. Bush was not really elected president: Americans thought that they were essentially electing Reagan for a third term. It was Reagan's mistake to pick somebody with no reform agenda and whose first act was firing every senior Reagan person in Washington.

The third mistake is more contentious. I am a supply-sider in that I believe in cutting taxes and regulations on the productive sector of the economy. However, many in the Republican Party have focused exclusively on tax cuts and growing the economy without dealing with the tougher job of limiting government to its proper size. Former representative Jack Kemp, for example, urged Republicans to cut tax rates, grow the private economy faster than the government sector, and thereby shrink government as a share of gross domestic product. Making the case for tax cuts, Kemp would say, "I'm not interested in cutting spending, I'm interested in growth."

That strategy has sadly oriented the party away from a focus on individual freedom and restoration of constitutional government. If we work toward a free society, economic growth will naturally follow, but growth should not be the primary focus. For one thing, supporters of an activist government also claim that their policies are good for the economy. Also, if Republicans concentrate just on growth and not on the proper role of government, the government will surely balloon because entrenched interests and ideological leftists are actively pressing for larger government all the time. James Buchanan, the Nobel laureate in economics, wrote in 2000:

> [C]lassical liberalism cannot secure sufficient public acceptability when its vocal advocates are limited to "does-it-work"

pragmatists. Science and self-interest do indeed lend force to an argument, but a vision, an ideal is necessary. People need something to yearn and struggle for. If the [classical] liberal ideal is not there, there will be a vacuum and other ideas will supplant it. Classical liberals have failed singularly in their understanding of this dynamic.[4]

Today, that vacuum has been filled by neoconservatives and other Republicans who are explicitly pro–big government. Writing in the *Weekly Standard,* Irving Kristol defined neoconservatives as "impatient with the Hayekian notion that we are on the road to serfdom. Neocons do not feel that kind of alarm or anxiety about the growth of the state in the past century, seeing it as natural, indeed inevitable."[5] In the article, Kristol pushes Goldwater aside and calls Presidents Franklin and Theodore Roosevelt "heroes" of neoconservatism.

Neoconservatives have had, regrettably, a huge effect in orienting American foreign policy toward foreign interventionism. Neoconservatives and fellow travelers in the GOP have likewise pushed for greater federal interventionism in domestic policy. In 1980, Reagan was elected on a platform of abolishing the Department of Education, but in recent years neoconservatives have sought greater federal intrusion in the nation's schools. Under President George W. Bush, Department of Education spending increased 80 percent between fiscal years 2001 and 2005.[6] Neoconservatives, such as Les Lenkowsky and Michael Joyce, have spearheaded Bush's faith-based initiative, which pushed the government into new spheres of activity that were previously private. The president's simplistic justification has been that there are a lot of souls to be saved, so the government ought to spend the resources to save them.

"National greatness" has been another neoconservative theme that has steered the Republican Party away from America's limited-government tradition and alienated it from many average citizens. In 1994, those citizens voted for smaller government and against grand national schemes such as Hillary Clinton's health care plan. Yet the neoconservatives, such as David Brooks, see it differently. He argues that we need:

> an emergence of a vigorous, One Nation Conservatism that will connect a revived sense of citizenship with a longstanding national greatness Americans hold dear . . . ultimately,

21

American purpose can find its voice only in Washington. Individual ambition and will power are channeled into the cause of national greatness, and in making the nation great, individuals are able to join their narrow concerns to a larger national project.[7]

Greatness Resides in Individuals, Not the State

Unlike the neoconservatives, I think Americans hold dear the ability to live, work, and pursue happiness as they please. They hold dear the greatness of living free from the censorship, arbitrary arrest, and wealth confiscation that still take place in many other countries. Many Americans view the goings on in Washington with disdain because little greatness is on display there.

Greatness can instead be found in the millions of individual efforts of the entrepreneurs, engineers, scientists, athletes, and others who put their minds to work to satisfy their own restless spirits. We do not need to submerge the individual into some larger, national project. The government does not create greatness, but confined to its proper place it can allow the rest of us to live free and fulfilling lives. I think 1994 captured some of that spirit, but we need a more thoroughgoing revolution to deliver to Americans the honest, limited, and constitutional federal government that they desire and deserve.

Notes

1. Rexford G. Tugwell, "Rewriting the Constitution: A Center Report," *Center Magazine*, March 1968, p. 18.

2. Barry Goldwater, *The Conscience of a Conservative* (Washington: Regnery, 1990, original print 1960).

3. Ed Gillespie and Bob Schellhas, eds., *Contract with America: The Bold Plan by Rep. Newt Gingrich, Rep. Dick Armey and the House Republicans to Change the Nation* (New York: Times Books, 1994), p. 7.

4. James M. Buchanan, "Saving the Soul of Classical Liberalism," *Wall Street Journal*, December 31, 1999, p. R29.

5. Irving Kristol, "The Neo-Conservative Persuasion," *Weekly Standard*, August 25, 2003.

6. *Budget of the U.S. Government, Fiscal Year 2005, Historical Tables* (Washington: Government Printing Office, 2004), p. 74.

7. David Brooks, "One Nation Conservatism," *Weekly Standard*, September 13, 1999, p. 23.

4. Same as the Old Boss? Congressional Reforms under the Republicans

John Samples

In 1992, two different groups studying Congress attended separate conferences to examine problems of the federal government. The first meeting included congressional staffers, Washington wonks, and college professors. That group concluded that the public's dissatisfaction with Congress was "wholly inaccurate and potentially dangerous." These elites and insiders suggested ways of insulating Congress from a fickle and unhappy public.

The second meeting comprised residents of a small Midwestern town. Those Americans saw things differently. They described members of Congress as "haughty, pampered, and out of touch." The small-town Americans had distinct ideas about reforming Congress, including "term limits, abolishing most staff positions, eliminating committees, and removing perquisites of office."[1]

The Midwesterners' views reflected a broad public dissatisfaction with Congress. The number of Americans expressing a great deal of confidence in Congress steadily declined from 1986 to 1994, after having risen in the years after Watergate.[2] One survey in the early 1990s found that 60 percent of Americans described their feelings toward members of Congress as "angry" or "disgusted," whereas only 14 percent chose the term "proud." Only 7 percent were angry or disgusted about Supreme Court justices, while about one-third felt that way about the president. One-third were proud of the members of the Court, but fully one-half felt the same about the president.[3]

In the early 1990s, public unhappiness with Congress reflected both frustrations regarding federal policies and skepticism about political power.

23

Congress in Trouble

Why did the public dislike Congress before 1994? A survey found substantial numbers of Americans agreed with the following statements:

- Congress is too far removed from ordinary people (78 percent).
- Congress is heavily influenced by interest groups when making decisions (86 percent).
- Members of Congress focus too much on events in Washington (70 percent).

Similarly, 57 percent of the respondents disagreed with the proposition that "Congress does a good job representing the diverse interests of Americans, whether black or white, rich or poor" and 78 percent disagreed that "members of Congress come back to their districts too often."[4]

When asked about specific events that fostered a dislike of Congress, many people mentioned a recent pay raise. Slightly more mentioned the House banking scandal of 1992. That scandal broke when the public learned that many members of Congress were writing checks on accounts in the House that had insufficient funds to cover the outlay. The members were, in effect, kiting checks with impunity. The scandal led to the retirement of several members. A similar number of respondents cited deficit gridlock as a reason for disliking Congress. A small, though significant, number also mentioned the recent Anita Hill–Clarence Thomas hearings as contributing to their dislike of the institution.[5]

Other surveys found similar results not only about Congress but also about the federal government. National Elections Studies found persistent declines in trust in government, in political efficacy, and in approval of Congress.[6] Each of those measures reached a long-term low in 1992 or 1994. The number of Americans who believed that government listened "a great deal" to the people also declined slightly to near-historic lows.[7]

Other indications of political change were in the air. In the early 1990s, public support for more government was dropping like a stone. The decline in support for more spending from 1991 to 1995 is the steepest recorded over the past 50 years.[8] That shift in underlying preferences was running up against the realities of partisanship and power. The Democrats, the party of more government and more spending, had controlled the House of Representatives for 40 years; in the Senate, only 6 of those 40 years had been under the Republicans. The public was rapidly moving in a direction that Congress could not accommodate for ideological and partisan reasons.

Normally we might expect that election returns would reflect the public's change of heart on spending, but by 1994, defeating a sitting member of Congress had become increasingly difficult—bordering on impossible. In the early 1990s, political scientists concluded that incumbency itself, apart from partisan considerations, was worth about 12 percentage points in an election, an advantage that had steadily increased since the 1960s.[9] At the time, informed opinion argued that the advantages of office (staff time, franking privilege, name recognition) translated into incumbency advantage.

The United States experienced an institutional and a policy crisis in the early 1990s. The public had turned sharply against government expansion. Congress and the president, especially after 1992, could not accommodate that change in outlook. That public frustration fostered a crisis in confidence in political institutions, which led to a movement to impose term limits on elected officials—an effort that drew broad public support.[10] At the polls, the public turned to outsiders like Ross Perot and the Republican minority to change the direction of the nation. How well did the Republicans respond to the policy and institutional concerns of the American people?

Promises and Performance

The Contract with America promised "smaller government with lower taxes and fewer services." If given power, the Republicans would "dramatically change the way Washington does business, and change the business Washington does."[11] The Republicans made the crisis of institutional confidence a central theme of their Contract with America. They criticized the high reelection rates of members of Congress and compared the House of Representatives to the British House of Lords, whose members are appointed for life. The advantages of incumbency, said the Contract, inhibit accountability and responsiveness: "Elected officials have become so entrenched and protected that they are unresponsive to the public they were elected to serve." The Contract denounced gerrymandering because it enabled public officials to choose their constituents rather than the other way around. The Contract argued that "the Democrats'

25

Figure 4.1
TOTAL FEDERAL OUTLAYS AS A SHARE OF GDP

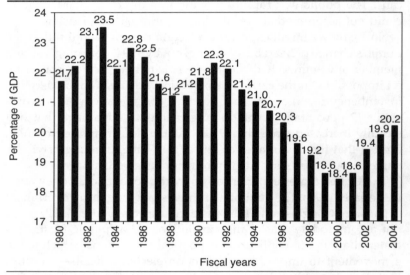

SOURCE: *Budget of the U.S. Government, Fiscal year 2005* (Washington: Government Printing Office, 2004).

iron-handed one-party rule of the House of Representatives over the last four decades led to arcane, arbitrary, and often secretive procedures that disenfranchised millions of Americans from representation in Congress." Congress held itself above the law and operated in secret. In response to this malaise, the Republicans promised to bring term limits to a vote, to impose term limits on party leaders, to ban gifts to members of Congress, and to apply civil rights and employment law to Congress.[12] In sum, the Republicans promised a smaller government and a more responsive Congress.

For a few years, the Republicans delivered on their promise to reduce spending, at least when measured as a share of gross domestic product, as shown in Figure 4.1. However, as documented in Chapter 6 of this volume by Stephen Moore, the end of the Cold War played a key role in spending restraint during the 1990s. By the end of the 1990s, spending began rising rapidly, wiping out earlier progress at restraint. Under President Bush and the Republican Congress, spending has soared on both post-9/11 national security and domestic programs.

The congressional Republicans in the mid-1990s did constrain federal spending, in line with the wishes of the public. We cannot know what the Democrats would have done had they retained power, but we can speculate. The Democrats almost certainly also would have phased down defense spending after the end of the Cold War. It is possible, however, that together with a Democratic president, congressional Democrats would have increased domestic spending above the Republican levels until the end of the decade. But during the past five years, it is hard to see how anyone could have outspent the Republicans, who have increased agency spending across the board, as noted by Moore.

On their first day in power, the House Republicans cut House staff, changed budgeting rules, enacted term limits for their leadership, banned proxy voting in committee, opened committee hearings to the public, required a three-fifths vote to increase taxes, started a comprehensive audit of the House, and applied anti-discrimination and workplace safety rules to Congress itself. Those reforms aimed at making Congress "more effective, deliberative, and accountable."[13] Did those reforms persist and change Congress? We turn first to the most radical of the proposed reforms, term limits on members.

The Republican House passed the Congressional Accountability Act, which made Congress subject to 11 federal laws applying to the private sector, among them the Occupational Safety and Health Act, the Americans with Disabilities Act, the Family Medical Leave Act, and the Federal Service Labor Management Relations Act. The law set up an Office of Compliance to implement the applicable laws and provide procedures for complaints and dispute resolution.[14] Congress had long maintained that separation of powers prevented such laws from being applied by the executive to the legislative branch. The Congressional Accountability Act was popular enough to pass overwhelmingly both chambers of Congress.

The purpose of making Congress obey its own laws was not to be narrowly legalistic or to improve the conduct of members on labor and civil rights issues. Some critics argued Congress legislated and regulated so broadly because it escaped the consequences of its actions. In theory, if Congress absorbed both the electoral benefits of passing regulations and paid the costs of complying with these rules, the nation might get less regulation.

After 1995, Congress initiated and enacted important agricultural and financial services deregulation bills. Other bills increased federal regulatory authority, such as minimum wage legislation and the Health Insurance Portability and Accountability Act of 1996.[15] Wayne Crews, Adam Thierer, and Jerry Taylor discuss the GOP record on regulations in more detail in this volume.

The new Congress passed additional disclosure requirements on lobbyists late in 1995. The Republicans also completely outlawed gifts to members of Congress or their staffs.[16] That absolute ban gave way in 1999 to a $50 per gift limit and a $100 ceiling on the total gifts from one source in a year. Later still, Congress allowed members to take all-expenses-paid trips to charity events.[17]

The Contract promised to bring congressional term limits to a vote within 100 days of taking power. The new Congress beat this self-imposed deadline by 15 days. However, political scientist James Gimpel notes that "the effort to pass term limits was the most disorganized and halfhearted operation of the first 100 days."[18] The Republican leadership was not enthusiastic about term limits, and many of the senior members of the GOP opposed them. By contrast, many of the more junior members strongly supported term limits.

By the time the 104th Congress addressed term limits, the Supreme Court had invalidated state limits on the terms of members of Congress. This ruling meant the House would have to vote on a constitutional amendment for term limits, which required 290 votes to pass. Success would have required unity among supporters of term limits (Republicans and the grass-roots movement behind limits) as well as about one-third of the Democratic caucus in the House.

The GOP initially put forth three separate versions of the term-limits amendment. The leadership eventually supported a proposal that limited House members to six terms along with a recommended two-term limit on senators. The bill also preempted any state laws that included a term limit of less than 12 years. (Later, a fourth version of the amendment appeared on the floor that included a 12-year limit without state preemption.) The generous limit on terms in the bill split the House Republicans from the grass-roots groups that had put term limits on the national agenda. In the end, the term-limits amendment fell 63 votes short of passage in the House.[19]

Lacking a legal constraint on members, the term-limits movement sought to persuade members to honor their pledge to leave office after three terms. Seven members did step down voluntarily in 2000 at the end of their third term.[20] Others did not, and the term-limits movement sought to make the breaking of the promise an electoral issue. This effort came to a head in 2000. George Nethercutt, a House member from Washington, had defeated former House Speaker Tom Foley in part because of the term-limits issue; Foley ran for reelection, thereby breaking his term-limit promise. Nethercutt handily won the 2000 Republican primary and general election.[21]

The Republicans in Congress did impose term limits on their committee and subcommittee chairmen. Newt Gingrich also imposed an eight-year limit on his own position, the Speaker of the House. Those limits led to the retirement of four committee chairmen in the House in 2000. A proposal to end the limits that same year went down to defeat by a vote of 141-27 in the House Republican Conference.[22] The limits have persisted also in the Senate, although they were weakened in 2002. Some committee chairman spent more than a year as ranking member after the Democrats took control in 2001; had the 1994 rules stayed in place, many would have had to step down as chairman in 2002. Term limits on committee chairmen in the Senate now include both six years as chairman and six years as a ranking member.[23] Congressional leaders also granted some chairmen exemptions from the limits. In early 2003, the House also removed the term limit on Speaker Hastert.[24]

The Public's Response

Republicans came to power during a period of great public dissatisfaction with the federal government in general and with Congress in particular. Has that changed? Does the public feel more in control of government since 1994? Specifically, has the American public felt that government is more responsive since 1994 than in the years prior to the Republican revolution? We have public opinion data to address these questions. The National Election Studies project has surveyed the public for some time to measure political efficacy, the perceived responsiveness of government, and trust in the federal government.

The NES political efficacy index measures the public's feeling it has a say in government.[25] Figure 4.2 shows the average index score for this measure over the past 50 years. Although the 1980s data show a lot of variation, in general, the efficacy shows a 30-year

Figure 4.2
POLICY EFFICACY INDEX

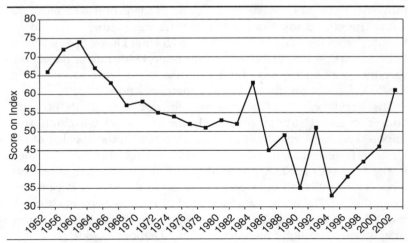

SOURCE: National Election Studies.

decline that began in 1960. The data also show a continual rise in the public's sense of efficacy from 1994 to 2002. Most analysts would be wary of attributing the rise only to the Republican ascendancy; nevertheless, the upward trend is striking.

The NES trust in government index tells a similar story, as shown in Figure 4.3.[26] The first 6 years of the Reagan presidency and the last 10 years are the only two periods that have seen rising trust in government since the mid-1960s. Because both Ronald Reagan and the freshman Republicans of 1994 stood for limited government, it is ironic that their elections would actually increase trust in the federal government. But that seems to be the case.

Finally, we might also examine survey responses to the question: "Do you approve or disapprove of the way the U.S. Congress has been handling its job?" Figure 4.4 shows that these data reflect well on the Republican Congress over the past 10 years. Public approval of Congress rises rapidly after 1994 and runs strongly counter to the trend after 1984. The changeover to Republican control seems related to increasing public satisfaction with Congress.

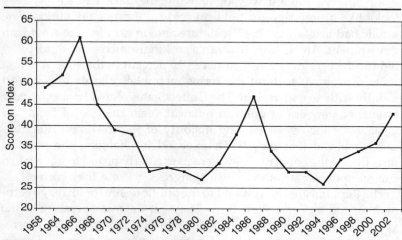

Figure 4.3
TRUST IN GOVERNMENT

SOURCE: National Election Studies.

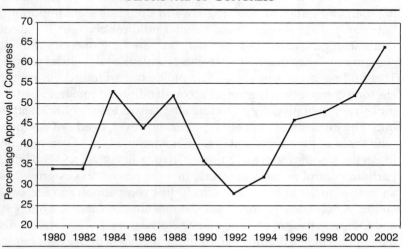

Figure 4.4
APPROVAL OF CONGRESS

SOURCE: National Election Studies.

Conclusion

Revolutions have a way of reviving the past. Even now, 1994 looks like a time ripe for political reform, if not a revolution. The public had lost faith in the legislature and, in general, the American government. An outsider had run a strikingly successful third-party bid for the presidency and garnered 20 percent of the vote. A grassroots movement to limit the terms of public officials had spread rapidly with no end in sight. The United States seemed poised finally to enter a new era of political renewal. Near the end of their first Congress, "the overwhelming majority of the freshmen [Republicans] believed that they had succeeded in changing the political direction of the country. They were particularly proud to have taken some important steps to reform Congress"[27] Were they correct?

The Republicans did respond to the public desire for lower government spending for a short time. They cut defense spending in the years following the end of the Cold War and held domestic discretionary spending below what it might have been under the Democrats for a few years. It would be a mistake, however, to call those changes a revolution, in part because the lower spending did not persist. Both defense spending and domestic spending rose sharply starting in the late 1990s. By Fiscal Year 2004, discretionary domestic spending was taking a larger share of GDP than in FY94.

The Republican record on congressional reform is underwhelming. Banning gifts and applying laws to Congress were important, but they fall far short of fundamental political change. The term limits struggle clearly indicated that the new GOP majority did not contain a majority that wished to enact fundamental political reform. This finding is not surprising. The public has an interest in robust electoral competition. It enforces accountability and constrains shirking by representatives by providing alternatives to the political status quo. The interests of the voting public, however, need not comport with those of their representatives who prefer a lack of competition in elections, some room for judgment in roll call voting, and enduring partisan control of the legislature. In sum, no one in Congress has an interest in the public interest, including competition and accountability. A new congressional establishment has replaced the old one, and Congress has not become a citizen legislature; politics still seems likely to become a lifetime job for many members of the Republican establishment.

House elections ended up less competitive in 2004 than they had been in 1994. A marginal seat in the House is subject to changes in party control. Seats where the incumbent received less than 55 percent of the vote in the last election are the most vulnerable to changes in party control. In 1994, the House had 79 marginal seats.[28] In 2004, the House will have 35 marginal seats at stake. Over 10 years, the number of marginals has declined by more than half. Other measures also show the number of competitive House seats declined from 1992 to 2000.[29]

The Republicans have been caught in what might be called the paradox of electoral competition. Before 1994, the Republicans had every reason to emphasize the stagnation of American politics and the institutional failures of Congress. Their vision of an open, accountable, and competitive Congress had great electoral appeal after two generations of rule by an entrenched majority. After the Republicans came to power, however, the appeal of robust electoral competition must have waned. Those who hold office have another name for competition: vulnerability to electoral defeat. The party in power seeks to stay in office by winning elections. Their leaders seek to limit electoral vulnerability in many ways. The Republicans in power have used partisan gerrymandering to prolong their control of Congress, a practice they denounced when the Democrats held power.[30] Not surprisingly, the new majority is acting much like the old one.

Judged from the distance of 10 years, the amount that Republicans' achievements actually changed Washington pale when measured against their own rhetoric in the Contract with America or the public aspirations and unhappiness of the early 1990s. They did respond to the public's desire for lower spending for a time and probably actually reduced discretionary spending beyond what it would have been otherwise. But the reductions were small and came to an end in 2000. The Republicans did make Congress live under the laws it passed but did not come close to limiting congressional terms or the power of incumbency. By 2004, congressional incumbents had become marginally safer than before the changeover. Having promised renewal, the revolutionaries of 1994 had settled for the *status quo ante*.

Notes

1. John R. Hibbing and Elizabeth Theiss-Morse, *Congress as Public Enemy: Public Attitudes toward American Political Institutions* (New York: Cambridge University Press, 1995), pp. xi–xii.

2. See Figure 2.1 in Hibbing and Theiss-Morse, p. 32.

3. Hibbing and Theiss-Morse, p. 58.

4. Ibid., p. 64.

5. Ibid., pp. 69–70.

6. Political efficacy is the individual's perception that government cares about and responds to his opinion. It is measured at National Election Studies by an index constructed using data from two questions: "People like me don't have any say about what the government does" and "I don't think public officials care much what people like me think."

7. National Election Studies, table 5C.1. Center for Political Studies, University of Michigan. (www.umich.edu/~nes/nesguide/nesguide.htm). Ann Arbor, MI: University of Michigan, Center for Political Studies [producer and distributor], 1995–2004.

8. See James Stimson's data on the public mood favoring more or less spending at www.unc.edu/~jstimson/.

9. Gary King, "Constituency Service and Incumbency," *British Journal of Political Science* 21, no. 1 (January 1991): 119–28.

10. In late 2004, surveys found that 62 percent and 76 percent of Americans favored term limits. See Gallup Poll, December 5, 1994, and Louis Harris and Associates, December 14, 1994. At the Roper Center at the University of Connecticut, Storrs, www.ruperrcenter.uconn.edu, these rules can be found as USGALLUP.94DC02.Q18 and USHARRIS.011295.R1. Eight years later, in the summer of 2003, 67 percent still said term limits were a good idea; see Hart and Teeter Research Companies, July 28, 2003, USNBCWSJ.03JUL26.R48.

11. Ed Gillespie and Bob Schellhas, eds., *Contract with America: The Bold Plan by Rep. Newt Gingrich, Rep. Dick Armey and the House Republicans to Change the Nation* (New York: Times Books, 1994), p. 22.

12. Ibid., pp. 157–59.

13. See David Dreier, "So Far, We're Not Off to a Good Start to an 'Open, Non-Partisan Congress'", *Roll Call*, January 9, 1995.

14. Nicol C. Rae and Colton C. Campbell, eds., *New Majority or Old Minority? The Impact of Republicans on Congress* (Lanham, MD: Rowman and Littlefield, 1999), p. 13. See also Alice A. Love, "President to Sign 'Accountability Act,' Bringing Hill under Workplace Laws," *Roll Call*, January 19, 1995.

15. William A. Niskanen, "The Clinton Regulatory Legacy," *Regulation* 24, no. 2 (Summer 2001): 42.

16. *CQ Almanac, 1995*, Vol. 51 (Washington: Congressional Quarterly Inc., 1996), p. 1–42.

17. Alexander Bolton, "House Ethics Task Force Looking to Tighten Rule on Members' Gifts," *The Hill*, October 22, 2003, p. 3.

18. James G. Gimpel, *Fulfilling the Contract: The First 100 Days* (Boston: Allyn and Bacon, 1996), p. 99.

19. Ibid., pp. 98–104.

20. Mathew Vita, "Political Appeal of Term Limits Appears to Wane; Movement Targets a Former Icon," *Washington Post*, July 17, 2000, p. A1.

21. See Michael Barone, Richard E. Cohen, and Grant Ujifusa, eds., *The Almanac of American Politics 2002* (Washington: National Journal, 2001), pp. 1613–14.

22. Ben Pershing, "Bid to End Panel Limits Rejected," *Roll Call*, November 16, 2000.

23. Noelle Straub, "Senate GOP Extends Term Limits," *The Hill*, June 6, 2001, p. 1.

24. Jim VandeHei and Juliet Eilperin, "GOP's Power Play; Goal of Reforms in House Gives Way to Tough Tactics Party Once Criticized," *Washington Post*, July 26, 2003, p. A1.

25. This index is constructed using data from questions measuring respondent agreement with the following statements: "People like me don't have any say about what the government does" and "I don't think public officials care much what people like me think."

26. This index is constructed using data from the following questions: "How much of the time do you think you can trust the government in Washington to do what is right—just about always, most of the time, or only some of the time?", "Would you say the government is pretty much run by a few big interests looking out for themselves or that it is run for the benefit of all the people?", "Do you think that people in the government waste a lot of money we pay in taxes, waste some of it, or don't waste very much of it?", "Do you think that quite a few of the people running the government are (1958–1972: a little) crooked, not very many are, or do you think hardly any of them are crooked (1958–1972: at all)?"

27. Nicol C. Rae, *Conservative Reformers: The Republican Freshman and the Lessons of the 104th Congress* (Armonk, NY: M. E. Sharpe, 1998), p. 202.

28. James G. Gimpel, *Legislating the Revolution* (Boston: Allyn and Bacon, 1996), p. 8.

29. Lew Irwin, "A 'Permanent' Republican House? Patterns of Voter Performance and the Persistence of House Control," *The Forum* 2, no. 1 (2004): 11. Irwin defines competitive seats as seats where the Republican candidate receives between 45 percent and 55 percent of the vote. The number of such seats declined by more than half from 1992 to 2000.

30. Gillespie and Schellhas, p. 157.

5. Social Policy, Supply-Side, and Fundamental Reform: Republican Tax Policy, 1994–2004

Chris Edwards

Cutting individual income taxes has been a key Republican policy objective in every session of Congress during the last decade. Tax cuts have provided a strong unifying goal in a diverse party whose elected members include social conservatives, defense hawks, libertarians, and others.

After promising tax cuts in the 1994 Contract with America, Republicans delivered substantial cuts in 1997, 2001, and 2003. This chapter looks at the tax proposals in the Contract and provides a chronology of Republican tax policies since 1995. Then the good news and bad news from a decade of GOP tax policy are discussed.

The Contract with America

The Republicans came to power in 1995 on the heels of tax increases under President Bill Clinton in 1993, President George H. W. Bush in 1990, and President Ronald Reagan in 1982, 1984, and 1987. House Republicans were eager to reestablish the GOP as the tax-cutting party in the tradition of Reagan's 1981 tax cut. The Contract included the following tax proposals:

- A $500 per child tax credit for families with incomes up to $200,000
- Marriage-penalty tax relief
- New "back-ended" Individual Retirement Accounts with $2,000 annual contribution limits, dubbed Roth IRAs when enacted in 1997
- A 50 percent cut in the capital gains tax rate cut for individuals and corporations, plus indexing to ensure that inflationary gains were not taxed

- Investment tax cuts in the form of inflation indexing for depreciation and capital expensing for the first $25,000 of equipment purchases
- A modest increase in the estate taxation exemption
- Various social policy tax breaks including refundable tax credits for adoption and elder care and a cut in taxation of Social Security benefits

The overall size of the cuts in the Contract was modest compared with the 1981 Reagan tax cut. The Contract cuts were scored at $370 billion over 7 years and $704 billion over 10 years.[1] The largest single cut was the child tax credit, which would save taxpayers $182 billion over 7 years.

The Contract's social policy tax cuts, including the child tax credit and marriage-penalty relief, were populist measures designed to aid particular constituencies. The supply-side tax cuts, including the capital gains tax cut, expanded depreciation deductions, and new IRAs were designed to reduce taxes on savings and investment as well as boost economic growth. The Contract's social policy and supply-side tax proposals dominated the Republican tax agenda for the rest of the decade.

Aside from these tax cuts, the Contract proposed that Congress pass a balanced-budget amendment (BBA) to the Constitution that included a 60 percent supermajority requirement for tax increases. The BBA was brought up for vote in the House and Senate numerous times but fell slightly short of passage. In January 1995, the BBA passed in the House by a 300-132 margin.[2] In the Senate, Robert Byrd (D-W.Va.) led the charge against the BBA. It was opposed by 34 members, thus falling a single vote short of passage. Six Democratic senators who had voted for the BBA in 1994 switched their vote to "no" in 1995.[3] After the budget went into surplus in 1998, momentum in Congress for a BBA dissipated.

Republican Tax Policy Year by Year

1995

Upon assuming control in the House, Republicans quickly began to move tax cuts through the chamber. Newt Gingrich championed a tax-cut package of $353 billion over seven years that included the Contract proposals within a plan to balance the budget by 2002. But

House Republicans immediately met resistance from Republican moderates in the Senate, including Budget Committee Chairman Pete Domenici (R-N.Mex.) and Finance Committee Chairman Bob Packwood (R-Ore.). The resistance to tax cuts by some important Senate Republicans, particularly Domenici, was to be a continuing problem for House tax-cutters the rest of the decade.

Ultimately, Congress passed a slimmed-down version of the Contract tax cuts valued at $245 billion over seven years.[4] The tax cuts came within a budget reconciliation package that also cut spending substantially compared to the baseline. Cuts included $270 billion to Medicare over seven years, $182 billion to Medicaid, and $190 billion to nondefense discretionary spending.[5]

President Clinton's February budget had proposed a continuation of large deficits throughout his five-year budget projection. The administration proposed that the fiscal year 1995 deficit of $193 billion remain essentially unchanged, and they projected a deficit of $194 billion for FY2000.[6] But under continued GOP pressure, Clinton changed course and introduced a revised budget plan in June 1995 that would balance the budget over 10 years.[7] As *Congressional Quarterly* noted on Clinton's move toward the GOP budget position in 1995, "Clinton's embrace of a balanced budget itself was a huge shift from the stand-pat stance he and Democrats took" after the 1993 budget deal.[8]

Nonetheless, the differences between Clinton and the Republicans on the budget were too large for an agreement to be reached. Clinton vetoed the GOP budget and tax package, which resulted in high-profile government shutdowns in November and December and a budget stalemate for the year.[9]

1996

In 1996, Clinton moved closer to the GOP budget position by agreeing to the goal of balancing the budget by 2002, not the longer time frame he had proposed. But on taxes, it was the GOP that compromised. After the prior year's tax-cut defeat, Republicans scaled back their proposal and the House and Senate agreed to a budget resolution that included room for $122 billion in tax cuts over six years. As it turned out, a substantial tax cut did not make it through Congress, and the year ended with only a small package of business tax cuts being enacted that were tied to a minimum wage bill. While this was the year that President Clinton declared in his State of the Union address that the "era of big government is over," Clinton would not support a deal that made substantial cuts in spending or taxes.

Nonetheless, there were some bright spots for tax policy in 1996. A staunch tax-cutter, Sen. Bill Roth (R-Del.), was now at the helm of the Senate Finance Committee. Also, Congress released a report by the National Commission on Tax Reform and Economic Growth that had been established by Republicans in 1995 and chaired by Jack Kemp.[10] The report endorsed replacing the income tax with a low-rate, pro-savings flat tax. Another bright spot in 1996 was the presidential campaign of Steve Forbes, who gained a lot of support with his proposal for a Dick Armey–style flat tax. During Bob Dole's presidential campaign, the senator proposed a 15 percent income tax rate cut. Dole's proposal indicated the popularity of tax-cutting, but he was unfortunately a poor salesman for tax-reduction policies.

1997

Political winds changed in 1997 with both Congress and the president determined to reach a budget deal to reduce the deficit to zero by 2002. Compromise was greatly aided by the booming economy, which was flooding Washington with tax revenues and sharply improving budget projections. In January 1995, the Congressional Budget Office baseline put the FY02 deficit at $322 billion.[11] By January 1997, the CBO projected that the FY02 deficit would be $188 billion. By the summer, it was clear that the deficit would be even smaller than that. (By September 1997 the projection for FY02 was a surplus of $32 billion, with about half the improvement since January resulting from the August budget deal and half from the improving economy and other factors.)[12]

A balanced-budget deal was signed into law in August that included cuts to baseline discretionary spending and Medicare of $196 billion over five years. Many of the budget savings were never to materialize because Congress soon started breaking spending caps with "emergency" supplemental bills and other techniques.[13] The budget deal represented a small positive step toward fiscal control, but it was mainly the strong economy that balanced the budget and not the 1997 budget deal. As the booming economy caused tax revenues to soar, the *Congressional Quarterly* joked in

1997; "Clinton and the Republican Congress were in a hurry to seal their deal before the budget balanced itself."[14]

As a twin bill to the 1997 budget law, the Taxpayer Relief Act of 1997 (TRA97) was signed into law by President Clinton in August. TRA97 was expected to save taxpayers $95 billion over 5 years and $275 billion over 10 years, representing a smaller cut than the House had proposed in 1995.[15] Nonetheless, TRA97 included versions of most of the Contract proposals, including a $500 per child tax credit, a cut in the capital gains tax rate from 28 percent to 20 percent (18 percent for investment holdings of 5 years or more), Roth IRAs, and modest estate tax reforms.

1998

After the 1997 tax cut and budget deal, the pendulum swung back to the left on fiscal issues. President Clinton and moderate Senate Republicans resisted calls for further tax and spending cuts. But the House was not giving up the fight yet. Under the leadership of Budget Committee Chairman John Kasich (R-Ohio), the House passed a budget plan that included $101 billion of spending and tax cuts over five years.[16] Kasich had a tough fight securing passage because some House Republicans saw the budget caps from the prior year's budget deal as a spending floor, and they were not interested in any further restraint.[17]

Kasich was one of the dwindling numbers of true believers in smaller government among the Republican revolutionaries. Many members gave up on spending reforms a year or two after the GOP took control of Congress in 1995. The elimination of the deficit in 1998 greatly weakened interest in spending restraint. But as Kasich noted in 1998, "Balancing the budget was never really the goal for me ... [instead it] was a very effective rallying cry to move the troops to be able to reduce the power of government."[18]

In the Senate in 1998, Budget Committee Chairman Pete Domenici, Appropriations Committee Chairman Ted Stevens (R-Alaska), and other deficit hawks and big spenders killed plans for tax and spending cuts after a bitter fight with Senate conservatives. Hard-charging John Ashcroft (R-Mo.) led the attack against Domenici's budget plan and pushed for a large tax cut. Ashcroft said that he was elected to "cut taxes, cut government, and cut the debt."[19] Ultimately, the Senate moderates prevailed, happy to sit on their laurels from the prior year's budget deal and eschew any further reforms.

One of the political dynamics in 1998 was that as large budget surpluses began to appear, conservative Republicans realized that it would be crucial to get the excess funds off the table with big tax cuts, otherwise the excess would be spent on expanded federal programs. Meanwhile, President Clinton's game plan was to fence off the emerging surpluses to foil any further GOP tax-cutting efforts. He did this by arguing that there was no money for tax cuts because the government must "save Social Security first." Clinton's rhetoric was politically effective, but it was empty. The administration did not introduce a serious plan to save Social Security, nor did the administration embrace any of the Social Security reform plans that were being introduced in Congress by members of both parties.

The large differences between the House and Senate budget plans could not be reconciled, and Congress passed no budget resolution in 1998 for the first time since 1974 when the modern budget rules were instituted. The lack of a budget, and President Clinton's opposition, meant that no tax cuts were passed in 1998.

The only bright spot for tax policy that year was the Internal Revenue Service Restructuring Act. The law was enacted after two rounds of congressional hearings that highlighted gross mismanagement at the IRS and the aggressive tactics the agency used in enforcement actions against small businesses and other taxpayers. The IRS legislation was put together following recommendations of the bipartisan National Commission on Restructuring the IRS, led by Sen. Bob Kerrey (D-Neb.) and Rep. Rob Portman (R-Ohio). The bill's new protections for taxpayers were modest but certainly a step in the right direction. The 1998 bill also included an important provision sponsored by Sen. Connie Mack (R-Fla.) to shorten the long-term capital gains holding period from 18 months to 12 months.

1999

The tax policy pendulum swung back to the right this year with strong momentum for tax cuts developing in both the House and Senate. Congress passed a substantial 10-year $792 billion tax cut bill, which included a 1 percentage point cut in individual income tax rates; marriage-penalty relief; a capital gains tax cut; an increase in IRA contribution limits; a phased-in repeal of the estate tax; and other business, education, and health care tax cuts.[20] The tax cut was vetoed by President Clinton in September.

In 1999, as in earlier years, Clinton feigned support for some tax cuts while actually blocking every Republican tax cut proposal. The president's tax policy in most years consisted simply of including an array of special-interest tax breaks in his annual budget proposal to gain support from particular narrow constituencies. Clinton's budgets for FY99 and FY2000 were typical, with numerous narrow tax breaks for education, health care, and energy efficiency.

Certainly, Republicans were just as guilty of supporting pro-complexity special-interest tax breaks. The difference between the parties was that the Republicans also pursued supply-side tax cuts to reduce tax code inefficiencies, and they put a substantial effort into consideration of fundamental tax reform. By contrast, the Clinton administration did not seem to view the complex, high-rate income tax code as a problem worthy of much policy attention. Major tax reform was of little interest to the administration, other than to oppose GOP reform efforts.

2000

After the veto of 1999's all-in-one $792 billion tax cut bill, Republicans changed their strategy. In 2000, they passed two separate and narrowly focused reconciliation tax-cut bills through Congress. A marriage-penalty relief bill would have saved taxpayers $90 billion over five years.[21] It was passed with the support of 51 Democrats in the House and 8 Democrats in the Senate but was vetoed by President Clinton. Similarly, the House and Senate passed a bill to repeal the estate tax with the support of 65 Democrats in the House and 9 Democrats in the Senate.[22] The president promptly vetoed that tax-cut bill as well.

2001

With a huge $5.6 trillion 10-year budget surplus awaiting him, President Bush came into office promising a tax cut of $1.6 trillion over 10 years.[23] His plan passed the House but got somewhat watered down in the Senate. Ultimately, a $1.35 trillion bill passed Congress and was signed into law in June.[24] The Economic Growth and Tax Relief Reconciliation Act was the largest tax cut since 1981 and included an across-the-board reduction in the individual income tax rates. Because of budget rules in the Senate, the president could not get the cuts enacted permanently, and they expire at the end of 2010 unless Congress acts to extend them.

The main elements of EGTRRA were as follows:

- Phased-in reduction of individual income tax rates from 15, 28, 31, 36, and 39.6 percent to 10, 15, 25, 28, 33, and 35 percent
- Phased-in increase in the child tax credit from $500 to $1,000
- Marriage-penalty relief in the form of adjustment of the standard deduction and the 15 percent tax bracket
- Phased-in reduction in estate taxes with a one-year repeal in 2010
- Eight narrow education tax breaks, including education IRAs
- Phased-in expansion of contribution limits for traditional and Roth IRAs to $5,000
- Substantial pension liberalization

EGTRRA's rules regarding when particular tax cuts phase in and phase out over time were absurdly complex. This complexity resulted from the modern congressional practice of beginning tax bill considerations with an overall dollar value first, then trying to fit as many cuts as possible into the legislation under the dollar ceiling. Unfortunately, the excessive focus on the dollar value of tax changes has made nearly every tax bill in recent years very complex. The focus on dollars comes at the expense of designing tax changes that simplify the tax code and improve its efficiency. But despite the complexity, the 2001 tax bill did pack a lot of reform punch as a generally supply-side package of rate cuts and pro-savings provisions.

2002

With concern about the economy in the wake of the 2001 recession, Congress enacted the Job Creation and Worker Assistance Act of 2002 in March. The act's main provision allowed businesses to expense, or immediately write off, 30 percent of the cost of eligible equipment in the year of purchase, on a temporary basis. The 10–year value of this investment tax cut was $16 billion, within an overall tax cut bill of $29 billion.[25]

Although the dollar value of the tax cut was small, partial expensing represents an important step toward converting the income tax to a consumption-based tax system. Consumption-based tax systems, such as the Dick Armey flat tax, would allow full expensing of capital purchases (in place of depreciating purchases over time). Expensing would greatly simplify the tax code and would spur investment by removing taxation on the normal returns to new capital purchases. The 30 percent expensing provision in the 2002 tax bill was subsequently increased to 50 percent in the 2003 tax bill. However, the future of this reform is uncertain because the Bush administration has proposed allowing it to expire at the end of 2004.

2003

With President Bush's leadership, Congress passed the Jobs and Growth Tax Relief Reconciliation Act of 2003 to cut taxes by $350 billion over 10 years.[26] The centerpiece of JGTRRA is reducing the maximum tax rate on capital gains from 20 to 15 percent and the maximum tax rate on dividends from 35 percent to 15 percent. The dividend tax cut was a long time coming; tax policy experts have been concerned about the distortionary effects of the excessive taxation of dividends since at least the 1930s.

JGTRRA included the following tax cuts:

- Reduced the maximum dividend and capital gains tax rates to 15 percent
- Made the phased-in tax rate cuts from the 2001 tax law effective immediately
- Increased capital expensing for business equipment from 30 to 50 percent
- Increased small business expensing from $25,000 to $100,000

Like the tax cuts enacted in the 2001 tax law, the capital gains and dividend cuts from the 2003 law will expire later in the decade unless they are extended by Congress. And, as noted, the 50 percent capital-expensing provision is scheduled to expire at the end of 2004. Most economists would agree that adopting temporary tax changes that phase in and phase out over time is a poor way to make tax policy. Recent tax changes have created planning difficulties for investors, businesses, and other taxpayers that will reduce the positive economic effects of the reforms. A priority for 2005 should be to revisit the Bush tax cuts and enact them permanently.

10 Years of GOP Tax Policy: Good News

Individual Taxes Were Cut

As a result of the 1990s economic boom and the tax rate increases of 1990 and 1993, tax revenues soared from 18.1 percent of gross domestic product in FY94 to 20.9 percent by FY2000, which ties the record high share of GDP set in 1944.[27] The 2001 recession and Bush tax cuts reduced revenues to 15.8 percent of GDP by FY04. Nonetheless, even if President Bush's 2001 and 2003 tax cuts are made permanent, revenues are expected to rise to more than 18 percent of GDP later this decade.[28] This rise is expected to occur partly because of a growing economy and partly because of a rapid increase in alternative minimum tax payments. Because the alternative minimum tax is not indexed for inflation, it will hit an increasing number of taxpayers in future years. If the 2001 and 2003 tax cuts are made permanent, the Congressional Budget Office estimates they would reduce federal revenues by about 1.7 percent of GDP annually by 2014.[29]

The highlights of the GOP's tax cuts include a modest cut in personal income tax rates, a cut in the top capital gains rate from 28 to 15 percent, and a cut in the top dividend tax rate from 39.6 percent to 15 percent. Also, Republicans have substantially cut taxes on savings. IRAs and pension vehicles have been liberalized, health savings accounts were created in 2003, and partial capital expensing (temporarily) was enacted. The crucial question is whether future Congresses will act to retain these pro-growth tax cuts.

Republicans Created a Tax-Cutting Brand Name

Republican leaders in Congress worked hard during the decade to make sure that the GOP gained a brand name as the tax-cutting party. Leading tax-cutters included Dick Armey (House majority leader, 1995–2002), Bill Archer (Ways and Means Committee chairman, 1995–2000), Bill Thomas (Ways and Means Committee chairman, 2001–2004), William Roth (Senate Finance Committee chairman, 1995–2000), and John Kasich (House Budget Committee chairman, 1995–2000). These key party leaders kept Congress focused on pro-growth cuts. In addition, some of these leaders and other members championed fundamental tax reform, including Sens. Richard Shelby (R-Ala.), Connie Mack (R-Fla.), Jon Kyl (R-Ariz.), and Richard Lugar (R-Ind.), and Reps. Billy Tauzin (R-La.), Phil English (R-Pa.), John Linder (R-Ga.), and Phil Crane (R-Ill.).

Bush Focuses on Supply-Side Tax Cuts

Before President Bush came to office in 2001, most GOP tax-cutting efforts were focused on social policy breaks, particularly child tax

Figure 5.1
MAJOR TAX BILLS COMPARED

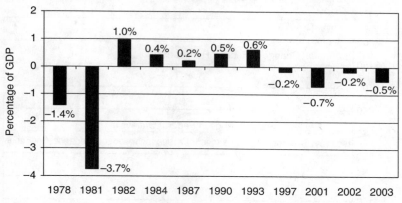

Revenue Effects during the First 5 Years as a Percentage of GDP

SOURCE: Author's calculations based on various Congressional Budget Office reports. The years shown are the years since 1978 that Congress enacted major tax bills. (The Tax Reform Act of 1986 was scored as having a minimal net revenue impact.) The analysis uses the official five-year estimates at the time of enactment of each bill.

credits and marriage-penalty relief. To Bush's credit, he changed course and followed the supply-side tax advice of his two key economists, chairman of the National Economic Council Larry Lindsey and chairman of the Council of Economic Advisors Glenn Hubbard. Although some of Bush's tax proposals have been narrow tax credit provisions, the bulk of his tax cuts have been pro-growth, pro-savings, and pro-investment.

Tax Hikes Are Averted

Before the 1997 tax law, the half-dozen previous major tax laws either imposed tax increases (1982, 1984, 1987, 1990, and 1993) or were roughly revenue neutral (the Tax Reform Act of 1986).[30] (See Figure 5.1.) In addition, the 1983 amendments to Social Security increased taxes. Without the change in policy direction that resulted from the 1994 election, Congress may have continued along the path of tax increases that had dominated recent budget policies. Indeed, in the 1990s Democrats and liberal Republicans led numerous efforts

47

Figure 5.2
FEDERAL REVENUE GROWTH VS. SPENDING GROWTH

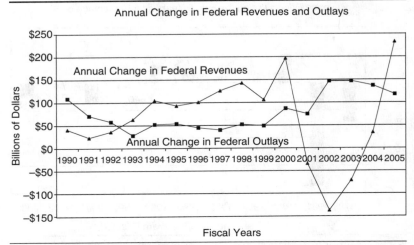

Annual Change in Federal Revenues and Outlays

SOURCE: Author's calculations based on Congressional Budget Office data.
FY05 is the CBO baseline estimate.

to increase cigarette taxes, gasoline taxes, and corporate taxes. These
were mainly averted. For example, President Clinton's FY2000 budget sought a cigarette tax increase of 55 cents per pack and proposed
dozens of corporate tax increase provisions.[31]

Tax Revenue Gusher Was Not All Spent

The economic boom of the 1990s caused income taxes, capital
gains taxes, and corporate profits taxes to pour into federal coffers.
Figure 5.2 shows that revenues were rising by roughly $100 billion
every year. For a few years in the mid-1990s spending increases
were limited to about $50 billion per year, thus preventing the full
gusher of rising tax revenues from being spent. Tax revenues as a
share of GDP rose from 18.5 percent of GDP in FY95 to 20.9 percent
in FY2000.[32] Yet as revenues rose, federal outlays fell from 20.7
percent of GDP to 18.4 percent during the same period. Most of
the reduction was in defense, but even nondefense discretionary
spending fell from 3.7 percent of GDP in FY95 to 3.3 percent by
FY2000. Alas, by 2004 President Bush and the Republican Congress
had completely blown the party's decent fiscal record of the 1990s.

Massive spending increases in recent years pushed outlays back up to 20 percent of GDP by FY04.

Dynamic Scoring Is Partly Instituted

During the last two decades, tax debates in Congress have put an excessive emphasis on the revenue effects of legislation. This trend has unfortunately shifted the policy focus away from the effects that legislation may have on economic growth and tax complexity. To compound the problem, official revenue estimates, which are presented as if carved in stone, have often been inaccurate because they ignored the effects of tax changes on the macroeconomy.

To begin addressing that problem, the Congressional Budget Office and Joint Committee on Taxation have begun to modernize their tax estimating apparatus by bringing macroeconomic modeling into the process.[33] One result should be to make revenue estimates more accurate. In addition, this greater focus on the economic effects of legislation should help sensitize Congress to the fact that tax changes are not just about gaining and losing money for the government budget; tax changes have serious consequences for economic growth and prosperity.

10 Years of GOP Tax Policy: Bad News

Corporate Taxes Have Not Been Cut

Aside from the temporary capital-expensing provisions enacted in 2002 and 2003, corporate taxes have not been substantially cut since 1981. The corporate tax bill enacted in 2004 was scored as being revenue neutral over 10 years and did not contain major reforms. Although many Americans seem to believe that corporations are big winners under Republican governments, that has not been the case. That fact is unfortunate because the U.S. corporate income tax desperately needs to be cut and simplified to adjust to the realities of the increasingly competitive global economy.

U.S. policymakers have been asleep at the switch while nearly every other industrial country has cut its corporate tax rate in recent years. The combined federal and average state corporate tax rate is 40 percent, which is 10 percentage points higher than the average of our 30 major trading partners.[34] Figure 5.3 shows that the average corporate tax rate in the 30-member Organization for Economic Cooperation and Development plunged from 37.6 percent in 1996 to 30.0 percent in 2004.

Figure 5.3
AVERAGE TOP CORPORATE INCOME TAX RATE IN THE 30 MAJOR
INDUSTRIAL COUNTRIES

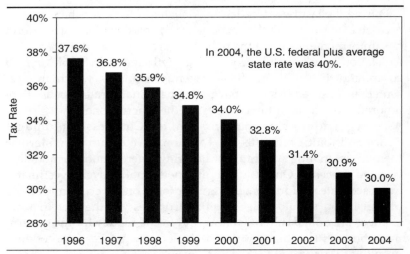

SOURCE: Author's calculations, based on KPMG data for the 30 Organization for Economic Coperation and Development countries, including national and subnational taxes.

America's high corporate tax rate creates many problems. In global markets, it causes U.S. companies to lose out to foreign businesses that face lower tax burdens. It also causes the American economy to lose investment to countries with more inviting tax climates. The high rate has also encouraged companies such as Enron to structure elaborate transactions to avoid corporate taxes.[35] Other U.S. firms have reincorporated abroad in low-tax countries to avoid the uncompetitive U.S. tax rules on foreign investment.

In an attempt to reduce such tax avoidance, U.S. policymakers have proposed and enacted numerous pieces of anti-shelter legislation in recent years, but these Band-Aid fixes just make the tax code more complex and more uncompetitive. A more fundamental response is needed to global tax competition. The U.S. corporate tax rate needs to be cut sharply, and policymakers should consider replacing the corporate income tax with a consumption-based cash-flow tax.[36]

Individual Tax Rates Are Too High

Today's top individual income tax rate of 35 percent is higher than the 28 percent rate achieved in the late 1980s. President Bush's tax cuts have not fully reversed the tax rate increases of Presidents George H. W. Bush in 1990 and Bill Clinton in 1993. The top tax rate is economically very important because of the concentration of small businesses, entrepreneurs, and investors in that rate bracket. Also, the income affected by the top tax rate is the most mobile of all income—as the rate increases, reported income tends to disappear.[37]

A related problem is that the overall income tax code is too progressive, or steeply graduated. For example, the average federal income tax rate (income tax liability divided by adjusted gross income) for those earning over $200,000 was 26 percent in 2002.[38] By comparison, the average tax rate of households earning between $50,000 and $100,000 was 11 percent. Thus, the income tax is vertically very unequal. To increase fairness and equality and to spur economic growth, the top statutory tax rates should be substantially reduced.

Tax Complexity Has Increased

Tax complexity has increased substantially during the past decade. Figure 5.4 shows that the total number of pages in the tax code, tax regulations, and related IRS rules increased almost 50 percent between 1995 and 2004. Table 5.1 provides various other indicators showing that tax complexity has increased under the Republican Congress. Tax forms and IRS instruction books are longer; more different tax forms exist; Americans are spending more money for tax preparation services; and the number of narrow tax breaks, or loopholes, has increased.

Despite occasional calls for tax simplification by members of Congress from both parties, when it comes to actually writing tax legislation, members usually support provisions that increase complexity. Members of Congress seem addicted to narrow tax credits, special deductions, and complex income limitations. For example, the Taxpayer Relief Act of 1997 contained 11 narrow education tax breaks for such items as student loan interest, a tuition tax credit, and an education IRA.[39] Each item has complex requirements related to income, eligibility, and administration.

In 2001, the Joint Committee on Taxation issued a 1,300-page report on simplifying the tax system that had been requested by

Figure 5.4
NUMBER OF PAGES OF FEDERAL TAX RULES

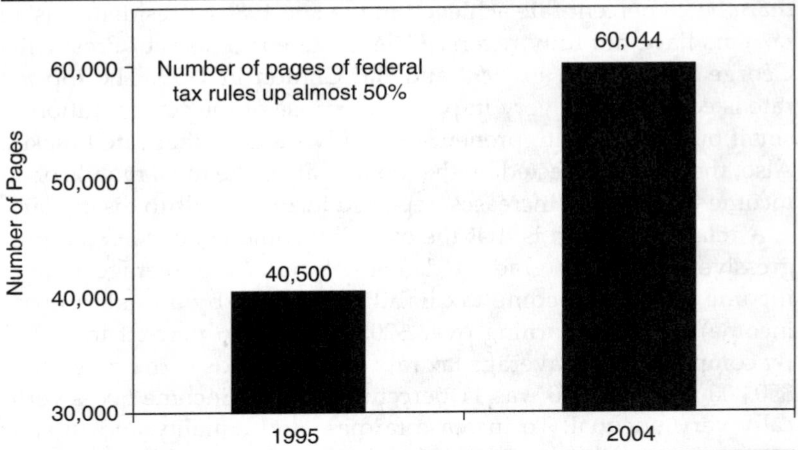

SOURCE: Number of pages in the CCH Inc. *Standard Federal Tax Reporter*, including the tax code, tax regulations, and IRS rulings.

Congress.[40] Despite the report's many useful recommendations, such as eliminating the individual and corporate alternative minimum taxes, Congress ignored it. Yet complexity continues to get worse each year. The alternative minimum tax problem, for example, is set to explode as the number of individuals paying this complex add-on tax rises from 3.7 million in 2004 to 30 million by 2010.[41]

High Deficit Creates Big Tax Threat

Although President Bush and Congress have passed some important tax cuts in recent years, they have let federal spending and the resulting budget deficits explode in size. Taxpayers face a big threat because future Congresses and presidents may use the deficit as an excuse to raise taxes, as President Clinton did in 1993. Federal outlays rose 29 percent under President Bush between FY01 and FY05.[42] This big-spending policy was remarkably irresponsible and short-sighted—both economically and politically—because the resulting deficits will create political pressure to let the 2001 and 2003 tax cuts expire, which would wipe out Bush's primary fiscal achievements.

Table 5.1
RISING TAX COMPLEXITY

Item	Initial Year	Recent Year
Total pages of federal tax rules[a]	1995 40,500	2004 60,044
Number of IRS tax forms[b]	2000 475	2004 529
Number of income tax loopholes for education and training[c]	1994 16	2004 28
Percent of taxpayers using paid tax preparers[d]	1995 50%	2003 62%
H&R Block U.S. tax preparation revenues[e]	1996 $740 million	2003 $1.9 billion
Hours Americans spend filling out tax forms[f]	1995 5.3 billion	2004 6.5 billion
Pages in Form 1040 instruction book[d]	1995 84	2003 131
Average time to complete Form 1040 and Schedules A, B, D[d]	1995 21.2 hours	2003 28.5 hours

SOURCE: Author's calculations, based on the following:
[a] CCH Inc. Including tax code, tax regulations, and IRS rulings.
[b] IRS, Tax Forms and Publications Division.
[c] Author's count of official "tax expenditures."
[d] National Taxpayers Union.
[e] H&R Block, annual reports for various years.
[f] Office of Management and Budget, Information Collection Budget of the U.S. Government, Fiscal Year 2004," www.whitehouse.gov/omb/inforeg/infocoll.html.

Fundamental Reform

The biggest Republican tax policy failure of the past decade has been the inability to move ahead with fundamental tax reform, despite high-level support in Congress. Consider this statement by Bob Dole and Newt Gingrich in the foreword to the 1996 report of the National Commission on Tax Reform and Economic Growth:

> The current tax system is indefensible. It is overly complex, burdensome, and severely limits economic opportunity for all Americans. We made clear on the very first day of the 104th Congress that our top priority would be to change the status quo and to bring fundamental change to America.

> And we agreed that there is no status quo that needs more
> fundamental changing than our tax system. [43]

Despite this top-level call for change, Dick Armey's leadership, the efforts of leading think tanks, and the enthusiasm of many citizens for reform, legislation to overhaul the tax system was not moved through the House or the Senate.

Within months of coming to power in 1995, Republicans began holding congressional hearings on fundamental tax reform, and many members introduced tax reform legislation. Most plans proposed replacing the individual and corporate income taxes with a simpler and more efficient consumption-based system. One leading reform idea was the consumption-based flat tax introduced by Dick Armey in June 1994, which was modeled on a 1981 plan by Hoover Institution economists Robert Hall and Alvin Rabushka. Following Armey's lead, Steve Forbes campaigned for president in 1996 with a flat tax as the centerpiece of his platform. Tax reform was so popular that even moderates, such as Arlen Specter, and liberals, such as Richard Gephardt, had their own flat tax plans (Specter's was a derivation of Hall-Rabushka; Gephardt's was a not-very-flat income tax).

A competing reform idea is replacing the income tax with a national retail sales tax. Senator Richard Lugar introduced his retail sales tax plan in April 1995. He was followed by Ways and Means Chairman Bill Archer (R-Tex.), who said he wanted to "tear out the income tax by its roots."[44] and replace it with a sales tax. Another reform idea is the pro-savings USA Tax proposal, currently championed by Rep. Phil English (R-Pa.). Many articles and books during the 1990s examined the economic growth and simplification advantages of consumption-based taxation, including early studies by the Cato Institute.[45]

Despite all the support for fundamental tax reform inside and outside the beltway, it has not happened yet. Why not?

- *Splits exist among tax reformers.* Nearly all the major tax reform plans of recent years, including the flat tax, retail sales tax, and the USA Tax proposal, have been economically similar in that they all rely on a savings-exempt or consumption-based structure. However, the reform plans have differed on key design features, such as the point of collection and the treatment of imports and exports. Those differences have been substantial enough to hold up agreement on a common Republican tax reform plan.

- *Big business has not gotten on board.* Corporations spend millions of dollars lobbying to gain narrow tax breaks and to defend against narrow tax increases. But most companies put little effort into supporting fundamental tax reform. Part of the problem is that the last major tax "reform" bill—the Tax Reform Act of 1986—imposed a substantial tax increase on corporations. Thus, businesses are justifiably concerned that "reform" means an increase for them. Nonetheless, corporations should consider that the past decade of lobbying for narrow provisions has gotten them little: the corporate tax is more punitive than ever. The corporate tax bill passed in 2004 contains only limited real reforms and does not solve major problems with the corporate tax. Big businesses need to rethink their strategy and work toward common reform goals that would benefit companies in all industries, such as an overall corporate tax rate cut.

- *Social engineering undercuts reform.* A good deal of the GOP's tax policy focus during the past decade has been on narrow social policy tax breaks. This focus diverted energy from consideration of fundamental tax reform, and it has made reform harder to achieve because narrow breaks create new constituencies against reform. For example, families with children may now be against any simple and neutral tax reform plan if it took away the recently enacted $1,000 child tax credit. Both parties deserve blame for social engineering in the tax code. Although the mortgage interest deduction and other special breaks were in code before the Republicans took control of Congress, the GOP's tax policies in some cases have made reform harder to achieve.[46]

- *Fewer Americans are paying income tax.* Since the 1980s, Congress has steadily reduced the constituency for tax reform by taking millions of moderate-income Americans off the tax rolls. Expansion of the earned-income tax credit in 1990 and 1993, the child tax credit, the new 10 percent tax bracket, and other provisions have had the effect of zeroing out income tax liability for millions of families. By 2003, 60 million of 150 million U.S. households (39 percent) did not pay a dime of federal income tax.[47]

Although it is good that many Americans have achieved tax freedom, the problem is that this policy has created a large group with a strong interest against any tax reform that asks them to pay even a simple low-rate tax.

- *Democrats oppose reform.* In the 1980s, tax reform was a bipartisan concern with prominent Democrats and liberal think tanks offering reform proposals. Former senator Dennis DeConcini of Arizona and representative Leon Panetta of California, both Democrats, first introduced versions of the Hall-Rabushka flat tax plan in Congress in early 1982, months after Hall and Rabushka crafted their proposal.[48] In 1985, the Brookings Institution's Henry Aaron and Harvey Galper proposed a comprehensive consumption-based tax plan.[49] But upon becoming the minority party in the 1990s, the Democrats have become very reactionary on tax policy. They have focused their energy on throwing darts at Republican tax reform plans, while offering no reform alternatives of their own. For tax reform to move ahead, it may be necessary for some forward-thinking Democrats to get on board the tax reform movement.

Conclusion

Despite the hurdles, one can bet that serious tax reform will come back onto the agenda in Washington. The last decade of tax debates has shown that both tax cuts and major tax reform ideas are popular with the general public. Tax cutting continues to be a key to the electoral success of the Republican Congress.

Dynamics in the tax system will also raise the profile of reform. Tax complexity continues to spiral upward and the alternative minimum tax will soon be hitting 30 million American households. These dynamics may spur a tax revolt and demands for a major tax-system overhaul. Also, the federal corporate income tax is headed for a train wreck as other countries continue to cut their statutory rates and investment capital becomes ever more globally mobile.

The tax reform ingredient that is missing right now is a new generation of Republican leaders to build on the efforts of Bill Archer, Dick Armey, and other reformers of the 1990s.

Notes

1. Joint Committee on Taxation (JCT), "Analysis of Estimated Effects on Fiscal Year Budget Receipts of the Revenue Provisions in the 'Contract with America'," JCX-4-95, February 6, 1995, www.house.gov/jct/pubs95.html.

2. *CQ Almanac, 1995,* vol. LI (Washington: Congressional Quarterly Inc., 1996), p. 2-34.

3. Ibid.

4. JCT, "Conference Agreement—Estimated Budget Effects of Revenue Reconciliation and Tax Simplification Provisions of HR 2491," JCX-53-95, November 16, 1995. www.house.gov/jct/pubs95.html.

5. *CQ Almanac, 1995,* vol. LI (Washington: Congressional Quarterly Inc., 1996), pp. 2-30, 2-33.

6. *Budget of the U.S. Government, Fiscal Year 1996* (Washington: Government Printing Office, 1995), p. 173.

7. *CQ Almanac, 1995,* vol. LI (Washington: Congressional Quarterly Inc., 1996), pp. 2-21, 2-28.

8. *CQ Almanac, 1997,* vol. LIII (Washington: Congressional Quarterly Inc., 1998), p. 2-18.

9. *CQ Almanac, 1995,* vol. LI (Washington: Congressional Quarterly Inc., 1996), p. 2-21.

10. National Commission on Tax Reform and Economic Growth, "Unleashing America's Potential," January 1996, www.empower.org/kempcommission/ kempcommission_toc.htm.

11. Congressional Budget Office, "The Economic and Budget Outlook, FY1996–2000," January 1995, www.cbo.gov/Pubs.cfm.

12. Congressional Budget Office, "The Economic and Budget Outlook, An Update," September 1997, Table 12, www.cbo.gov.

13. *CQ Almanac, 1997,* p. 2-27. In 1998, Congress busted the prior year's caps with a $21 billion supplemental bill and other spending increases. See *CQ Almanac, 1998,* vol. LIV (Washington: Congressional Quarterly Inc., 1999), p. 2-117.

14. *CQ Almanac, 1997,* vol. LIII (Washington: Congressional Quarterly Inc., 1998), p. 2-18.

15. JCT, "Estimated Budget Effects of the Conference Agreement on the Revenue Provisions of HR 2014," JCX-39-97, July 30, 1997, www.house.gov/jct/pubs97.html.

16. *CQ Almanac 1998,* p. 6-12.

17. Ibid., p. 6-9.

18. Ibid., p. 6-11.

19. Ibid., p. 6-6.

20. The bill was titled the Taxpayer Refund and Relief Act of 1999. See JCT, "Estimated Budget Effects of the Conference Agreement for HR 2488," JCX-61-99R, August 5, 1999, www.house.gov/jct/pubs99.html.

21. JCT, "Estimated Revenue Effects of the Conference Agreement for HR 4810," JCX-79-00, July 19, 2000, www.house.gov/jct/pubs00.html.

22. *CQ Almanac, 2000,* vol. LVI (Washington: Congressional Quarterly Inc., 2001) p. 18-2.

23. Office of Management and Budget, *A Blueprint for New Beginnings: A Responsible Budget for America's Priorities* (Washington: Government Printing Office, 2001), pp. 186, 194.

24. JCT, "Estimated Budget Effects of the Conference Agreement for HR 1836," JCX-51-01, May 26, 2001, www.house.gov/jct/pubs01.html. This figure represents the 11-year revenue change, FY01 to FY11.

25. JCT, "Estimated Budget Effects of the Job Creation and Worker Assistance Act of 2002," JCX-13-02, March 6, 2002, www.house.gov/jct/pubs02.html.

26. JCT, "Estimated Budget Effects of the Conference Agreement for HR2," JCX-55-03, May 22, 2003, www.house.gov/jct/pubs03.html.

27. *Budget of the U.S. Government, Fiscal Year 2005, Historical Tables* (Washington: Government Printing Office, 2004) p. 34.

28. Congressional Budget Office, "An Analysis of the President's Budgetary Proposals for Fiscal Year 2005," March 2004, p. 3, www.cbo.gov.

29. Ibid.

30. CBO, "Projected Federal Tax Revenues and the Effect of Changes in Tax Law," December 1998, www.cbo.gov.

31. *Budget of the U.S. Government, FY2005*, p. 374.

32. Ibid., *Historical Tables*, p. 34.

33. For background, see David Burton, "Reforming the Federal Tax Policy Process," Cato Institute Policy Analysis no. 463, December 17, 2002.

34. Chris Edwards, "The Corporate Income Tax and the Global Economy," Cato Institute Tax & Budget Bulletin no. 18, September 2003, as updated to 2004. Based on data from KPMG.

35. For a thorough discussion, see Chris Edwards, "Replacing the Scandal-Plagued Corporate Income Tax with a Cash-Flow Tax," Cato Institute Policy Analysis no. 484, August 14, 2003.

36. Ibid.

37. For a summary of the literature, see Chris Edwards, "Economic Benefits of Personal Income Tax Rate Reductions," Joint Economic Committee, April 2001.

38. Internal Revenue Service, "Individual Income Tax Returns: Preliminary Data, 2002," *SOI Bulletin*, Winter 2003–2004, p. 6.

39. JCT, JCX-39-97, July 30, 1997.

40. JCT, *Study of the Overall State of the Federal Tax System and Recommendations for Simplification*, JCS-3-01 (Washington: Government Printing Office, April 2001).

41. JCT, JCX-55-03, May 22, 2003.

42. CBO, "Analysis of President's Budgetary Proposals FY05," p. 3.

43. National Commission on Tax Reform and Economic Growth, "Unleashing America's Potential," January 1996, www.empower.org/kempcommission/kempcommission_toc.htm.

44. As quoted by Dick Armey in "Caveat Emptor: The Case against the National Sales Tax," *Policy Review* no. 73, Summer 1995.

45. For example, see Laurence J. Kotlikoff, "The Economic Impact of Replacing Federal Income Taxes with a Sales Tax," Cato Institute Policy Analysis no. 193, April 15, 1993.

46. It is also true that the GOP's tax rate cuts and pro-savings changes have made tax reform easier because they move the tax code toward a low-rate consumption-based system.

47. JCT, "Estimates of Federal Tax Expenditures for Fiscal years 2004–2008," JCS-8-03, December 22, 2003, p. 30.

48. Robert Hall and Alvin Rabushka, *The Flat Tax*, 2d ed. (Stanford: Hoover Institution Press, 1995), p. 47.

49. Henry Aaron and Harvey Galper, *Assessing Tax Reform* (Washington: Brookings Institution, 1985). Aaron and Galper called their plan a "cash flow income tax." The plan would have combined a personal consumed-income tax, a business cash flow tax, and a tax on estates and gifts.

6. The Federal Budget 10 Years Later: The Triumph of Big Government

Stephen Moore

The Contract with America that helped sweep Republicans into power a decade ago promised a bold agenda to change the government. It included reforms in 10 policy areas such as welfare, term limits, tax cuts, congressional governance, and, most important, budget reduction. Rep. Newt Gingrich (R-Ga.) promised that Republicans would make the government smaller and smarter and get rid of programs, not just start them.

I will never forget when I first heard of the Contract with America in 1994. My boss at that time, Rep. Dick Armey (R-Tex.), the second most powerful House Republican, told me that the Contract would help sweep Republicans into the majority for the first time in 40 years. I had a hard time not laughing. The idea of a Republican majority seemed as improbable as my beloved Cubs winning the World Series. But I got to work helping construct the tax and budget provisions of the Contract.

It is chic these days to criticize the Contract and write off the Republican revolution as a failure. That is a misreading of history. Much of importance was accomplished during the first 100 days in 1995. For the first time, Republicans required Congress to live by the rules that it imposed on the rest of the nation. Term limits were imposed on House committee chairs. The first steps toward meaningful litigation reform were taken. Perhaps most impressive, the budget was balanced, not in seven years as originally planned, but in three years.

The new Republican majority saw other triumphs. Perhaps the biggest was strong-arming President Bill Clinton into signing the most historic social reform bill of the last 50 years: the 1996 welfare reform law. Since 1996, welfare caseloads have been cut by more than half, and many people previously on welfare are now leading productive lives in the work force.

Even in the fight to cut the federal budget, there were some early victories. By fiscal year 1999, real discretionary outlays were actually lower than when Republicans came to office in FY95.[1] Even real nondefense outlays were initially reduced. There was a new ethic of fiscal restraint in Congress—at least temporarily—rather than fiscal expansion.

In March 1995 House Majority Leader Dick Armey asked me to edit a book for the House Republicans titled *Restoring the Dream: The Bold New Plan by House Republicans*.[2] It was a follow-up to the *New York Times* best seller of 1994, *Contract with America*.[3] This project gave me a front-row seat in the budget battles of 1995, which included the high-stakes showdown between Gingrich and Clinton and the subsequent government shutdown. Those were heady days for Republicans. We felt that we really could "change the way government operates before Easter," as Gingrich put it. We felt that Clinton was irrelevant to the budget and that he would give in quickly in any showdown. Polls at that time showed that public discontent with government was at 70 percent.[4] One poll showed that Americans believed that roughly 50 cents of every dollar sent to Washington was wasted.[5] Cutting the budget seemed easy because the public was demanding it.

I was proud to work with the young and energetic House Budget Committee chairman, John Kasich (R-Ohio), who put together the original Contract with America budget for FY96. It was a remarkable document—something we have not seen the likes of since. Kasich's budget slated more than 200 programs for termination. Some programs were little more than political slush funds for special interest constituencies, such as the Legal Services Corporation, bilingual education funding, and President Clinton's program for an army of AmeriCorps "volunteers." That budget also tried to defund programs that Ronald Reagan had tried to kill, such as the Economic Development Administration, Amtrak subsidies, federal transit grants, the Appalachian Regional Commission, and maritime subsidies. Most impressive of all, the FY96 House budget called for the elimination of three cabinet departments: Commerce, Education, and Energy.

Ultimately, politics triumphed over fiscal common sense and most of the proposed budget cuts were not made. The following sections review what happened in the war against big-government spending.

The Fiscal Revolution

Arguably Newt Gingrich's finest hour as Speaker of the House was when he persuaded House Republicans to adopt a seven-year balanced budget plan. Balancing the budget was a key promise of the incoming Republicans—a fundamental change in direction after 25 consecutive years of budget deficits. But many in the GOP caucus thought that eliminating the $200 billion deficit could not be achieved by 2002—especially with tax cuts also in the budget package. Yet, Newt Gingrich cajoled House members into adopting a balanced budget plan that cut taxes by $245 billion over seven years.[6]

The House budget called for cutbacks in most domestic agencies and it even sought to trim Medicare. Democrats went all out to thwart the cuts, charging that the Republicans were going to defund Medicare, Medicaid, and environmental programs. Republicans said they were only going to cut the growth rate of Medicare, but even that modest reform was politically difficult with the Democrats running a "Medi-scare" political campaign. As Ronald Reagan learned in the 1980s, Democrats will demagogue even small reforms to entitlement programs for seniors. When Bill Clinton vetoed the Republican budget for FY96, which led to brief government shutdowns, the Democrats charged that Medicare reforms were aimed at financing "tax cuts for the rich."

Even though Republicans "lost" the budget showdown with Clinton, they still accomplished some of what they set out to do. In 1996, for the first time in years many federal agencies saw a decline in their budgets, and nondefense discretionary spending fell slightly.[7] Unfortunately, the new ethic of fiscal restraint was short-lived.

Although House budgets at the start of the GOP revolution called for the elimination of hundreds of programs, most of those programs are still flourishing today. A Cato Institute study in 2000, "The Return of the Living Dead: Federal Programs That Survived the Republican Revolution," found that very few programs were killed, and combined spending on programs that had been slated for termination was higher than when the GOP took over Congress.[8] During George W. Bush's presidency most of these programs expanded even further. Here are some examples of unreformed programs:

- *AmeriCorps.* One of President Clinton's pet projects, AmeriCorps has seen its outlays quadruple from $127 million in FY94 to

$503 million in FY03. AmeriCorps is part of the government's Corporation for National and Community Service (CNCS), which had outlays of $609 million in FY04. CNCS outlays are set to jump to $990 million under President Bush's budget for FY05.[9]

- *Amtrak.* The government passenger rail system was supposed to be financially self-sufficient by FY02, but the taxpayer subsidies continue. The railroad received $1.2 billion in FY04.[10]

- *Medicare.* Runaway entitlement programs are a key cause of the ongoing budget crisis. But what began as a Republican crusade to cut Medicare costs in the 1990s ended in 2003 with a Republican law to expand the program by $534 billion over 10 years with a new prescription drug benefit. The GOP drug plan is more than three times more costly than the drug plan proposed by Clinton in his FY01 budget.[11]

- *Department of Education.* Ronald Reagan in the 1980s and the Republicans in the 1990s argued that this department should be shut down because it has no demonstrated effect on school performance and the nation's schools are properly a state, local, and private responsibility. Department outlays increased from $31 billion in FY95 to $36 billion by FY01.[12] Outlays exploded under President Bush, reaching $63 billion by FY04, or double the level when the GOP came to power. Republicans now boast openly of outspending the Democrats on education.

- *Pork-barrel spending.* Another disturbing trend has been the reemergence of the very kind of wasteful pork-barrel spending that the Republicans would deride when they were in the minority. There is a rising trend of earmarked pork programs for particular states and congressional districts. The omnibus spending bill that passed in early 2004 contained an enormous 7,931 earmarked pork projects—about twice the number that the Democrats typically included when they held power.[13] Projects included $50 million for an indoor rainforest in Iowa, $200,000 for the University of Hawaii to produce a documentary on hunting techniques of the Kalahari Bushmen, and $200,000 to the Rock and Roll Hall of Fame in Cleveland for the "Rockin' the Schools" program.[14] The Bush administration urged passage of the bill.

The first few Republican budgets did slow the growth of spending, which helped balance the budget in FY98, four years ahead of the

Table 6.1
THE "PEACE DIVIDEND" GETS SPENT

Fiscal Years	Defense Spending	Social Spending
	Billions of 2000 Dollars	
1989	400	883
2001	298	1,322
2004	413	1,585
	Change	
1989–2001	−102	439
2001–2004	115	263
	Percentage Change	
1989–2001	−26	50
2001–2004	39	20

SOURCE: *Budget of the U.S. Government, Fiscal Year 2005 Historical Tables* (Washington: Government Printing Office, 2004), p. 126.
NOTE: Social spending includes all nondefense, noninterest spending.

original schedule. In FY94 the budget deficit was $203 billion and was expected to stay that high for years to come. Yet after five years of Republican control of Congress, the surplus reached $236 billion in FY2000.[15]

The budget improvement, however, resulted mainly from the strong economic expansion of the late 1990s and record high tax revenues. Also, cuts to the defense budget after the end of the Cold War helped offset nondefense increases. Table 6.1 shows what happened to the "peace dividend"—the excess of funds that materialized as defense spending fell. Between FY89 (the peak year for real defense spending in recent decades) and FY01, real defense spending fell by 26 percent. During that same period, all other federal spending (excluding interest) rose 50 percent. Clearly, the peace dividend was more than spent.

In recent years, both defense and nondefense spending have risen rapidly. The trend of ever larger domestic budgets under Republicans is demoralizing. Figure 6.1 shows that recent Congresses have increased spending at rapid rates. The 104th Congress cut real spending, but by nowhere near as much as Ronald Reagan and the 97th Congress did. During the 10-year period FY95–FY05, real nondefense discretionary spending increased 39 percent.[16]

Figure 6.1
PERCENTAGE CHANGE IN REAL NONDEFENSE DISCRETIONARY
OUTLAYS

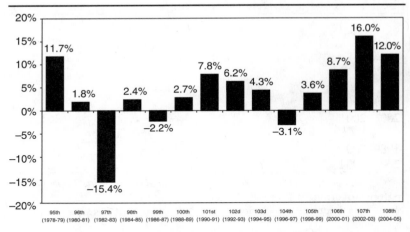

Congress and Related Budget Fiscal Years

SOURCE: *Budget of the United States, FY2005, Historical Tables* (Washington: Government Printing Office, 2004).

The fiscal metamorphosis of the GOP into a big-spending party was described by Jeff Flake (R-Ariz.), who was elected in 2000. He complained that "every vote I have taken in my first 6 months in Congress was to increase spending. There was not one vote to save money."[17] The National Taxpayers Union reported that in 1995 and 1996 more than 500 members of Congress cast votes to cut spending. But by the late 1990s, only 2 members' overall votes would cut spending on net, James Sessenbrenner (R-Wis.) and Ron Paul (R-Tex.).[18] NTU data show that most Republicans and Democrats now sponsor dozens of bills to raise federal spending for each bill they sponsor to reduce spending.

Republicans Break the Bank under President Bush

Under President Bush (and a Republican Congress) federal outlays increased 28 percent between FY01 and FY05.[19] Nondefense discretionary spending increased 34 percent during these four years. That fiscal policy is exactly the opposite of what was promised by Republican leaders when they first came to power in the 1990s.

When spending started speeding up in the late 1990s, Republicans blamed it on Bill Clinton. Yet the president is not capable of spending a single dime without congressional approval. In any case, Newt Gingrich and other Republican leaders said that when the GOP had the White House, the budget would be cut in short order. But in just the first two years under President Bush, the real nondefense discretionary budget grew by more than during Clinton's eight years in office.[20] Both Bush and Congress share the blame. Although Congress has the main control over spending, Bush has not vetoed a single bill, which would have sent a strong message to Congress that spending is too high. If Bush is displeased with big spending in Congress, he has shown no sign of it.

How much of the recent spending spree is a result of the war on terrorism? Recent nondefense spending increases include some money for homeland security. But the recent spending spree is spread across many federal agencies, whether or not they have a security function. Besides, nondefense spending was rising rapidly even before September 11, 2001. Also note that pork-barrel special projects aimed at particular congressional districts have skyrocketed.

Increased war spending should lead to smaller, not larger, domestic budgets. During national security crises in the past, domestic agency budgets have shrunk so that every available dollar could be devoted to protecting America. But just the opposite has happened since September 2001, with special interest groups and congressional appropriators trying to wrap every parochial spending request in Old Glory. Figure 6.2 shows that spending on both guns and butter is rising. Meanwhile, the budget surpluses of the late 1990s that Republicans fought hard to achieve have turned into budget deficits of more than $400 billion. Under Bush, the Grand Old Party has become the Grand Old Spending Party.

The Farm Bill Fiasco

Congressional Republicans no longer have an anti–big government agenda. Nowhere is that more evident than in federal farm policy. One of the top accomplishments of the Republican Congress was the "Freedom to Farm" Bill of 1996. It was designed to phase out crop subsidies over seven years so that farmers could produce for the market rather than Uncle Sam.

65

Figure 6.2
GUNS AND BUTTER: REAL DISCRETIONARY SPENDING EXPLODES

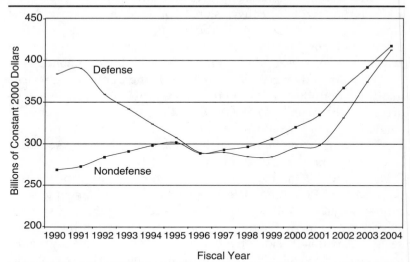

SOURCE: *Budget of the U.S. Government Fiscal Year 2005, Historical Tables.*

That legislation was eviscerated by the 2002 Farm Bill. That bill increased farm subsidies—which were already too high—by $87 billion over 10 years.[21] Florida citrus growers received more subsidies; the infamous wool and mohair subsidy was resurrected; Connecticut oystermen received an emergency bailout; and the loan program for Florida sugar plantations was made more generous. Avocado farmers in California will receive funds from a new tax on imported avocados to fund research and marketing campaigns. And the federal government will purchase $30 million a year of cranberry juice, benefiting big companies such as Ocean Spray.

The Market Access Program annually hands out more than $100 million to farm-related businesses to pay for their foreign marketing expenses.[22] This program received a doubling of funds under the Republican farm subsidy law of 2002.[23] The program subsidizes entities such as the Hop Growers of America, the Wine Institute, Welch's, the Popcorn Board, and the Pet Food Institute.

The strange resurrection of the wool and mohair subsidy in the 2002 bill is symptomatic of the collapse of budget restraint. Created in the 1950s during the Korean War, this subsidy was said to be vital for national security because it would ensure that there was enough domestic wool production to put uniforms on soldiers. Starting in the 1960s the Pentagon switched to cotton and synthetics for uniforms, thus eliminating the national security rationale for wool and mohair subsidies.

But the subsidies did not disappear. Over the next 30 years, federal taxpayers continued to fund America's sheepherders and goat herders. In the 1990s, the program started getting bad publicity as it became clear that taxpayers were getting fleeced. The *Wall Street Journal* famously reported in 1995 that the third-largest recipient of wool subsidies in Lincoln County, New Mexico, was sheepherder Sam Donaldson of ABC news.[24] Donaldson had pocketed as much as $97,000 in subsidy payments, with the checks sent to his suburban Virginia home. Congress finally voted to phase out the subsidies.

However, in recent years wool and mohair subsidies rose from the dead. The 2002 Farm Bill reestablishes subsidies for mohair producers.[25] Clearly, the lunacy of federal farm policies remains intact 10 years after the Contract with America. Farmers are still not operating in the free-market environment that most other businesses confront every day. When the 1996 farm reform law was passed, the Congressional Budget Office projected that $47 billion would be spent on direct farm subsidies over 7 years.[26] Instead, farm subsidies ended up costing $117 billion over 7 years.[27] No doubt the new farm subsidy bill will cost taxpayers far more than was promised as well.

Is Trying to Cut the Budget Futile?

Fiscal conservatives in Congress made only slight and temporary progress in slowing government growth. After 10 years of Republican control, the business-as-usual approach to budgets has triumphed. Democrat appropriators ("cardinals") on Capitol Hill have simply handed over the reins of power to pro-spending Republican cardinals.

Some analysts conclude that the goal of limiting government is futile because politicians are simply giving the voters what they want. That conclusion is wrong. By two-to-one margins Americans still say that they prefer less government and lower taxes to more government and higher taxes. Two-thirds of voters consistently say they think their taxes are too high, not too low. The goal of cutting the budget is not flawed, but the game plan has been. The GOP's budget strategy has failed for five reasons:

1. Since the Tim Penny–John Kasich effort to eliminate wasteful programs in 1993, there has not been a bipartisan effort to cut spending. Republican budgets have been devised in a partisan way that fails to reach out to moderate "blue dog" Democrats, some of whom are more fiscally conservative than old-bull Republicans. One lesson of both the Reagan and Gingrich eras is that cutting wasteful programs is much easier if there is bipartisan support.

2. Would-be budget cutters need to recognize that the budget process is severely biased in favor of increased spending. Fiscal conservatives in Congress have devoted insufficient attention to institutional reforms—changing the fiscal rules of the game to end the pro-spending tilt.

3. Advocates of limited government in Congress need to constantly remind voters of all the inept ways that Washington spends their money. For example, Michigan Republican Pete Hoekstra publishes a monthly "Tale of Bureaucracy" with easily digestible horror stories of Washington waste. Many federal agencies cannot pass a simple financial audit and cannot account for billions of dollars. When Americans realized how much waste there was in the Pentagon in the 1980s—auditors discovered $300 hammers and $600 toilet seats—they were outraged. That created political momentum to begin weeding out some of the Pentagon waste.

4. Budget reduction plans need to be perceived as fair-minded by the public. One of the reasons that Republicans have not gained more traction for cuts is that the GOP's budget knife usually spares corporate welfare, yet it does sometimes go after programs for the poor. Back in 1995, the *Washington Post* assessed the budget plan of the new GOP Congress by declaring, "Everything seems to get cut—but not corporate welfare."[28]

5. Budget-cutting proposals should not rely exclusively on deficit reduction as a rationale. One lesson of the 1990s is that focusing on deficit reduction as the reason for controlling spending risks a collapse of restraint when the deficit is falling or eliminated.

Budget cutters need to convince the public that there is a financial and freedom dividend from smaller government. The crusade for smaller government should be linked to pro-growth tax cuts.

Lessons Learned in the War against Big Government

What lessons can be learned from the Contract with America and its aftermath? First, despite the failure of Republicans to tame the budget, there were major domestic policy accomplishments. The 1994 elections launched one of the most successful political reform eras in American history. Welfare reform, the balanced budget, tax cuts, the new congressional ethics laws, and the cleanup of the corrupt practices of prior Congresses were true victories. The Newt Gingrich and Dick Armey–led revolution furthered the goals of the 1980s Reagan revolution.

The stock market roared back to life almost on the day that the Republicans were elected to the majority. In November 1994, the Dow Jones Industrial Average was less than 4,000; by 1999 it had topped 10,000. This was a period of unparalleled wealth creation and prosperity. Whatever the Republicans did, the bulls in the financial markets clamored their approval.

Nonetheless, one lesson is that political revolutions in America are short-lived. Reformers come in and change course, but soon the forces of inertia overwhelm the change agents. The Gingrich Republicans ran out of gas. Similarly, the Reagan administration accomplished its major economic victories in its first two years. Some critics look back and say that Republicans tried to do too much, too quickly. That view is completely wrong. The window of political opportunity shuts rapidly, thus it is best to do as much as you can while the opposition is in disarray.

The two most important elections in the past 50 years were the 1980 election of Reagan and the 1994 congressional elections. The Gingrich Republicans were a heroic bunch. They did a great service in changing course after two years of Clintonomics, which included anti-growth tax hikes and a proposed national health care plan. The Contract with America contained policies that sharply changed direction.

The tragedy is that many of the Republicans who led the revolution have settled into power, become too comfortable with their perks and authority, and are now mirror images of what they replaced. The Republicans are now spending money faster than the Democrats ever did and have forgotten why voters put them in power in the first place. Perhaps it is time for fiscal conservatives to start plotting the next revolution.

Notes

1. *Budget of the U.S. Government, Fiscal Year 2005, Historical Tables* (Washington: Government Printing Office, 2004), p. 126.

2. Stephen Moore, ed., *Restoring the Dream: The Bold New Plan by House Republicans* (New York: Times Books, 1995).

3. Ed Gillespie and Bob Schellhas, eds., *Contract with America: The Bold Plan by Rep. Newt Gingrich, Rep. Dick Armey and the House Republicans to Change the Nation* (New York: Times Books, 1994).

4. Dan Balz, "Dole Must Conquer Time and History; Hurdles Jam Path to White House," *Washington Post*, July 7, 1996, p. A1.

5. Karlyn Bowman, "Flat Tax Fever? Depends on What the Pollsters Ask," *Roll Call*, February 5, 1996.

6. For the tax cut score, see Joint Committee on Taxation, "Estimated Budget Effects of Revenue Reconciliation and Tax Simplification Provisions of HR 2491," JCX-53-95, November 16, 1995, www.house.gov/jct/pubs95.html.

7. *Budget of the U.S. Government, Fiscal Year 2005, Historical Tables*, p. 125.

8. Stephen Moore and Stephen Slivinski, "The Return of the Living Dead: Federal Programs That Survived the Republican Revolution," Cato Policy Analysis no. 375, July 24, 2000.

9. *Budget of the U.S. Government, Fiscal Year 2005, Analytical Perspectives*, p. 114.

10. Ibid., p. 83.

11. *Budget of the U.S. Government, Fiscal Year 2001* (Washington: Government Printing Office, 2000), p. 401. The Clinton plan cost $167 billion over 10 years.

12. *Budget of the U.S. Government, Fiscal Year 2005, Historical Tables*, p. 76.

13. Taxpayers for Common Sense, "Statement by Jill Lancelot on the Omnibus Spending Bill," January 22, 2004, www.taxpayer.net.

14. Taxpayers for Common Sense, "Statement on Omnibus Spending Bill," December 8, 2003, www.taxpayer.net.

15. *Budget of the U.S. Government, Fiscal Year 2005, Historical Tables*, p. 22.

16. Ibid., p. 126.

17. Jeff Flake, personal communication with author. See Stephen Moore, "Who Lost the Big Economic Dividend?" *Washington Times*, January 27, 2002, p. B1.

18. Jeff Dircksen, "A Reality TV Show out of Touch with Fiscal Realities," National Taxpayers Union Foundation, Policy Paper no. 151, Vote Tally Report 108-1, June 17, 2004. See also Vote Tally data at www.ntu.org/main/components/congressby-num/vt106_c2.pdf.

19. *Budget of the U.S. Government, Fiscal Year 2005, Historical Tables*, p. 125. Also see Congressional Budget Office, "An Analysis of the President's Budgetary Proposals of FY2005," March 2004, www.cbo.gov.

20. *Budget of the U.S. Government, Fiscal Year 2005, Historical Tables*, p. 126.

21. Congressional Budget Office, "Pay-As-You-Go Estimate," for HR 2646, Farm Security and Rural Investment Act of 2002, May 22, 2002 (Washington: Congressional Budget Office, 2002).

22. U.S. Department of Agriculture, press release, June 6, 2003, www.usda.gov/news/releases.

23. Ibid.

24. Bruce Ingersoll, "As Congress Considers Slashing Crop Subsidies, Affluent Urban Farmers Come under Scrutiny," *Wall Street Journal*, March 16, 1995.

25. See U.S. Department of Agriculture, "Wool and Mohair Marketing Assistance Loan and Loan Deficiency Payment Program," April 2003, www.fsa.usda.gov/pas/publications/facts/html/woolmoh03.htm.

26. Cited in David Orden, Robert Paarlberg, and Terry Roe, *Policy Reform in American Agriculture: Analysis and Prognosis* (Chicago: University of Chicago Press, 1999), p. 152.

27. *Budget of the U.S. Government, Fiscal Year 2005, Historical Tables*, p. 57. This number is the seven-year total (1996–2002) for Farm Income Stabilization.

28. Brian Kelly, "The Pork That Just Won't Slice; Everything Gets Cut—but Not Corporate Welfare," *Washington Post*, December 10, 1995, p. C1.

7. A Decade of Republican Trade Policy: A Modest Record of Accomplishment

Daniel Griswold

The Contract with America did not explicitly mention trade policy, but the GOP's stated commitments to freer markets and reducing regulation implied a policy of greater freedom for international trade. This chapter assesses whether the Republican Congress moved the nation closer to limited government on trade issues and how the GOP record compares to what the Democrats might have done.

The first section describes the evolving role of Congress in fashioning trade policy. The second section examines the expectations for trade policy when Republicans captured control of Congress in 1994. The third section evaluates the Republican record on trade compared to both those expectations and the ideal of free trade. The final section compares the Republican record to what might have occurred if Democrats had retained control of Congress.

The Changing Role of Congress in U.S. Trade Policy

The U.S. Constitution empowers Congress to legislate our nation's international trade policy. Article I, section 8, grants Congress exclusive authority "to lay and collect taxes, duties, imposts and excises" and "to regulate commerce with foreign nations." One of the first acts of Congress was to impose duties on a range of goods in order to raise revenue and protect certain domestic producers. For the first 150 years or so, Congress exercised its authority over trade more or less independently of the executive branch. It set tariffs and other conditions on trade the way it levied taxes domestically, raising tariffs and imposing new barriers in one Congress, lowering or repealing barriers in a subsequent Congress. Trade bills were initiated by Congress and patched together through the standard practices of compromise and logrolling. And they were enacted unilaterally, without negotiating with other nations for mutual reductions.

During the 19th century, Congress used its power to maintain relatively high barriers to trade, punctuated by a few, brief periods of tariff cutting typically under Democrats. That approach reached its zenith, or more accurately its nadir, with enactment of the Trade Act of 1930, known as the Smoot-Hawley tariff bill. (The bill's main sponsors were Rep. Willis Hawley of Oregon and Sen. Reed Smoot of Utah, both Republicans). Smoot-Hawley was the final gasp of old-style trade policy. As the nation began to slip into recession in 1929 and early 1930, the Republican Congress responded with a tariff bill aimed at protecting U.S. employment. The process became a feeding frenzy, with every industry and constituency demanding, and usually getting, high tariffs against foreign competition.

The result was legislation, eagerly signed into law by President Herbert Hoover, that dramatically increased tariffs on a broad range of imports, including some, such as cashew nuts, that were not even produced in the United States at the time.[1] The real-world impact was a reduction in imports and retaliation from U.S. trading partners, who raised tariffs against U.S. exports. World trade spiraled downward from 1929 to the depths of the Great Depression in 1933. It would be inaccurate to say Smoot-Hawley caused the Great Depression, but it certainly failed to protect U.S. jobs as promised and almost certainly deepened and prolonged the economic crisis in the United States and abroad. By 1932, the Republicans had been swept from power in Washington and "protectionism" suffered a political blow from which it has not recovered.[2]

What followed was the most significant turning point in congressional trade policy in the nation's history. In a profound institutional shift, Congress ceded a significant share of its trade policy authority to the executive branch. Under the Reciprocal Trade Agreements Act of 1934, Congress authorized the president of the United States to negotiate mutual tariff reductions of up to 50 percent with other foreign governments. The reductions were preapproved and automatically became U.S. tariff policy without final approval from Congress. Over the next decade, under the pro-trade leadership of Secretary of State Cordell Hull, the Roosevelt administration negotiated dozens of agreements under the RTAA. The result was a drop in the average U.S. tariff rate comparable to the sharp rise under Smoot-Hawley.

After World War II, trade negotiations became multilateral through the General Agreements on Tariffs and Trade. As with

RTAA agreements, the executive branch negotiated with other GATT members through a series of rounds to mutually reduce trade barriers. The lower rates were applied to imports from all GATT members, with every member facing the same nondiscriminatory rate offered to the "most favored nation." In a modification of the RTAA approach, agreements signed by the executive branch were then presented to Congress for approval.

Another new development in postwar trade policy was the emergence of a bipartisan consensus. Democrats had been the party of free trade because of the benefits to consumers and workers; Republicans had been the party of protection because of the benefits for certain farm producers and domestic manufacturers. But as the chill of the Cold War shaped U.S. decisionmaking, both parties rightly grasped that trade was an important tool of U.S. foreign policy that could knit together Western European allies with the United States.

In the Trade Act of 1974, Congress instituted "fast-track" authority, committing itself to vote in a timely manner on trade agreements submitted by the executive branch and to vote up or down without amendment so that Congress could not pick apart complicated agreements. Fast-track authority was renewed several times during the next two decades, enabling the United States to sign and implement the Tokyo Round (1979) and Uruguay Round (1994) Agreements of GATT, bilateral agreements with Israel (1986) and Canada (1988), and the North American Free Trade Agreement (NAFTA) with Canada and Mexico (1993). Fast-track authority expired at the end of 1994, just as the new Republican Congress was about to assume power.

The GOP Victory and Expectations on Trade

Trade was not mentioned specifically in the Contract with America, but it was one of the more controversial issues confronting Congress at the time. In November 1993, Congress approved NAFTA after a bitter public debate and a close, final vote in the House. In spring 1994, the Clinton administration signed the ambitious Uruguay Round Agreement with the other members of GATT, which set the clock ticking for a vote in Congress before fast-track authority expired at the end of the year. Meanwhile, anxieties about Japan's trade prowess were still running high.

The "promises" of the Republican Party on trade on the eve of the 1994 election, although not as explicit as those made in the Contract, were nonetheless real. The party routinely endorsed freer trade in its platforms, and recent Republican presidents and congressional leaders generally supported trade expansion in word and deed. NAFTA was negotiated during the Republican presidency of George H. W. Bush and became law because the Republican leaders who were about to take control of Congress—Newt Gingrich, Dick Armey, and others—worked with a Democratic president, Bill Clinton, to enact the agreement when they were in the minority. The Uruguay Round began under the Republican presidency of Ronald Reagan and progressed toward final agreement under the first Bush administration. As the party most identified with free markets, multinational businesses, and the expansion of global capitalism, the Republicans were expected to support trade liberalization.

Nonetheless, Republicans were not eager to make trade a central issue in the 1994 campaign. The party did not want to alienate followers of Pat Buchanan or the independent H. Ross Perot, who were harsh critics of NAFTA and trade liberalization in general. Nor did they want GOP candidates to commit themselves to voting against the Uruguay Round Agreement Act, scheduled for a November 29 vote in a lame duck session. A month before the vote, then minority leader Bob Michel (R-Ill.), whip Newt Gingrich, (R-Ga.), and Ways and Means Committee ranking minority member Bill Archer (R-Tex.) told House Republicans to "keep your powder dry" by not taking a stand on the GATT agreement.[3]

The GOP's attitude on trade at the time was reflected in its national platform of 1996.[4] In the section "Promoting Trade and International Prosperity," it declared, "Free-market capitalism is the right model for economic development throughout the world. The Soviet model of a state-controlled economy has been discredited, and neither stage of development nor geographic location can justify economic authoritarianism." Yet the platform could only bring itself to endorse "free and fair trade." Its emphasis was on expanding trade through exports, without a word about the benefit of lower prices through import competition. It chastised the Clinton administration for allowing the trade deficit to rise, "siphoning American wealth into the hands of foreigners." It endorsed the vigorous use of various administrative trade tools, including antidumping laws and the

"Super 301" threat of sanctions against foreign trade barriers. It proposed abolishing the U.S. Department of Commerce.

Has the GOP Congress Advanced the Freedom to Trade?

The record of the Republican Congress on trade liberalization has been modestly positive. Its legislative record since 1995 contains no sweeping or historic turns in favor of trade liberalization or against it. There was good reason why the Republican Congress did not consider major trade legislation during the 1990s. Significant trade liberalization was already built into the process because of action in the last Democratically controlled Congress with the passage of NAFTA in 1993 and the Uruguay Round Agreements Act in 1994.

Both of those milestone agreements passed with strong support from the Republican minority, in cooperation with a pro-trade Democratic president and what then was a sizeable number, if not always a majority, of pro-trade House Democrats. Days after the election of 1994, outgoing House Ways and Means Committee Chairman Sam Gibbons (D-Fla.) accurately predicted that approval of the Uruguay Round legislation in the closing days of the Democratic Congress would preclude any other major trade legislation in the near future. "I think when we finish this we'll have about finished the agenda for the rest of the decade," Gibbons told reporters on November 16. "It will take about five or six years just to absorb the Uruguay Round."[5] Those words proved to be prophetic.

The following five sections look at the Republican record on trade, including legislation enacted that advanced trade liberalization, legislation rejected that would have restricted trade, legislation enacted that restricted trade, opportunities missed to advance liberalization, and actual growth in trade during the past decade.

Major Accomplishments

Permanent Normal Trade Relations

Passage of permanent normal trade relations (PNTR) with China in 2000 cleared the way for the entry of China into the World Trade Organization in 2001. The Clinton administration successfully negotiated an agreement with China in 1999 that committed China to sweeping reductions in trade barriers across a broad swath of industries as a condition of its entry into the WTO. The United States agreed to remove China from the list of nations whose trade status must be renewed annually under the 1974 Jackson-Vanik amendment. That Cold War–era amendment to the Trade Act of 1974 denies most-favored-nation status to any Communist country that does not allow free emigration. Its central purpose in the 1970s had been to pressure the Soviet Union into allowing Jewish refuseniks to emigrate freely.

Because China fit the definition of a communist nonmarket economy under the law, the president was required to declare a waiver to the law each year, subject to rejection by Congress. But such a review violates the nondiscrimination clause of the WTO's basic agreement, so the United States could not enjoy the increased market access to China without lifting the Jackson-Vanik sanctions and granting China permanent normal trade relations. On May 24, 2000, 74 percent of House Republicans joined with 35 percent of the chamber's Democrats to pass the China PNTR legislation by a final vote of 237-197. On September 19, the Senate, by an overwhelming vote, approved the legislation 83-15. In the years leading up to the vote on PNTR, the Republican Congress had easily turned away annual efforts to revoke China's trade status.[6]

Continuing normal trade relations with China is hugely important for America's economy and foreign policy interests. After two decades of rapid growth, China has become America's third-largest trading partner, behind only Canada and Mexico. China is the number three source of imports to the United States, and the number six destination for U.S. exports. By ushering China into the WTO, the Republican majority in Congress—working with a Democratic president and significant numbers of Democrats in both chambers—took a major step toward bringing more economic freedom and the rule of law to the world's most populous country. Revocation of normal trade relations would have caused tariffs on Chinese imports to the United States to rise dramatically, biting into the daily budgets of tens of millions of American families who buy shoes, clothing, toys, consumer electronics, and other goods made in China. It would also set back efforts to create a larger and more independent middle class in China and to secure China's cooperation in containing North Korea and in other security matters. Despite domestic political pressure, the Republican Congress refused to compromise America's economic and security interests by jeopardizing normal trade relations with China.

Trade Promotion Authority

The other major accomplishment of the Republican Congress has been enactment of trade promotion authority (TPA), previously known as fast track. Passage came at a high price (see the later section on "Backsliding"), but it has opened the door for important trade agreements. On December 6, 2001, the House leadership engineered the slimmest majority possible to pass a version of TPA by a vote of 215-214. The victory was made possible only by holding the vote open long after the usual 15 minutes and then by promising concessions on textile trade to certain Republicans from North and South Carolina. The vote was heavily partisan, with 89 percent of Republicans but only 10 percent of Democrats voting in favor.

The Senate was under control of the Democrats when it considered trade promotion authority in 2002. Institutionally and historically the Senate has been less partisan and more trade friendly than the House, but the Democratic leadership waited several months after the House vote to bring TPA up for a full vote. On May 22, 2002, the Senate voted decisively to approve its version of TPA, with 89 percent of Republicans joining 49 percent of Democrats to pass the bill by a vote of 66-30. On July 27, 2002, the House passed the final, conference-committee version of TPA by a still slim and deeply partisan margin of 215-212, and the Senate followed suit five days later, approving the same legislation by a vote of 64-34.

After a long lapse of eight years, Congress again granted the president the authority to negotiate free-trade agreements under rules for expedited consideration. Within a year, the 108th Congress, with the Senate back under Republican control, approved two major bilateral trade agreements with Chile and Singapore. The Chile agreement had been in the works since the mid-1990s. As the leading free-trade and free-market reformer in Latin America, Chile has been eager to expand its trade with the United States. For the United States, the agreement rewards and encourages trade liberalization in the Western Hemisphere. The Singapore agreement deepens America's economic ties to a leading free-trade nation strategically situated in Southeast Asia. On July 24, 2003, the House voted decisively in favor of both the Chile and Singapore free-trade agreements. A large majority of Republicans joined with more than one-third of Democrats to approve the agreements. A week later, the Senate approved both agreements by 2:1 margins. TPA will be necessary to approve any final agreements in the Doha Round of WTO negotiations, the Free Trade Area of the Americas, or any of the bilateral and regional trade agreements that have been, or are being, negotiated.

Other Accomplishments

Other positive steps the Republican Congress has made toward greater trade liberalization include the following:

- *Enacting the African Growth and Opportunity Act.* In May 2000, strong bipartisan majorities in both the House and the Senate approved a unilateral reduction in U.S. trade barriers on certain imports from certain sub-Saharan and Caribbean countries.

- *Allowing exports of U.S. food and medicine to Cuba and other sanctioned countries under certain conditions.* As part of the 2001 agricultural appropriations bill, Congress mandated the lifting of unilateral sanctions on the export of food and medical supplies to Cuba and other rogue regimes. Sales to Cuba must be cash-only or financed by a party outside the United States. The provision was one of the rare exceptions granted to the virtually total trade embargo that has been in force against Cuba for more than 40 years.

- *Moderating or rolling back other unilateral sanctions.* After reaching a peak in the mid-1990s, the number of new economic sanctions imposed by Congress has been declining and a number of previously imposed sanctions have been repealed or allowed to expire. New sanctions are more narrowly targeted.[7]

- *Approving normal trade relations with Vietnam.* In July 2000, the Clinton administration signed a bilateral trade agreement with the government of Vietnam, a necessary step to grant normal trade relations and make Vietnamese imports eligible for the lower tariff rates extended to imports from all but a handful of countries. In 2001 and 2002, the House rejected by wide majorities legislation that would have revoked normal trade relations with Vietnam.

- *Opening Alaskan oil for export.* In 1995, Congress approved the export of oil from Alaska's North Slope. Export of the oil had been banned in the past under the mistaken belief that exporting the oil reduced America's energy independence. The Senate voted to lift the export ban in May 1995 by a vote of 74-25. The House voted to lift the ban in November by a vote of 289-134.

Saying No to Most Protectionist Proposals

Also belonging on the positive side of the balance sheet are proposals that were considered and rejected by the Republican Congress. Even during the recession of 2001 and the recovery that followed, the Congress came nowhere close to passing legislation that would have restricted trade in any major way. No major protectionist bills other than the 2002 Farm Bill (discussed in the next section) made their way to the president's desk.

One of the high points of the past decade was the Senate's rejection, in June 1999, of comprehensive quotas on imported steel. A bill to impose quotas had passed the House in March of that year by a lopsided 2:1 margin, with 94 percent of Democrats teaming up with a sizeable 42 percent of Republicans to vote in favor of the ban. But the Senate, with the backing of the Clinton White House, rejected a similar ban by a margin of 42-57. (Ironically, tariffs were eventually imposed temporarily on steel imports, not by Congress, but by the Republican Bush administration.)

Other trade-restricting proposals considered but rejected by the Republican Congress included measures to require less-developed countries to enact higher environmental, labor, and human rights standards as a condition of trade; allow private antidumping suits; require reciprocal tariff reductions before lowering barriers to imports from poor countries; support presidential action to impose sanctions against Japan if automobile market-access talks failed; and require a separate vote on any provision in multilateral trade agreements that affect U.S. antidumping laws.

Backsliding on Farm Subsidies, Export Subsidies, and Cuba

On the negative side of the ledger, the GOP Congress's most blatant departure from free-trade principles was the expensive and trade-distorting farm bill of 2002. The Farm Security and Rural Investment Act of 2002 marked a repudiation of the more market-oriented approach Congress adopted in the 1996 Freedom to Farm Act. The 1996 legislation cut direct farm subsidies and expanded the freedom of American farmers to decide for themselves what crops to plant based on market signals. But sagging global farm prices beginning in 1997–98 spurred the Republican Congress to pass a series of supplemental appropriations bills that dramatically increased spending on farm subsidies from the baselines established in the 1996 act. The 2002 Farm Bill codified those increases, committing the federal government to spend nearly $200 billion in the next decade, an 80 percent increase over baseline subsidy levels. The bill targets the biggest subsidies on eight "program" crops—cotton, wheat, corn, soybeans, rice, barley, oats, and sorghum—while maintaining subsidies and protective quotas for domestic beet and cane sugar.

The 2002 Farm Bill's market distortions did not end there. The bill also requires that the country of origin be labeled for meat, fish, peanuts, and other imported produce starting in the fall of 2004. The so-called COOL regulations (for country-of-origin labeling) serve no legitimate public safety need but merely add to the costs of selling imported produce. The regulations will also make it more difficult for the United States to oppose regulations in the European Union to require labels on imports of U.S.-produced genetically modified foods.[8] The COOL regulations passed the House with majority support of both parties. The farm bill also doubled subsidies for export promotion through the Market Access Program. The final version of the farm bill was supported by two-thirds of Republicans and Democrats in the House but not by a majority of Republicans in the Senate.

Such huge farm subsidies are antithetical to free trade. By artificially boosting domestic production, subsidies drive down global prices below free-market levels. U.S. subsidies also undercut the U.S. bargaining position in WTO talks by undermining U.S. calls for others to liberalize and antagonizing many less-developed countries. The Doha Development Round has stalled since its launch in 2001 in significant part because of continuing rich-country subsidies to agriculture. The effect has been to deny potential breakthroughs for market access for U.S. exporters.

Another area of anti-market policy for the Republican Congress has been export and investment subsidies through the Export-Import Bank and the Overseas Private Investment Corporation. Supporters of those programs claim they promote foreign trade and investment, but in fact they distort commerce by channeling activities according to politics rather than markets. The Export-Import Bank, for example, can raise demand for exports produced by certain U.S. multinational companies that benefit from its loans. But the increased production spurred by the extra exports raises costs for other, less-favored export industries competing for the same labor, capital, and intermediate inputs. They also crowd out unsubsidized exporters as foreign buyers bid up the price of U.S. dollars on foreign-exchange markets to buy the more-attractive subsidized U.S. exports. Export subsidies also impose a higher burden on taxpayers. Nonetheless, the Republican Congress has consistently voted to continue large subsidies for certain exporters and foreign investors.

A third area of backsliding has been trade with Cuba. By any reasonable measure, the four-decade-old embargo against Cuba has failed to yield positive results. Indeed, the embargo may be keeping Fidel Castro in power by providing him a handy excuse for the failure of his socialist experiment. But instead of repealing or even loosening the embargo, the Republican Congress tightened the screws with the Cuban Liberty and Democracy Solidarity Act of 1995. Known as the Helms-Burton Act, after its two Republican cosponsors, the legislation imposed sanctions not only against Cuba but also against non-U.S. companies that allegedly profit from property or trademarks confiscated by the Cuban government. The House and the Senate have separately passed amendments that would ease the ban on travel to Cuba, but those amendments passed primarily because of overwhelming support from Democrats and have been kept out of final legislation by the Republican leadership and veto threats from the Republican administration. In fact, the same legislation that allowed cash-only sales of food and medicine to Cuba and other sanction targets codified the travel ban, making its future repeal more difficult.

Opportunities Missed

Another shortcoming of the Republican Congress on trade has been its failure to aggressively seize and create opportunities to advance the freedom of Americans to trade in the global economy. Republicans have been thoroughly conventional in this respect, passively demanding that other countries first reduce their own trade barriers to U.S. exports before the United States will even consider lowering its barriers.

Congress has done virtually nothing to reform our protectionist antidumping laws. Those laws interfere in free trade by imposing high duties on certain imports found to be traded "unfairly." The law itself is unfair, however, because it punishes foreign producers for engaging in competitive pricing practices that are perfectly legal and routine among domestic U.S. producers. Antidumping law allows certain favored U.S. producers to cripple their foreign competition, raising prices for American families and for import-consuming U.S. industries.[9]

Instead of restricting the use and abuse of antidumping law by U.S. companies, Congress has resisted efforts by the administration to subject those laws to serious negotiation among WTO members. In November 2001, as WTO members were about to meet in Doha, Qatar, to launch a new round of trade negotiations, the House voted 410-4 for a resolution stating that the president "should preserve the ability of the U.S. to enforce its trade laws" while ensuring that "U.S. exports are not subject to the abusive use of trade laws by other countries."[10] Although the resolution was correct to point out foreign abuses of antidumping law, it expressed reluctance to tackle similar abuses of U.S. law. In May 2002, 61 Senators approved the so-called Dayton-Craig amendment, which would have required a separate vote on any trade-agreement provisions that would limit U.S. antidumping law. The amendment, which was eventually dropped in conference committee, would have radically compromised the president's ability to negotiate international curbs on the use and abuse of protectionist antidumping laws. In February 2003, 70 Senators signed a letter to President Bush pledging to resist any efforts to change the so-called Byrd amendment, even though the amendment has been found by the WTO to be in violation of international rules the United States has agreed to follow. Although none of the actions by Congress have expanded the use of the antidumping law, together they have sent the unmistakable signal that Congress has no plans to reform the deeply flawed law.

Finally, the Republicans have arguably missed an opportunity to preserve bipartisanship on trade. Of course, it takes two to dance that tango, and the Democratic Party for its own reasons has drifted away from its historical commitment to expanding trade. But the Republican majority has made it difficult for more Democrats, especially in the House, to join them in supporting trade agreements. Relations between the parties have become strained in the all-important House Ways and Means Committee. The relationship between the current Republican chairman, Bill Thomas of California, and the ranking Democrat, Charles Rangel of New York, is far more combative and contentious than was the relationship between their previous counterparts. Nor has the Republican leadership been above using trade in an overtly political fashion. In September 1998, the leadership held a floor vote in the House on trade promotion authority even though it lacked President Clinton's blessing at the time and the chances of passage were slim. Instead, the aim of the vote was to force Democrats running for reelection to make an awkward choice between the interests of business and their core labor-union constituency. The bill failed by a vote of 180-243, with a paltry 29 Democrats joining a solid but inadequate majority of Republicans. The vote further politicized the trade debate and probably locked some Democrats into opposing trade who may have been persuadable under less politically charged circumstances. Other factors have been equally if not more important in deepening the gulf between the two parties on trade, but the Republican leadership must bear a share of the blame.

America's Growing International Trade

Another way to measure the Republican record on trade is by measuring the actual freedom to trade, as reflected in average tariff rates and levels of trade. By either measure, the freedom of Americans to engage in global commerce has expanded under the Republican Congress.

By several measures, the level of taxes imposed on imports to the United States has continued its long postwar decline under the Republican Congress (see Figure 7.1). Duties collected on imports, as a share of total imports, have declined from just over 3 percent before the party took control of Congress to half that rate in 2003.[11] According to the WTO, the simple average applied tariff rate fell from 6.4 percent in 1996 to 5.1 percent in 2002, although the average rate on farm goods remained twice as high and dropped only slightly, from 10 to 9.8 percent.[12] Similar calculations from the World Bank and the Fraser Institute's *Economic Freedom of the World* report show the average tariff rate falling from about 6 percent before the Republican Congress to about 4 percent by 2001–2002.[13] Most of that liberalization resulted from implementing NAFTA and the Uruguay Round Agreements.

By most measures, Americans are trading and investing more with the rest of the world today than a decade ago. U.S. imports

Figure 7.1
AMERICA'S DECLINING TARIFF RATES
(average U.S. tariff rate on dutiable imports, 1823–1999)

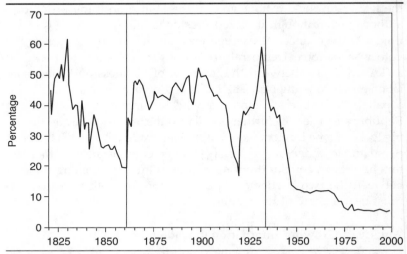

SOURCE: Douglas A. Irwin, *Free Trade under Fire* (Princeton University Press, 2002), p. 147.

and exports of goods and services, plus payments and receipts of investment income, totaled $3,189 billion by 2000, compared with $1,817 billion in 1994. America's trade dropped sharply between 2000 and 2002 because of the U.S. recession and slow growth abroad, but it began to rebound in 2003. By 2003, the total amount Americans paid for imports of goods and services and payments on foreign investments in the United States was $1,767 billion, compared to $948 billion in 1994. The total amount earned from exports and payments on U.S. investments abroad in 2003 was $1,294 billion, compared with $868 billion in 1994.[14]

As a percentage of gross domestic product, imports rose from 13.4 to 16.1 percent from 1994 to 2003, while exports declined slightly, from 12.3 to 11.8 percent. Total two-way trade and investment income as a percent of GDP rose rapidly in the 1990s, peaking in 2000 at 32.5 percent before declining through the recession to a level that was still higher than in 1994. Whatever judgment one makes about the legislative record of the Republican Congress on trade, there is no evidence that anything Congress has done has noticeably impeded the freedom of Americans to earn and spend money in the global marketplace.

How Would a Democratic Congress Have Differed on Trade Policy?

To compare the Republican record on trade with what a Democratic Congress might have done under similar circumstances requires that we briefly review the trade record of the last Democratically controlled Congress. The striking fact when comparing the record of the Republicans with that of the Democrats before them is not the differences but the continuity. Whether Democrats or Republicans controlled Congress, congressional leaders have worked with presidents of both parties to pass bipartisan legislation to liberalize trade.

The Democratic Congresses of 1987–94 compiled a generally positive record of advancing trade liberalization while resisting significant backsliding. In fact, the Democratic leadership worked with the Republican minority and presidents of both parties to pass some of the most significant trade-expanding legislation in a generation. In 1988, Congress overwhelmingly approved the U.S.-Canada Free Trade Agreement, which has eliminated virtually all trade barriers with our largest trading partner. Congress renewed fast-track negotiating authority in 1991 and then approved the milestone North American Free Trade Agreement with Canada and Mexico in late 1993 and the Uruguay Round Agreements Act in late 1994. Along the way, Congress eliminated high tariffs on imported minivans in March 1993. Granted, Democratic leaders and committee chairs were more supportive of trade liberalization than were rank-and-file Democratic members of Congress. On the contentious NAFTA vote, for example, a majority of House Democrats voted against the agreement, but Democratic leaders worked with Democratic President Bill Clinton and a solid majority of Republicans to make NAFTA a reality.

Even the Omnibus Trade and Competitiveness Act of 1988, despite the protectionist rhetoric that surrounded it, did not on balance interfere in the freedom of Americans to trade with the rest of the world. The focus of the bill was on promoting exports through, for example, more aggressive use of Section 301. It also extended fast-track authority through 1991. The House version of the bill did contain the protectionist Gephardt amendment, which would have raised tariffs against imports from countries with which the United States ran persistent bilateral trade deficits, but that provision was wisely jettisoned from the final bill.[15]

Throughout the 1990s and into the new century, however, the Democratic Party has continued to drift further away from its pro-trade tradition. In the House, especially, the number of Democrats who can be counted upon to support pro-trade legislation has declined steadily from 40 to 50 percent of the caucus in the 1980s and early 1990s to well under a third today. One explanation is the growing dominance of organized labor within the party. Labor unions, led by the AFL-CIO and the Teamsters, have made opposition to trade agreements a virtual litmus test for Democratic candidates. And as fewer and fewer congressional districts remain competitive between the two parties, satisfying core party constituencies and avoiding a primary challenge has become more important for most Democratic House members than appealing to a broader constituency that would be more favorable to trade liberalization.

Taking all those factors into account, a Democratic Congress would probably have been more open to calls for such protectionist measures as steel tariffs and would have been less inclined to pass permanent normal trade relations with China and trade promotion authority. But those differences would have been incremental and perhaps not decisive. A Democratic Congress could conceivably have enacted PNTR and TPA using the same formula that worked for NAFTA and the Uruguay Round Agreements—Democratic leaders working with a pro-trade president and Republican minority to push the legislation through. But it is equally conceivable that a Congress under control of the Democrats would have reached a tipping point where a large and growing majority of trade-skeptical Democrats would join with a sizeable enough minority of like-minded Republicans to be able to block all major trade-expansion legislation. The Republican Congress has so far managed to keep the pro-trade coalition in the majority.

Conclusion

The Republicans have largely kept their stated and implied promises on international trade in the decade since they took control of

Congress. After digesting the monumental NAFTA and Uruguay Round agreements, Republican leaders further expanded the freedom of Americans to trade by shepherding the passage of PNTR with China and presidential TPA, along with other, more incremental trade-expanding legislation. The most glaring exception, of course, has been the party's weakness for farm-sector subsidies and protection.

By the broadest measures, Americans are more free and able to trade and invest in the global economy than they were a decade ago. Congressional trade policy under a decade of Republican rule largely continued the policies enacted previously under Democratic rule, but the Democrats' historical commitment to trade liberalization has continued to erode in the past decade. As a consequence, congressional trade policy under the Republicans has almost certainly been more trade friendly than it would have been under continued Democratic control.

Former Alabama governor and independent presidential candidate George Wallace famously complained that there wasn't a dime's worth of difference between the two major political parties on the most important issues of the day, and many chapters in this book bear witness to that fact. But on trade policy, there remains more than a dime's worth of difference between the two parties.

Notes

1. Jagdish Bhagwati, *Protectionism* (Cambridge, MA: MIT Press, 1988), pp. 20–21.

2. For a more detailed discussion of the evolution of U.S. trade policy, see I. M. Destler, *American Trade Politics,* 3d ed. (Washington: Institute for International Economics, 1995).

3. *Inside U.S. Trade,* "Republican Leadership Warns against Campaign Promises on GATT," October 14, 1994.

4. 1996 Republican National Platform, section on "Promoting Trade and International Prosperity," available at www.nvra.com/1996_national_platform.htm.

5. "Gibbons Says Trade Agenda Largely Set through End of Decade," *Inside U.S. Trade,* November 18, 1994.

6. For congressional voting on this and other trade-related bills, see Daniel T. Griswold, "Free Trade, Free Markets: Rating the 107th Congress," Cato Trade Policy Analysis no. 22, January 30, 2003; "Free Trade, Free Markets: Rating the 106th Congress," Cato Trade Policy Analysis no. 13, March 26, 2001; and "Free Trade, Free Markets: Rating the 105th Congress," Cato Trade Policy Analysis no. 6, February 3, 1999, all available at www.freetrade.org.

7. Barry Carter, "Study of New U.S. Unilateral Sanctions, 1997–2001," USA*Engage, 2002, available at www.usaengage.org/literature/2002/2002sanctions/index.html.

8. Dan Ikenson, "Uncool Rules: Second Thoughts on Mandatory Country-of-Origin Labeling," Cato Institute Free Trade Bulletin no. 7, January 16, 2004.

9. For a thorough look at what is wrong with U.S. antidumping law, see Brink Lindsey and Dan Ikenson, *Antidumping Exposed* (Washington: Cato Institute, 2003).

10. Griswold, "Free Trade, Free Markets," January 30, 2003, p. 8.

11. Calculations based on figures from the U.S. International Trade Commission Dataweb, http://dataweb.usitc.gov.

12. World Trade Organization, *Trade Policy Review of the United States* (Geneva, Switzerland: World Trade Organization, 2003), Table III.1, "Structure of Applied MFN Tariffs in the United States, 1996–02."

13. James Gwartney, *Economic Freedom of the World: 2003 Annual Report* (Vancouver, Canada: Fraser Institute, 2003); and World Bank, Data & Statistics Section, available at www.worldbank.org/trade.

14. Council of Economic Advisors, *Economic Report of the President 2004* (Washington: Government Printing Office, 2004), Table B 103, p. 402.

15. Destler, pp. 92–98.

8. The Long, Winding Road to Social Security Reform

Michael Tanner

Support for allowing younger workers to invest part of their Social Security taxes into private accounts is becoming Republican orthodoxy. This has not always been the case; Republicans after 1994 were initially quite tepid in supporting reform. Indeed, Social Security reform prompted a struggle within the GOP, pitting politics against principle and sometimes leaders against backbenchers. The battles within the GOP have not ended, but the proponents of reform have now gained the upper hand.

Although Social Security's financial troubles were well known, and groups such as the Cato Institute had long advocated private accounts, Social Security reform was not a major part of the 1994 campaign. Indeed, the Contract with America mentioned Social Security only in the context of removing the "earnings cap" and repealing President Bill Clinton's tax increase on Social Security benefits.[1]

The Republican capture of Congress gave new impetus to calls for market-based Social Security reform. But a few months after the Republican majority took control, House Speaker Newt Gingrich warned Republicans against any effort to reform Social Security. "Every liberal in America would love for us to touch Social Security," Gingrich said in a press briefing.[2] He went on to say that, perhaps some day in the future, "if we balance the budget, if we create the level of change necessary, if people decide we're real ... we can have a dialogue about the future of retirement for Baby Boomers."[3]

It is understandable that Republicans were reluctant to tackle Social Security. After all, Democrats had used the issue as a political weapon for decades. But for Gingrich, who frequently cited President Franklin Roosevelt as a hero, the reluctance to make changes to Social Security seemed more than tactical. Gingrich even publicly opposed a plan by Democratic Senator Bob Kerrey of Nebraska to allow younger workers to privately invest two percentage points of their payroll taxes. In response, Kerrey told *Time* that if Gingrich were willing to duck Social Security's problems because they are 25 years away, "don't give any speeches saying how concerned you are about your children and grandchildren."[4] He added that Gingrich, "like many Democrats, calculates that he can't tell people the truth about Social Security."[5]

By 1996, the political climate had shifted considerably. Public confidence in Social Security, especially among young people, was declining rapidly. A famous poll showed that young people believed they were more likely to see a UFO than a Social Security benefit check, and reform efforts gathered momentum. The Advisory Council on Social Security recommended major reforms, and a plurality of panel members supported individual accounts. Cato launched its Project on Social Security Privatization, and other think tanks urged reform.

The Republican leadership lagged behind, but Gingrich started shifting his position. He advocated a bipartisan national commission to study the issue, including ideas for individual accounts.[6] But there was still much old-guard thinking in the party. Sen. Robert Dole, the Republican presidential nominee, attacked Steve Forbes in the 1996 primaries over the issue and frequently claimed that Social Security needed nothing more than minor tinkering. Dole ran television ads warning, "Steve Forbes plans to end Social Security as we know it."[7]

Nonetheless, many Republicans were reformers. Reps. Jim Kolbe (R-Ariz.), Mark Sanford (R-S.C.), and John Porter (R-Nev.) were outspoken in favor of reform. They were joined by some Democrats, and even the Clinton White House was interested in reevaluating Social Security. In his 1998 State of the Union Address, President Clinton called on Congress to "save Social Security first." Clinton was trying to forestall Republican tax cuts, but his announcement helped jump-start the movement for Social Security reform. Clinton provided a clear diagnosis of Social Security's problems while traveling the country for a series of town hall meetings, and he helped convince the public that Social Security was facing financial disaster. He also spoke respectfully of individual accounts, helping move the idea from the fringes to the mainstream of the debate. Indeed, many observers believe that if the Monica Lewinsky scandal had not forced

Clinton to shore up his support among liberals in the Democratic Party, he would have endorsed individual accounts.[8]

Clinton's tactics galvanized Republican support for individual accounts. Republicans were not about to be outflanked on the political right over Social Security. Moreover, they recognized the roadblock that an unreformed Social Security system posed to tax cuts and other elements of the Republican agenda. In the late 1990s, the political climate was well suited for reform, with a rising stock market, budget surpluses available to finance transition costs, and a growing body of academic support for individual accounts. Public opinion polls showed large majorities of voters supporting individual accounts.

By mid-1998, Gingrich was inching toward reform. Early that year he gave an "off the record" speech to the World Economic Forum in Davos, Switzerland, where he laid out the case for individual accounts.[9] Within a few months, he had become an enthusiastic convert to the cause and was giving speeches extolling the benefits of young people's earning compound interest in private accounts over their lifetimes. Nonetheless, his proposal for Social Security Plus Accounts did not go all the way. They would have been funded through general budget surpluses rather than a carve-out from payroll taxes, and he still supported a bipartisan commission to come up with a final proposal.

By the end of 1998, Gingrich had resigned as Speaker, and his brief replacement, Robert Livingston, seemed no more anxious to exhibit leadership on the issue. Upon taking the speakership, Livingston announced that his number-one priority was not Social Security reform but a proposal to create a "lock box" for Social Security. Lock boxes were all the rage and provided Al Gore with a key campaign plank in 2000, but they would have done nothing to actually fix Social Security.

Livingston was replaced by Dennis Hastert, who was no more dynamic than his predecessors on the issue. His few public pronouncements on the issue ran toward advocacy of a Social Security lock box and issues such as the Social Security earnings test.[10]

Yet more and more rank-and-file Republicans were supporting partial privatization by the late 1990s. Republican members outside the leadership were introducing bills, some for full privatization, and polls showed Republican voters shifting strongly in favor of the idea. Indeed, polls showed majorities of Democrats and Independents also in favor of individual accounts.

The 2000 Republican presidential primary was very different from the one in 1996. With the exception of Gary Bauer, every candidate supported individual accounts—there was no Bob Dole defending the status quo. In fact, the Dole in this primary, Elizabeth, strongly supported personal accounts. George W. Bush was particularly strong in his support. While contemplating a run for the presidency, then Governor Bush had been briefed on Social Security by Cato's Jose Piñera and Ed Crane. Bush came away from that meeting expressing support for the concept of individual accounts but expressing concerns about its political viability.

During the 2000 campaign, Bush stuck to his support for individual accounts in the face of withering attacks by Al Gore and allied groups. In campaign commercials and stump speeches, Gore hammered Bush for threatening the benefits of current elderly recipients of Social Security. Special-interest groups from labor unions, to the American Association of Retired Persons, to the National Committee to Preserve Social Security and Medicare weighed in with phone banks, mailings, and newspaper ads, pouring millions of dollars into an effort to electrify the third rail of American politics. The actor Ed Asner even provided recorded phone calls to seniors in an attempt to scare them into the voting booth.

Despite weeks of high-volume attacks on the issue against Bush, election exit polls showed that 57 percent of voters supported Bush's vision of individual Social Security accounts. Even more remarkably, more than one-third of those who said they voted for Gore also supported individual accounts. These results led pollster John Zogby to declare, "The third rail has been broken."[11]

The same trends were visible at the congressional level; a survey conducted by Cato found that nearly all Republican candidates supported individual accounts.[12] A postelection tally found that candidates supporting individual accounts had racked up impressive victories throughout the country.

Once in office, Bush appointed a bipartisan commission to study proposals for "modernizing" Social Security. The commission, chaired by former senator Daniel Patrick Moynihan (D-N.Y.) and AOL/Time Warner Chief Operating Officer Richard Parsons, operated within a simple set of guidelines:

- Modernization must not change Social Security benefits for retirees or near retirees.
- The entire Social Security surplus must be dedicated only to Social Security.
- Social Security payroll taxes must not be increased.
- The government must not invest Social Security funds in the stock market.
- Modernization must preserve Social Security's disability and survivors' insurance programs.
- Modernization must include voluntary personal retirement accounts, which will augment Social Security.

Although the commission was ostensibly open to any potential way to fix Social Security, both supporters and critics agreed that it was heavily inclined toward support for individual accounts.[13] The commission held a number of public hearings designed to educate voters about the problems facing Social Security and build support for individual accounts. Behind the scenes, commissioners began to develop concrete proposals for giving workers the opportunity to invest at least a portion of their Social Security payroll taxes. Everything seemed to be moving toward a dramatic legislative confrontation in 2002.

Then, after the terrorist attacks of September 11, 2001, federal priorities changed overnight. Foreign policy, national defense, and the war on terror became the central political issues. Domestic issues in general, and Social Security in particular, went to the back burner. The commission dutifully issued its final report as scheduled on December 11, putting forward three alternative proposals for creating individual accounts, but no one was really listening.

The environment for Social Security reform grew worse during the spring and summer of 2002. A series of corporate scandals swept across the news headlines. A stock market already reeling from the end of the tech bubble and September 11 fell to five-year lows.

Although public opinion polls showed continued strong public support for individual accounts, some of the most timid Republicans on Capitol Hill began a full-fledged retreat from the idea. The leader of this "flight not fight" brigade was National Republican Congressional Committee (NRCC) Chairman Tom Davis of Virginia. Davis denied that support for individual accounts was a "Republican position," stating on NBC's *Meet the Press*, "We have a number of our members that are not going to support that."[14] Davis devoted enormous effort to purging the word "privatization" from the GOP lexicon and did everything he could to prevent candidates from discussing the issue. Under his guidance, Republican congressional candidates actually attacked Democrats who had suggested openness to private investment. The NRCC even threatened to cut off funding of candidates seen as too aggressive on the issue.[15]

Fortunately, Senate Republicans showed far more backbone, and as a result, Social Security reform became a key issue in several important Senate races. Hans Reimer of the anti–private account Campaign for America's Future called the North and South Carolina races bellwethers that would hinge on the issue of Social Security reform. Neither Elizabeth Dole in North Carolina nor Lindsey Graham in South Carolina made any attempt to hide their support for individual accounts. Indeed, when accused of supporting "a risky scheme," both counterattacked, pointing out that their Democratic opponents had no proposals of their own to fix the program's looming financial crisis. Dole campaigned showing a blank piece of paper as the "Bowles Social Security Plan." Voters chose both Graham and Dole by large margins.

Several other prominent supporters of individual accounts won important Senate races as well, including Saxby Chambliss in Georgia, Norm Coleman in Minnesota, John Cornyn in Texas, Jim Talent in Missouri, and John Sununu in New Hampshire. Sununu was top target for anti-account activists, who poured money into an effort to defeat him. Ads accused him of wanting to privatize Social Security to benefit his "wealthy Wall Street backers."

In the House, those few candidates who defied Davis and refused to tone down their support for individual accounts were also successful. Few representatives were as outspoken in their support for individual accounts as Pat Toomey (R-Pa.), despite the fact that his Democratic-leaning district has high concentrations of both senior citizens and union workers. Opponents of individual accounts poured money and manpower into the district trying to defeat Toomey, yet he won by a larger margin in 2002 than he had in 2000. Reps. Clay Shaw (R-Fla.) and Shelley Moore Capito (R-W.V.) also ran campaigns in which Social Security was a major issue and won by larger margins than in 2000. Former representative Jill Long Thompson may have been the first candidate in the country to air an ad attacking her opponent, Chris Chocola, for supporting privatization. Chocola won, picking up an open seat previously held by Democrats. In New Mexico, Steve Pearce, another strong supporter of individual accounts, won a newly created seat in a competitive district.

The success of pro-reform candidates in the 2002 elections may well have put the final nail in the coffin of Tom Davis–style Republican obstructionism. Although the War on Terror and the war in Iraq continue to keep domestic issues off the front pages, there has been more congressional interest in Social Security reform than at any time since before 9/11. Several individual account bills have been introduced, including a bill sponsored by Reps. Sam Johnson (R-Tex.), Pat Toomey (R-Pa.), and Jeff Flake (R-Ariz.), based on Cato's proposal to allow workers to privately invest half (6.2 percent) of the Social Security payroll tax through individual accounts. That bill has 14 cosponsors, more than any Social Security reform bill in recent years.

Several candidates in the 2004 election are running on the issue of Social Security reform, notably Rep. Jim DeMint, the Republican candidate for Senate in South Carolina. Although the House leadership and new NRCC chief Tom Reynolds have kept the issue low profile, they have not taken active measures to discourage candidates from talking about it. The issue is also expected to feature prominently in the presidential campaign.

The Republican revolution of 1994 did not bring to power a party dedicated to reforming Social Security. But, over time, the interaction of politics and principle within the GOP has fostered a working majority that favors pro-market changes to Social Security. It has been a long and winding road, but Republicans are finally coming around to full support of an issue that they were long ago assumed to have embraced.

Notes

1. Ed Gillespie and Bob Schellhaus, eds., *Contract with America: The Bold Plan by Rep. Newt Gingrich, Rep. Dick Armey and the House Republicans to Change the Nation* (New York: Times Books, 1994).

2. Michael Pearson, "Gingrich Says Hearings on Flat Tax Plan Could Begin Soon," *Associated Press*, April 1, 1995.

3. Ibid.

4. Dan Goodgame, "Reining in the Rich," *Time*, December 19, 1994. p. 35.

5. Ibid.

6. In a typical Gingrich twist, he proposed that the commission conduct its deliberations through the Internet. "Speaker of the House Holds News Conference on Social Security Reform," *Dow Jones News Service*, April 1, 1996.

7. "Social Security Skirmish," *CNN AllPolitics*, February 9, 1996, www.cnn.com/ALLPOLITICS/1996/news/9602/09/soc.sec/index.shtml.

8. Clinton even appointed a secret Treasury Department task force to study how individual accounts might be implemented. David Wilcox, Douglas Elmendorf, and Jeffrey Liebman, "Fiscal Policy and Social Security during the 1990s" (paper, *American Economic Policy in the 1990s* conference, Kennedy School of Government at Harvard University, June 27–30, 2001), www.ksg.harvard.edu/cbg/Conferences/economic_-policy/elwrevisedcbg.pdf.

9. Jodie Allen, "Can Newt Gingrich Save Social Security?" *Slate*, March 27, 1998, http://slate.msn.com/id/2497.

10. Ceci Connolly, "Plain-Spoken Hastert Poised to Be Speaker," *Washington Post*, December 21, 1998.

11. Susan Page, "Eight Lessons Learned from the Campaign," *USA Today*, November 7, 2000.

12. Cato Institute, "Congressional and Senatorial Candidates' Positions on Social Security Reform," www.socialsecurity.org/election00/congress/index.html, 2000.

13. There was a heavy Cato influence on the commission. Two commission members, Sam Beard and Tim Penny, were members of Cato's Project on Social Security Choice. A third, Lee Abdnor, was a former Cato vice president. Andrew Biggs, assistant director of Cato's project, took a leave of absence to become a senior staff member of the commission, and the commission's press secretary was also a former Cato employee.

14. Tom Davis, interview by Tim Russert, *Meet the Press*, NBC, September 12, 2002.

15. Michael Barone, "Too Clever by Half," *US News & World Report*, August 14, 2002.

9. Welfare Reform: The Biggest Accomplishment of the Revolution

Ron Haskins

In January 1995 Republicans took control of Congress for the first time in four decades. The Republicans intended to dramatically change American domestic policy based on their promises in the Contract with America. The Contract included a compendium of 10 bills that House GOP members promised to pass if they were elected. Analysts disagree about how much the Contract influenced the election, but there is no question that it provided a blueprint for legislative action after Republicans were in power.

This chapter examines the 1996 welfare reform legislation that was one of the key planks of the Contract with America. The Contract promised that Republicans would overhaul the welfare system to "reduce illegitimacy, require work, and save taxpayers money."[1] After rejecting President Bill Clinton's welfare reform proposal and surviving two Clinton vetoes of its own bill, the GOP succeeded in enacting welfare reform in August 1996.

The results of the reform have been impressive and are examined in detail here. The seven major policy changes in the 1996 law are described, followed by an examination of data to measure the effects of each of them. To put the success of welfare reform in context, a few words are in order first regarding the overall effect of the Republican revolution.

Background on the GOP Revolution

In one of the great acrobatic feats of modern congressional history, House Republicans passed all 10 pieces of Contract with America legislation in the first 100 days of the 104th Congress. Democrats had lost the election in part because they demonstrated little discipline in managing Congress. By contrast, Republicans were initially a well-oiled legislative machine that showed more majority-party discipline than Congress had seen in decades.[2]

In retrospect, numerous parts of the GOP agenda were not particularly revolutionary. The tax cuts, crime-fighting provisions, and regulatory reform proposals were modest changes and not revolutionary. A number of other parts of the Contract were not signed into law.[3] In stark contrast, welfare reform was signed into law and was as big a success as the Republicans had promised, as discussed below.

The Contract also promised a balanced-budget amendment (BBA) to the Constitution, which would have been revolutionary. However, it failed to pass in the Senate by a single vote in 1995. Nonetheless, Republicans were determined to balance the federal budget, with or without the BBA. Pursuing that goal led to battles with President Clinton, who initially had no plans for zeroing out the deficit. His fiscal year 1996 budget, released in February 1995, foresaw $200 billion deficits as far as the eye could see. The budget battles caused Clinton and congressional Republicans to allow the government to shut down twice as the GOP refused to pass even an interim budget until Clinton committed to the Republican balanced-budget plan.

After absorbing a beating in the media, Republicans twice backed down and allowed the government to open again.[4] However, the president eventually agreed to a balanced-budget plan, and balance was ultimately achieved in three years. Looking at the data, outlays in the mid-1990s increased more slowly than in previous years while revenues increased dramatically. When outlays and revenues are viewed as a percentage of gross domestic product, outlays declined continually after 1991 and revenues increased steadily after 1992.[5] Thus, the budget trends that would balance the budget were in place before Republicans captured Congress. Even so, it appears that Republicans forced President Clinton to help them moderate spending even as revenue was flowing rapidly into federal coffers. The balanced budget was a major, but temporary, achievement.

Everything changed when the economy went south in 2001. The Republican Congress and Republican President George W. Bush failed to moderate spending and substantially reduced taxes, causing the deficit to reappear in 2002. It seems likely that the deficit will continue at high levels (between 4 and 5 percent of GDP) for many years.[6] Cutting taxes is a major goal of the Republican Party, but so is reducing the size of government and maintaining a balanced budget. If recent policy actions by Republicans are any indication, Republicans value tax cuts much more than reducing the size of government or maintaining a balanced budget. In any case, the reappearance of continuing deficits shows that the balanced budgets of the late 1990s were not a lasting achievement. Similarly, inasmuch as Republicans failed to eliminate a single government agency or to actually reduce spending, as measured in nominal outlays, in even one year since 1995, it is difficult to credit the Republican revolution with leading to permanent changes in the size or scope of the government. The most that can be claimed is that Republicans temporarily slowed the growth of spending. Thus, Republicans did not achieve the central goal of the Contract to end "... government that is too big, too intrusive, and too easy with the public's money."

Welfare Reform as the Apocalypse

Welfare reform is a blazing exception to the lack of lasting GOP reforms. The 1996 welfare reform law (the Personal Responsibility and Work Opportunity Reconciliation Act) radically changed the principal federal welfare program, which provides grants to state governments for cash assistance to poor families. The law replaced Aid to Families with Dependent Children (AFDC) with Temporary Assistance for Needy Families (TANF).

The welfare reform legislation was first passed by the House in March 1995, was then twice vetoed by President Clinton, but ultimately signed into law by Clinton on August 22, 1996. It was a radical change in federal policy and it provoked a furor from the American left as it was being considered in Congress.

The onslaught from the left began in House committees and then continued on the floors of the House and the Senate. Liberal members of Congress claimed that the bill would make hoards of children homeless and find them "sleeping on grates" (Sen. Daniel Patrick Moynihan);[7] cast a million children into poverty (numerous members of Congress);[8] render parents incapable of supporting their children and force them to give up kids for adoption (Sen. Carol Moseley-Braun);[9] destroy "the basic guarantees of our democracy" (Rep. Patsy Mink);[10] amount to a "callous, coldhearted and mean-spirited attack on this country's children" (Rep. Cardiss Collins);[11] and punish children "for a lifetime" by depriving them "of food, of clothing, of housing, of education, of love" (Rep. Sam Gibbons).[12]

The Republican welfare reform bill reminded Rep. John Lewis of Georgia, a hero of the American civil rights movement, of the German Nazi government before and during World War II. Lewis recalled the words of the theologian Martin Niemoller, who pointed out that when the Nazis "came for" the Communists, the Jews, the trade unionists, and the Catholics, no one spoke up for them and all were soon dead. Lewis argued that Republicans were "coming for the children," "coming for the poor," and "coming for the sick, the elderly, the disabled." According to Lewis, only Democrats had the power to "stop this onslaught."[13] Rep. William Clay of Missouri also invoked Hitler and the Nazis, claiming that Republicans were using the "big lie" in attacking the poor. "What is next," he wondered on the floor of the House, "Castration? Sterilization?"[14]

Liberals outside Congress were equally bitter in their denunciation of the Republican bill. A choice example is provided by Jill Nelson, writing in the August 26, 1996 *Nation*:

> The welfare bill will destroy [America's] state of grace. In its place will come massive and deadly poverty, sickness, and all manner of violence. People will die, businesses will close, infant mortality will soar, everyone who can will move. Working- and middle-class communities all over America will become scary, violent wastelands created by a government that decided it has no obligations to its neediest citizens. In such a landscape, each of us becomes either predator or prey.[15]

Marian Wright Edelman, head of the Children's Defense Fund in Washington and an icon of liberal social policy, invoked the highest authority of all in condemning the Republican bill in an op-ed article in the *Washington Post*. After comparing the bill to burning Vietnamese villages to save them, she held that it violated "God's mandate to protect the poor and the weak and the young."[16] Even God, it seemed, was against those dastardly Republicans.

Nor were those stentorian outbursts the only signs of distress on the left. Three senior officials in the Clinton administration resigned in response to their president's placing his signature on the Republican legislation. All three were professionals with substantial reputations and extensive knowledge of welfare programs, including Wendell Primus, a Ph.D. economist and accomplished Washington insider; Mary Jo Bane, a noted professor of social policy at Harvard University; and Peter Edelman, a distinguished law professor and former adviser to Bobby Kennedy. What prompted these unprecedented reactions? The answer is clear: welfare reform was the most fundamental realignment of American social policy since enactment of the Social Security Act in 1935.

Welfare before the 1996 Reforms

On the eve of the great welfare reform debate of 1995–96, House Republicans asked the Congressional Research Service, a nonpartisan arm of Congress, to estimate the number and spending level of all federal welfare programs. CRS found 338 programs of eight types (cash, education and training, health, food support, and so forth).[17] As documented by Vee Burke of the CRS and Robert Rector of the Heritage Foundation, welfare spending soared between the early 1960s and early 1990s.[18] Total welfare spending rose almost fivefold as a share of gross domestic product between 1960 and 1993—from 1.1 percent to 5.1 percent.

It was not simply the increased spending on welfare that accounted for growing Republican criticism. In addition, there was abundant evidence that the programs did not work as advertised. National data make it difficult to show that the explosion of government programs and spending over the period from the 1960s to the mid-1990s was accompanied by any progress against social problems. Between President Lyndon Johnson's declaration of the War on Poverty in 1964 and the Republican takeover of Congress in 1995, poverty had grown, crime was up, nonmarital births had grown wildly, and more Americans than ever were on welfare.[19]

Charles Murray made a huge splash with his 1984 book *Losing Ground*, which argued that high welfare spending was correlated with poor social outcomes.[20] Murray cited substantial research evidence that the expansion of social programs was a major cause of higher poverty, higher crime, and falling educational achievement. Social programs, according to Murray, often make things worse.

Consider two examples. Progress against poverty since Johnson's War on Poverty had been very uncertain. Child poverty dropped during the 1960s, a period when federal and state spending on social programs was still quite modest. But by the early 1970s, progress against child poverty was at a standstill. During the next quarter century as programs and spending expanded rapidly, child poverty moved up and down somewhat, but its general drift was up. Throughout the 1970s, child poverty was in the range of 15 to 16 percent, but between 1981 and 1995 child poverty was above 20

Table 9.1
MAJOR COMPONENTS OF THE 1996 WELFARE REFORM

1. Temporary Assistance for Needy Families
2. Reducing nonmarital births
3. Streamlining child care
4. Strengthening child-support enforcement
5. Ending welfare for noncitizens
6. Ending welfare for drug addicts and alcoholics
7. Reducing Supplemental Security Income eligibility for children

percent in all except two years.[21] It would be very difficult to conclude that the increased number of programs and spending that characterized this era helped reduce poverty.

Nonmarital births provide an equally compelling case. Nonmarital births among all women and among black women rose modestly between the end of World War II and roughly the mid-1960s. But after the War on Poverty began and welfare spending exploded, so did the number and rate of nonmarital births. By 1994, nearly one in three children—and a shocking seven in ten black children—were born outside marriage.[22] Studies showed only a modest connection between welfare and measures of illegitimate birth and marriage.[23] But in the Republican view, supported by Murray's provocative volume, the growth of welfare spending, welfare dependency, family dissolution, crime, and nonmarital births were inextricably linked. Increasingly, Republicans saw poverty programs as the nexus of a tangle of growing social pathologies in America.

The 1996 Welfare Reform Law

Within days after the 1994 election, House Republicans were meeting with Republican governors to work out the details of a welfare reform bill. The starting point was a bill written by a House Republican task force before the 1994 election as part of the Contract with America. When Congress opened on January 4, 1995, Republicans were ready. On that day, they introduced the most radical welfare reform legislation ever introduced by the majority party of Congress. Although the bill was modified as it worked its way through Congress, almost all the major provisions were intact when the bill was signed into law in August 1996.

The sweeping legislation contained substantial reforms of seven major areas of policy, as summarized in Table 9.1 and considered in turn below. Reform of any one of these seven areas would have constituted major legislation. Taken together, the reforms represented a fundamental shift in American social policy away from entitlement welfare, and toward limited welfare, personal responsibility, and work-based benefits.

Temporary Assistance for Needy Families

The most important and well-publicized of the 1996 reforms were to AFDC. AFDC was abolished and replaced with the aptly named Temporary Assistance for Needy Families. The most far-reaching change was that the "entitlement" to cash benefits was replaced by a cash benefit contingent on work or work preparation. Many critics, including Sen. Daniel Patrick Moynihan of New York, the greatest student of welfare in the Congress and an implacable opponent of the bill, saw this change as the most fundamental. The central idea was that no longer would the nation guarantee income to young people who had babies outside marriage and did not work. Moynihan and many Democrats wrongly saw the end of entitlement as the end of the federal commitment to helping the poor, but Republicans saw entitlement as the embodiment of all that was wrong with welfare because it guaranteed benefits without imposing any obligations on recipients. Entitlement welfare, Republicans believed, was incompatible with self-sufficiency.

The new law gave states immense flexibility to design their own TANF welfare-to-work programs. States had always played a role in the AFDC program, especially by setting their own benefit levels, but Republicans now proposed to give them almost total control over cash welfare and work preparation. Led by Republicans Tommy Thompson of Wisconsin and John Engler of Michigan and Democrat Tom Carper of Delaware, governors flocked to Washington to argue for greater state control. In their appearances before the House Committee on Ways and Means in January of 1995, governors presented a spirited case for transferring major responsibility for welfare to the states.[24] The heart of their argument was that people closest to the problem could design the best solutions. The governors argued that Congress had to realize that one-size-fits-all, cookie-cutter solutions to welfare were ineffective and out of date.

The mechanism for giving control to the states was the block grant. Whereas AFDC had provided a federal guarantee for a reimbursement to the states of between about 50 and 80 percent of the

105

cash benefits for every family that states admitted to the rolls, TANF provided states with a flat funding level for six years. This level was set at the highest level of federal funding that each state had received in prior years for AFDC and several programs associated with AFDC.

The difference in financial incentives presented by the old funding system and the new block grants was important. Under AFDC, states received more federal dollars if they added recipients to the rolls and fewer dollars if they helped parents leave the rolls, even if parents left the rolls for work or marriage. By contrast, the flat funding level of the TANF block grants means that if states help families leave welfare, the state has more money per family remaining on the rolls because the same number of dollars serves fewer families. This surplus money can then be reinvested in work-preparation programs or child care so that still more families can leave the rolls.

Nonetheless, for all their enthusiasm about state flexibility, Republicans were not about to simply turn welfare over to the states. Their goal was a complete overhaul of the nation's approach to welfare, and cash welfare was their primary vehicle for change. Republicans were willing to allow states to design their own programs, but every state was required to meet specific requirements to create true welfare reform. One of those requirements is that states must place a given percentage of their caseload in work programs. The percentage began at 25 in 1997 and rose to 50 percent in 2002. Previous welfare reform laws had contained supposed work requirements, but there are several major differences in the approach taken by Republicans in 1996. Ending entitlement cleared away many obstacles to imposing serious work requirements. States, for example, would now be unimpeded in their use of sanctions. Indeed, the law requires states to use sanctions by reducing or even terminating cash benefits of adults who do not meet work requirements.

Another difference between the 1996 law and previous attempts to impose a work requirement on recipients was that Republicans devised a more stringent definition of work. Under prior law, states could fulfill work requirements by putting recipients in an education program, often a GED program that could lead to a high school equivalency degree. This time, however, Republicans actually meant work. To the astonishment of Democrats, the Republican bill contained a distinct bias against education and training in the form of strict limits on how much education could count toward fulfilling the work requirement. The rallying cry of the new approach was soon dubbed "work first." Forget education. Forget training. Give welfare recipients a one-week course in how to prepare a resume, fill out a job application, look for a job, interview with a prospective employer, and behave after they got the job. The underlying theory of this approach, firmly established as effective by scientific research, was that the best way to break welfare dependency was to work, and the best way to learn to work was to get a job.[25]

Finally, given the overriding importance of ending welfare dependency, the law took the most straightforward approach possible. It simply declared that families could not remain on cash welfare for more than five years. Since at least the Elizabethan-era Poor Laws, conservatives have expressed concern that adults would become dependent on public welfare handouts, as indeed an impressive body of research showed that many did.[26] The conservative solution was simple—limit the length of time adults could receive government welfare. If that policy were implemented by states, the nature of welfare would be utterly changed. Instead of a mass of able-bodied adults watching soap operas or working off the books while waiting for their next government check, welfare programs would be suddenly populated by young adults who knew that they must achieve independence by working or by marrying someone who works—or both.

Welfare time limits drew fierce criticism. The criticism was hardly surprising because the time limit meant that some families would lose and never again qualify for cash welfare. But Republicans held that the best way to send a persuasive message that welfare was truly temporary was to establish and enforce a time limit. Thus, states that allowed more than 20 percent of their recipients to violate the five-year time limit were themselves subject to financial sanctions.

Those major provisions—end of the entitlement structure, block grants, work requirements, sanctions, and time limits—constituted the most fundamental reform of any major welfare program in American history. They also cast the nation's major cash welfare program into a sea of uncertainty. Were states capable of successfully mounting work programs? Could a welfare system designed to calculate eligibility for cash payments convert itself to a jobs program? Would the American economy generate enough jobs? And most of all, were low-income mothers with little education or work experience capable of getting jobs and holding them?

Reducing Nonmarital Births

One of the more fascinating and controversial features of the new law was the unprecedented breadth of the attack on nonmarital births. Children born outside marriage are at a yawning statistical disadvantage in America. They are more likely than children born to married parents to live in poverty, to be subject to abuse, to have education problems including dropping out of school, to commit crimes, and to experience a host of other problems. Republicans believed that illegitimacy was a major cause of domestic problems such as school failure, unemployment, crime, and welfare use, and they believed that those problems were handed from generation to generation under the old welfare system.[27]

A modest problem that Republicans faced in formulating policy to reduce nonmarital births was that there was virtually no evidence that any policy would be effective. But Republicans were not distracted by the mere lack of evidence that anything would work. Their solution was simple—try everything. As a result of that approach, the new law contained at least 15 provisions directed at reducing illegitimacy.

Among the most remarkable was the policy of ending or reducing welfare benefits for children born outside marriage. House Republicans included two stripped-down versions of Charles Murray's sweeping policy of welfare termination in their initial bills.[28] The first version grew from a set of proposals offered by conservative House Republicans led by Jim Talent of Missouri and Tim Hutchinson of Louisiana that would have ended cash AFDC and food stamps for all illegitimate children. After intense debate among themselves just before the 1994 elections, a House Republican task force agreed on a policy to end just cash welfare for illegitimate children and their mothers if the mother was under age 18. When the mother turned 18, the cash benefit would be restored. Democrats savagely attacked this radical policy idea. Even so, it was supported by nearly all House Republicans and was included in the bill the House sent the Senate in March 1995. But in a direct vote on the Senate floor in September 1995, a majority of Senate Republicans and nearly all

Democrats rejected the policy.[29] This policy remains an option for states, but no state has adopted it.

A second and milder form of the Murray termination proposal was to end the practice of providing additional cash benefits to mothers who have babies while they are on welfare. This policy, which came to be known as the "family cap," enjoyed overwhelming support among House Republicans and was also a major feature of the bill they sent the Senate in March 1995. But this policy too came to an abrupt end on the Senate floor.[30] Even so, because of the broad flexibility granted to states by the TANF block grant, eventually about half the states adopted the family cap without federal prodding.[31]

Several other policies directed against nonmarital births were important. First, the tough work requirements and time limits imposed by the TANF program were seen by many Republicans and policy analysts as a discouragement to childbearing outside marriage. If young women know that they cannot depend on welfare as they have in the past, they might take steps to avoid having babies that they would have to work to support.

Second, child-support enforcement was seen as a deterrent to male participation in creating pregnancy outside of marriage. If young men know that a nonmarital birth is nearly certain to result in 18 years or more of making child-support payments, they might be more cautious in their sexual encounters. To the extent that child-support reforms made it more difficult for fathers to avoid paying child support, child-support enforcement became a kind of birth control. Especially important in this regard were the very strong paternity establishment requirements included in the TANF program. Mothers with nonmarital children had to identify the father by supplying names, addresses, places of employment, and other information or have their cash benefit ended. That policy, which put a premium on coercion, was buttressed by also requiring that states establish a voluntary paternity establishment program that operated in hospitals. Research showed that most fathers of illegitimate children had a serious relationship with the mother and often visited the mother and baby in the hospital at the time of birth.[32] Thus, states were required to approach the fathers at this propitious moment and ask them to acknowledge paternity.

Perhaps the most innovative feature of the Republican attack on illegitimacy was the creation of a $50 million per year abstinence education program. Each state is given a share of the federal grant money based on its percentage of the nation's poor children. States can spend the money only on abstinence programs, which are defined to exclude any use of the money to promote birth control or family planning. Abstinence, according to the Republican definition, means that youngsters should be exposed to adults who give them a pure abstinence message.

This approach to sex education is a substantial departure from the approach taken by most curriculums used in public schools both then and now. Those curriculums tend to treat sex as something in which all adolescents are expected to participate. One curriculum recommends that teachers instruct students in the use of condoms by dividing their class into two teams and conducting a relay race to see which team would be the fastest in having each participant put a condom on a cucumber. Other "safe sex" curriculums discuss various ways to have sex without having intercourse. Those methods included "outer course" in which kids simulate sex while wearing clothes, reading sexy material to each other, oral sex, and mutual masturbation.[33] The GOP focus on abstinence represented a sharp break with this sex education approach. It is based on the adult value judgment that kids should not be involved with sex, period.

Taken together, these and several other provisions in the new law—such as a cash bonus to states that reduced their illegitimacy rate—constitute the broadest and most serious attack ever mounted against illegitimate births.

Streamlining Child Care

The work requirements of the welfare reform law mean that child care is a necessity. To accommodate the need for child care, Republicans made fundamental changes in federal child care programs. The defining characteristics of the federal child care system had been laid down by welfare reform and child care legislation enacted in 1988 and 1990, respectively.[34] Surprisingly, the child care policy established by those two laws reflected basic Republican views and explicitly rejected federal control, even though both laws were enacted before the GOP majority.

The heart of federal child care policy is the use of vouchers through which parents can make their own choice of child care facility. For two decades liberals had pushed to establish a national policy that would favor center-based care in which professional child care workers would provide care that met federal standards. But Republicans opposed federal standards and the professionalization of child care by ensuring that states give parents the right to select their own provider through use of vouchers and by allowing state and local governments to set their own regulations. Research and experience had shown that many parents were more likely to select an informal neighborhood provider or a relative than a child care center. The child care provisions in the 1996 welfare law affirmed those policies of parental choice and no federal regulations.

The vital child care innovation of the 1996 legislation is the simplification of the system of funding child care. Republicans simply ended several programs and poured the money into a single program. The approach eliminates lots of state paperwork and opens the possibility of states having a single, coordinated child care program that can provide financial assistance to poor and low-income families whether they are on welfare or working. Because of the expected increased need for child care, Republicans, with prodding from governors and congressional Democrats, increased the amount of day-care funding by $4.5 billion over the six years between 1997 and 2002. These child care reforms mean that states can now serve many more families and do so more efficiently than under prior law. After modest levels of partisan bickering, especially over funding, the child care reforms enjoyed nearly universal support.

Strengthening Child-Support Enforcement

Originally enacted in 1975, the child support program aims to locate absent parents, establish paternity if necessary, obtain court orders for child support, and collect money. If a family has never been on welfare, the custodial parent (usually the mother) and children receive all the funds collected. However, if the family is still on welfare, nearly all the collections are retained by the state and federal governments. If the family has left welfare, collections equal to or less than the amount of the monthly child-support order are given to the family; any amount above the monthly child-support order is split between the family and the government.[35]

The 1996 reforms to the program were the most important since 1975. New means of locating income, new methods of collecting money, new information-processing requirements, and new databases were established. Perhaps the most significant provision for

111

increasing collections was requiring that employers report identifying information on every person hired. Employers report to their state database, which in turn feeds into a national database. That new data system, which would soon contain the name and address of the employer of almost every person hired in the country, was expected to greatly reduce the ability of noncustodial parents to hide their income. Another major reform required every state to develop procedures for locating and extracting money from accounts held in financial institutions by parents who owed child support. The provision that caused the most angry telephone calls and letters to members of Congress required states to have laws that permitted states to terminate the driving, hunting, and fishing licenses of fathers who owed overdue child support. Raiding a man's bank account is one thing, but interfering with his ability to hunt or fish was radical!

Notwithstanding those important changes, the biggest reform affected the way that child-support collections were split between families and the government. Under the new policy, after mothers leave welfare they are given about half the funds collected by states on overdue child support. This reform represented a sharp break with the original program conceived by Sen. Russell Long (D-Ga.), but was consistent with the overall thrust of the 1996 legislation. Before the 1996 reforms, a major purpose of the child-support program had been to reimburse government for providing welfare payments to families. But that purpose was now superseded by the importance of helping mothers supplement their earnings in order to avoid welfare. In this new world, policies were aimed at helping mothers sustain themselves in employment. Hence child-support collections were aimed at mothers and not the government.

Ending Welfare for Noncitizens

Although the child care and child-support reforms enjoyed some bipartisan support, the Republican determination to end welfare for noncitizens was bitterly contested. From the earliest colonial times, noncitizens had generally been excluded from government assistance programs.[36] When the federal Congress first enacted legislation addressing welfare for noncitizens in the 1870s, immigration officials were charged with ensuring that no immigrants be admitted unless they could support themselves. Congress later strengthened that

112

provision to require that noncitizens who became "public charges," that is, dependent on welfare, be deported. The clear implication of those provisions was that noncitizens should not receive government welfare benefits. The principle behind that policy was that taxpayers should not be required to subsidize benefits for people who came to America for opportunity. Public opinion polls in the 1990s showed that 60 to 70 percent of Americans supported the policy of barring welfare for noncitizens. A Roper poll conducted in December 1994, for example, found that 64 percent of Americans favored a policy to "limit or deny welfare aid to noncitizens."

Nonetheless, beginning in the 1960s noncitizens managed to obtain federal and state welfare benefits in increasing numbers. By 1995, Census Bureau data showed that households with noncitizens were actually more likely to receive welfare than households composed entirely of citizens. The case of Supplemental Security Income (SSI) was especially notable. SSI provides cash benefits to the elderly and the disabled poor. The number of noncitizens receiving SSI exploded in the 1980s and early 1990s, rising from about 120,000 in 1982 to nearly 700,000 by 1993.[37] Growth in SSI for the elderly, which quadrupled to 440,000 in the decade after 1983, led the way. Apparently, immigrants who had established themselves in America were encouraging their parents to immigrate as well. Having never worked in the United States, elderly noncitizens could obtain a visa to establish residence for the purpose of family reunification, live here for the mandatory five-year waiting period, and then qualify for SSI cash and health insurance. The former provided about $8,000 per year (including the cash supplement provided by most states); the latter provided a benefit that was potentially worth much more than the cash benefit.

Republicans saw this policy as unfair to taxpayers because America already offered immigrants the best deal in the world: immigrants could enjoy the world's best economy and the most individual freedom. But in exchange, the GOP said that noncitizens should obey our laws and not go on welfare. When immigrants become citizens, they are eligible for welfare benefits just like any other citizen. Given the certainty that some immigrants would face unemployment, sickness, and injury, Republicans wanted most immigrants to have a sponsor before they could enter the country. Upon entry, noncitizens are now told that they are not eligible for welfare but that they should rely on their sponsor if they fall on hard times. Sponsors are required to sign a legally binding agreement accepting responsibility for providing assistance if the noncitizen faces destitution.

An even more fundamental reform was that noncitizens were barred from receiving nearly all welfare benefits for five years after entry. Thus, only immigrants who intend to live by their own labor or who have a sponsor willing to support them are now likely to enter the country. Exceptions are made for natural disasters, communicable diseases, medical emergencies, and similar extreme circumstances. Refugees are also exempted from the ban because they are often forced from their native country and usually arrive destitute. But in all other circumstances, immigrants need to rely on their own resources or those of their sponsor. After five years, states have the option of providing benefits through TANF and Medicaid. But the ban on food stamps, SSI, and housing continues beyond five years, until the immigrant becomes a citizen.

One exception to those new rules is notable. Because the main goal of the 1996 law was to promote self-sufficiency, Republicans maintained the eligibility of noncitizens for most programs that provided education, training, or work support. Even though most programs have limited funding and do not serve all eligible citizens, Republicans nonetheless believed that immigrant children should be given every chance to obtain a good education by enrolling in Head Start, Title I public education programs, and other education programs. Similarly, noncitizen adults retain their eligibility for a host of education, training, and work-support benefits, including child care and the Earned Income Tax Credit. The EITC alone was worth up to $3,500 annually in 1995 ($4,500 today) for immigrant families that worked. If the family has come to America to pursue opportunity, Republican policy includes them in a network of programs that provide support. But welfare for noncitizens who do not work was all but ended, despite the strong protests of Democrats.

Ending Welfare for Drug Addicts and Alcoholics

Another aspect of federal welfare that Republicans were determined to reform was the policy of providing drug addicts and alcoholics with a guaranteed annual income and medical coverage. Addicts could get these benefits through SSI, Social Security Disability Insurance (SSDI), Medicaid, and Medicare. The Social Security

Administration (SSA) had determined that addiction was a disabling condition and was therefore eligible for coverage under both SSI and SSDI. In addition to the monthly cash benefit, SSI and SSDI coverage automatically included health coverage under either Medicaid or Medicare. For addicts with health problems secondary to their addiction, health coverage could be even more costly to taxpayers than the SSI cash benefit of about $8,000 per year.

There actually were fewer SSI recipients with the primary diagnosis of drug addiction or alcoholism in 1986 than there had been in 1975 when the program was established. But after 1986, enrollment increased rapidly. Between 1986 and 1990 the enrollment increased by an average of about 4,000 addicts per year. But between 1991 and 1995, enrollment increased by an average of more than 20,000 per year. Just before the welfare reform legislation was signed in 1996, there were 119,000 SSI recipients with the primary diagnosis of addiction to drugs or alcohol.[38] Indeed, the SSA, under orders from Congress, was actively recruiting additional addicts and alcoholics to the program. Apparently, the word was getting around that the government would provide cash and health care to citizens (or even noncitizens) who could prove they were addicted to alcohol or drugs, regardless of whether they had physical or mental disabilities.

Republicans were convinced that this program for addicts and alcoholics should be terminated. If addicts had secondary conditions that could qualify them for SSI or SSDI, such as sclerosis of the liver or mental health problems, then they could receive benefits. No Democrats appeared to champion either the SSI or SSDI programs for addicts and alcoholics. For Republicans, these were the quintessential welfare programs. Republicans believed that welfare caused or at least supported nonwork and illegitimacy, and they were even more convinced that it was irresponsible to give welfare to people who violated the norms of society and, in the case of drug addicts, broke the law. The programs died with barely a whimper of opposition.

Reducing SSI Eligibility for Children

The Republican changes to the SSI program for children were potentially the most explosive and dangerous of all the welfare reforms. The goal of the reforms was reducing the number of children with mild problems that should not be considered disabilities

115

who nonetheless received disability payments. This politically risky goal virtually invited attacks from Democrats and children's advocates. The nightmare scenario for Republicans was that Democrats would bring a child with severe physical disabilities into a hearing as the poster child for the cruel lengths to which Republicans would go to save money. On May 23, 1996, in a Ways and Means Committee hearing, Democrats took precisely that politically charged action.[39]

Even so, Ways and Means Republicans, under the leadership of Reps. Clay Shaw of Florida and Jim McCrery of Louisiana, insisted on tightening the children's eligibility requirements for SSI. Republicans argued that hundreds of thousands of children were being admitted who had only modest problems, usually in the form of mild behavioral disorders like attention deficit disorder and mild mental retardation. As a result of the loose eligibility requirements, enrollment of children in SSI had tripled to nearly one million in just five years.[40] In testimony before the Ways and Means Committee, a General Accounting Office official agreed that the criteria for children's disability were so loose that children with only mild problems were admitted to the program. Indeed, the GAO official told the committee that the criteria were so loose that children who simply behaved in an age-inappropriate way were often qualified for benefits.[41] Clay Shaw remarked that by this criterion, half the members of Congress were qualified for SSI.

The 1996 law contained three substantial reforms of the children's SSI program. First, the definition of childhood disability was changed so that only physical or mental impairments that resulted in "marked and severe" limitations in ability to think, talk, or interact with others would qualify for benefits. As part of that reform, a test then used by the SSA to determine disability was eliminated because it detected disability where none existed. Second, the SSA was required to review all childhood cases for improvement on a regular basis, especially cases in which infants had been admitted because of low birth weight. Third, children were required to have their eligibility redetermined using adult criteria when they reached age 18.

Results of Welfare Reform

It has been almost a decade since the welfare reform law was signed by President Clinton amid predictions of disaster from the political left. A tremendous volume of information bearing on the effects of the legislation has been produced in recent years. The legislation itself provided funding for research,[42] private foundations have funded research,[43] state data have been accumulated, and Census Bureau data have provided many insights into the effects of the legislation.

The most interesting and important outcomes are those for the TANF welfare-to-work program. The results of TANF and the other six major policy changes are discussed in turn.

Temporary Assistance for Needy Families

A major outcome of the new TANF program has been remarkable and widespread changes in local welfare offices. An aspect of federal policymaking that is often overlooked is that many federal edicts lead to modest or undetectable changes at the state and local levels. As an irreverent graduate student once put it, "They passed a law in Washington, and no one noticed." And yet, as a number of observers, including Professor Richard Nathan and his colleagues at the State University of New York at Albany, have shown in careful studies, the changes in local welfare offices have been pervasive.[44]

Most states have developed a course, lasting a week or less, that might be called "Jobs 101." Those courses, which nearly all welfare applicants must take, help clients develop a resume, instruct them how to contact employers, and review the basics of job interviews. Some programs have recipients role-play job interviews; other programs provide tips for dressing in a professional manner; some even provide a free business suit to help welfare recipients make solid first impressions. Most of the courses also review the elements of being a good employee, including showing up on time, getting along with co-workers, and taking directions. In most states, the philosophy of the new welfare-to-work programs has been to get mothers a job as quickly as possible and not to provide education or training. It is remarkable how quickly former welfare offices from New York to California and Florida to Washington converted themselves into job centers.[45]

Because a majority of states were busy implementing their own welfare-to-work reforms by 1994, it seems wise to examine the effects of the 1996 reforms, not by using 1995 as the comparison year, but by using 1993, the year before most states began to implement their

Figure 9.1
AFDC/TANF CASELOAD

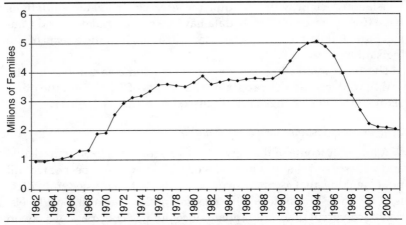

NOTE: 2003 is preliminary based on January-September data.
SOURCE: U.S. Department of Health and Human Services, Indicators of Welfare Dependence: Annual Report to Congress, 2003 (Washington: Government Printing Office, 2003).

reform programs, as the comparison year. Thus, most of the following analyses compare information on welfare use, work, income, and poverty for 1993 and 2002, the most recent year for which abundant information is available.

If the reforms have had their intended effect, a key indicator of success should be a declining welfare caseload. TANF data reported by states to the federal government show that caseloads began declining in the spring of 1994. The decline picked up steam after the federal legislation was enacted in 1996, as shown in Figure 9.1[46] Between 1994 and 2003, the caseload declined about 60 percent nationally. The number of families receiving cash welfare is now the lowest it has been since 1971. These results are dramatic.

Although it is often reported in the media that cash welfare caseloads increase during economic recessions and decline during recoveries, that claim is mostly false. In the 41 years between 1953 and 1994, the number of families on AFDC declined in only five years. Only once did the caseload decline two years in a row (between 1977 and 1979 it declined by about 2 percent). By contrast, 2003 was

118

the ninth year in a row that the caseload had declined. Clearly, we are in a new era of reduced welfare use.

Critics charge that caseload decline should not be the major consideration in determining whether welfare reform has succeeded. Agreed. Another test of welfare reform is whether mothers leaving welfare are now working. Again, there is abundant information to answer this question from three lines of evidence. First, dozens of scientific studies have been conducted since the 1980s to examine the effects of various programs designed to promote work.[47] Both before and after enactment of the 1996 reforms, those studies almost uniformly show reductions in caseloads and increases in employment attributable to work requirements, especially job-search requirements. Second, since 1996 more than 40 studies have been conducted by states of adults who left welfare. On average, these "leaver" studies show that about 60 percent of the adults leaving welfare are employed at any given moment, and that over a period of several months about 80 percent have held at least one job.[48]

Third, the most definitive data are on adult employment for the nation as a whole from the Bureau of Labor Statistics.[49] Between 1993 and 2000, the percentage of employed single mothers grew from 58 percent to nearly 75 percent, an increase of almost 27 percent, as shown in Figure 9.2. Even more pertinent to assessing the effects of welfare reform, the subgroup of working never-married mothers grew from 44 percent to 66 percent over the same period. Before 1996, never-married mothers were precisely the ones most likely to drop out of school, go on welfare, and have long welfare spells of over a decade or more. Yet their employment over this period grew by almost 50 percent. As with the caseload decline, these changes in employment by low-income single mothers—especially never-married mothers—are without precedent.

Figure 9.2 shows that there was a small decline in employment among never-married mothers in 2001 as well as a small decline among all single mothers in 2002. Those declines were almost certainly caused by the recession that began in March of 2001. The decline for never-married mothers in 2001 was slightly more than one percentage point, but employment among this most-disadvantaged group of mothers completely recovered in 2002. The decline in 2002 for all single mothers was also about one percentage point. By historical standards, those declines in employment during a recession are modest. An analysis by the Economic Policy Institute shows

119

Figure 9.2
PERCENTAGE OF SINGLE AND NEVER-MARRIED MOTHERS WHO
ARE WORKING

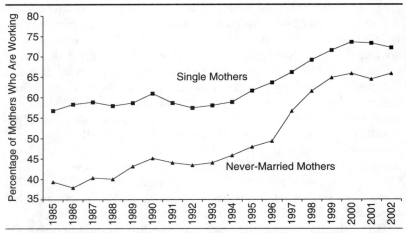

SOURCE: U.S. Bureau of Labor Statistics, http://stats.bls.gov/cps/home.htm

that unemployment among workers with less than a high school education was much less during or following the 2001 recession than during or following the two previous recessions. Specifically, unemployment among these workers declined by 1.8 percentage points and 2.6 percentage points in the 1981 and 1990 recessions, respectively, compared with a 0.4 percentage point decline during the 2001 recession.[50] The reasons for these differences are not well understood, but it is clear that the 2001 recession had a modest effect on employment of low-income mothers.

If the welfare rolls have fallen and work has increased, it stands to reason that income patterns for female-headed families should have changed. Census Bureau data on income for the 40 percent of mother-headed families with children at the bottom of the income distribution (those below about $21,000 in 2000) show that the pattern of income for these families has indeed shifted dramatically since 1993.[51] The income data can be grouped into four categories: earnings, welfare (cash, food stamps, housing, school lunch), the Earned Income Tax Credit, and other income (including social insurance and child-support payments). In 1993, earnings accounted for 29 percent of the income of low-income mother-headed families

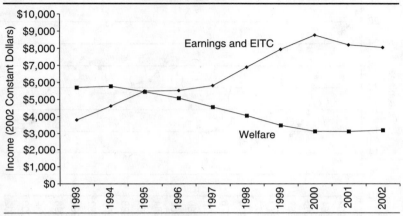

Figure 9.3
EARNINGS AND WELFARE FOR THE BOTTOM TWO-FIFTHS OF
FEMALE-HEADED FAMILIES

NOTE: Welfare income is cash, school lunch, food stamps, and housing.
SOURCE: Richard Bavier, Office of Management and Budget.

whereas welfare payments accounted for nearly 50 percent. By 2000, that pattern had reversed: earnings in dollars had leaped while welfare income fell, as shown in Figure 9.3. As earnings grew, income from the EITC more than doubled. In total, overall income of these families increased by more than 22 percent during the period despite a large drop in welfare income.

Rising earnings and falling welfare are the precise goal of welfare reform. Changes in income of this magnitude over such a short period for low-income families are unprecedented in the history of Census Bureau records. The bottom line is that female-headed families with children are financially better off primarily because the mothers work and earn more money, despite the fact that their income from welfare has fallen. Even without welfare, taxpayers make a contribution to the well-being of these families through the EITC and other programs.

The increased earnings of female-headed families has had a substantial effect on poverty rates. Child poverty dropped smartly during the 1960s, but after the early 1970s child poverty gradually drifted upward, primarily because an increasing percentage of American children were being reared in female-headed families. But child

Figure 9.4
PERCENTAGE OF U.S. CHILDREN IN POVERTY

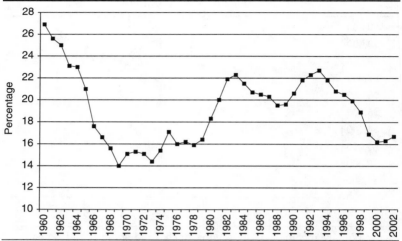

SOURCE: Bernadette D. Proctor and Joseph Dalaker, *Poverty in the United States: 2002* (Washington: Government Printing Office, 2003).

poverty fell every year between 1993 and 2000 and reached lows not seen since 1978, as shown in Figure 9.4. Even better, the poverty rate of black children reached its lowest level ever. The percentage of families in deep poverty, defined as half the poverty level (about $7,000 for a mother with two children in 2000), has also declined substantially, reaching the lowest level ever recorded in 2000.[52]

These declines in child poverty after 1993 were disrupted by the recession of 2001. Child poverty increased by about 0.1 percentage point in 2001 and 0.4 percentage point in 2002. But those increases were very slight compared with the effects of the recessions in the early 1980s and early 1990s. In the first year following those two recessions, poverty among children in female-headed families increased by 3.5 and 2.6 percentage points, respectively. By contrast, the poverty increase in the year after the 2001 recession was only 0.6 percentage point. Any increase in child poverty is unfortunate, but by historical standards the effect of the 2001 recession on child poverty has been modest.[53]

Although welfare reform is a major cause of the decline in welfare dependency and child poverty as well as the dramatic rise in earnings of female-headed families, at least two other factors are important. First, the economy of the 1990s was exceptionally strong. Statistical studies have been conducted to determine the relative contribution of the economy, of welfare reform, and of other factors to the dramatic increases in work and earnings by low-income mothers.[54] Those studies all show that both welfare reform and the booming economy were important, but there is little agreement about the relative contributions of each factor. It might be noted, however, that previous economic booms did not lead to either the reduction in welfare rolls or the increase in work by low-income mothers heading families that were seen in the 1990s. Without welfare reform pushing mothers into the growing market economy, there would have been a more modest effect on the employment and earnings of these mothers.

Another important factor contributing to the decline of welfare and the rise of employment and earnings is a series of changes in government programs that support working families. Numerous pieces of legislation enacted since the mid-1980s have created new programs and expanded existing ones to help low-income working families. These programs included expansions in child care funding, creation of the child tax credit, larger standard deductions and personal exemptions in the income tax code, expansions of Medicaid coverage, and several major expansions of the EITC.

A 1998 study by the Congressional Budget Office provides an idea of the magnitude of these changes.[55] The study examined several major programs that aid low-income working families, including child care, the State Child Health Insurance Program, the child tax credit, Medicaid, and the EITC. CBO estimated the benefits that would have accrued to low-income working families in 1999 from these programs both as they existed in 1984 and as they existed in 1999 after numerous expansions. The findings were surprising: if the programs had remained as they were in 1984, working families in 1999 would have received around $6 billion in benefits. But because Congress expanded the programs, CBO estimated they would provide nearly $53 billion in support to working families in 1999 (see Figure 9.5). Those amazing numbers lead to the conclusion that the nation's social policy to help low-income families has shifted from one that provided most of its benefits to families dependent on welfare to one that provides enormous benefits to working families.

123

Figure 9.5
GOVERNMENT SUPPORT FOR WORKING FAMILIES INCREASES
DRAMATICALLY

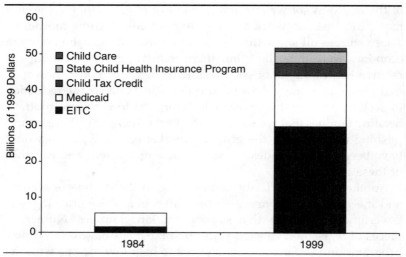

SOURCE: Congressional Budget Office, "Policy Changes Affecting Mandatory Spending for Low-Income Families Not Receiving Welfare, " 1998.

Reducing Nonmarital Births

Trends in nonmarital births and the composition of American families are modestly good. One of the most important indicators of family composition is the rate of teen births. Annual data from the National Center for Health Statistics indicate that the teen birthrate has been declining since the early 1990s. By 2002, after 11 years of continuous declines, the rate of teen births had reached 43.8 births per 1,000 females aged 15–19, the lowest ever for this age group.[56] This development is exceptionally welcome. Although the decline began in the early 1990s, showing that factors other than welfare reform play a role, welfare reform may also be contributing to the continuing declines.

After decades of increases, the nonmarital birthrate for women of all ages has roughly stabilized since 1994, as shown in Figure 9.6. The rate for blacks has actually declined since 1994. For whites the percentage of nonmarital births has continued to increase, although at a slower pace since the mid-1990s. Again, given the timing of the

Figure 9.6
PERCENTAGE OF BIRTHS TO UNMARRIED WOMEN

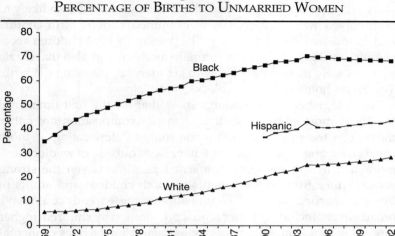

SOURCE: Stephanie J. Ventura et. al., "Nonmarital Childbearing in the United States, 1940–99," *National Vital Statistics Reports*, vol. 48, no. 16 (Washington: National Center for Health Statistics, 2000), and "Revised Pregnancy Rates, 1990–97, and New Rates for 1998–99 in the United States," *National Vital Statistics Reports*, vol. 52, no. 7 (Washington: National Center for Health Statistics, 2003).

decline among blacks and the overall stabilization, the role of welfare reform in producing these trends is ambiguous: other factors are certainly involved, but welfare reform could be playing a role in the continuing decline for blacks and moderating the increases for whites and Hispanics.

The most widely studied change in family composition since the 1996 reforms is the percentage of children living with single mothers. Researchers seem to agree that this indicator has declined. Conversely, the percentage of children living with two adults has increased, although it is not clear that this figure always means mothers are living with the fathers of their children. Most investigators also conclude that because those changes have occurred primarily among low-income parents, welfare reform appears to be a causal factor.[57]

Recent careful analyses by Richard Bavier of the Office of Management and Budget show that the fraction of children living with married parents has increased since the mid-1990s, and that the change is especially large for blacks, a demographic group likely to be involved with welfare. Bavier examined various birth cohorts and found that for birth cohorts beginning in 1994 children were slightly less likely to be born to single mothers, and also that single mothers were increasingly likely to get married following the birth. This trend holds for whites, blacks, and Hispanics.[58]

Taken together, these findings show that for the first time since the 1960s most of the measures of family composition are either moving in the right direction or no longer deteriorating. If those trends continue, fewer children will be born outside of wedlock and more will live in two-parent, married families. Given the strong research literature on the benefits for both children and adults of living in married families,[59] continuation of these trends could have broad effects, including better school preparation by children, higher rates of school completion, less delinquency, lower rates of mental health problems, lower poverty rates, and further declines in welfare use.

It is too early to be confident that the favorable trends in family composition will continue or that the desirable outcomes these should produce will actually materialize. But for the first time in several generations, modest optimism is warranted. As welcome as these trends might be, only modest evidence exists that welfare reform is a major cause. Indeed, some researchers claim that welfare is not affecting family composition.[60]

Streamlining Child Care

The child care reforms in the 1996 law are widely seen as a success. States have used all the $4.5 billion in new child care money provided by the 1996 reforms. And in a development that no one predicted, states are using a substantial portion of their TANF funds for child care, a move made possible by the flexibility of the TANF block grant. In 2005, for example, states are expected to use about $3.6 billion of their $16.5 billion TANF funds for child care, in addition to the nearly $5 billion from the federal child care funds and another $3.3 billion of state matching funds.[61] Overall, the combined total of state and federal dollars for child care has doubled since the 1996 reforms, as has the number of families receiving assistance. Welfare reform has produced an outpouring of government child care funds for poor and low-income families.

In addition to dramatic increases in spending, the emphasis on vouchers and regulatory flexibility—features of previous child care legislation that were retained in the 1996 reforms—have ensured the continuation of a diverse child care market. Parents using child care subsidies are purchasing center-based care, informal care in neighborhoods, and care by relatives such as grandparents. The preservation of parent choice and modest state regulation of care has meant that lots of relatively inexpensive care is used, thereby keeping down the overall costs of welfare reform and helping the pocketbooks of all low-income families. Notwithstanding, many child development researchers worry that much of this care provides inadequate support for optimum child development.[62]

Strengthening Child-Support Enforcement

The child-support reforms have proven to be just as successful. Most states have aggressively implemented the child-support reforms, including expanded databases, new collection methods, and more efficient data processing. The immediate outcome is that the nation's child-support program has joined the electronic age. In many states the child-support program may well be the most sophisticated and modern of all government services. In part as a result of those reforms, child-support collections have nearly doubled since 1995, rising from $10.8 billion to more than $20 billion. Equally impressive, paternity establishment has increased substantially, rising from about 0.9 million in 1995 to above 1.5 million every year after 1997.[63] This remarkable success seems to be caused by the carrot of voluntary paternity establishment programs in hospitals and the stick of requirements on welfare mothers with nonmarital children to provide information on fathers or lose their benefits.

Although the improvements in the child-support program are remarkable, the number of low-income mothers who receive child support and the amount they receive is somewhat discouraging. The approximately four million mothers heading families with children who have total income of less than $21,000 received an average of only about $620 in child-support payments in 2000. Probably because of the growing effectiveness of the child-support program, this amount was about 50 percent greater than in 1995.[64] Single mothers are now receiving more child support than in the past, but the modest amount received per family shows that many low-income mothers cannot expect major income boosts from child support in the near future, especially because only about one-quarter of these mothers received any child-support payments in 2000. Perhaps the most that can be said about the child-support program is that the mothers who receive payments enjoy a substantial income supplement, but even after extensive reform and substantial government investments, three-quarters of low-income mothers still receive no help at all.

Ending Welfare for Noncitizens

The effects of the 1996 reforms on welfare for noncitizens have been exactly what Congress intended. Data from the Census Bureau show unequivocally that use of welfare by noncitizens has declined rapidly. Research by Michael Fix and colleagues at the Urban Institute, based on the Census Bureau data, shows that between 1994 and 1999 the receipt of TANF cash welfare by noncitizens declined 60 percent, food stamp receipt declined 48 percent, and SSI receipt declined 32 percent.[65] More recently the CRS found that those declines were maintained through 2001.[66] Although legislation passed in 1997 allowed most of the noncitizens receiving welfare benefits when the 1996 law passed to retain their benefits, the number of noncitizens receiving welfare is nonetheless clearly headed downward. For those who believe that noncitizens should not qualify for welfare, the reforms have been a major success.

Few areas of social policy present such a stark example of the importance of values in policy choice as that presented by welfare for noncitizens. Republicans generally believe welfare raises dependency—with its associated evils of nonwork and illegitimacy—no matter who receives it. Democrats are willing to risk dependency as a reasonable price to pay to ensure that destitute mothers, children, immigrants, addicts, and other groups have guaranteed benefits. In addition to the concern with dependency, Republicans believe that noncitizens should be ineligible for welfare until they become citizens because the basis of immigration policy should be the opportunity and freedom provided by our private economy, not government handouts. By contrast, Democrats believe that the need to ensure a basic level of economic security trumps the self-sufficiency principle of immigration. The 1996 legislation seems not to have changed the reasoning of either side. Rather, Republicans used their control of

Congress to muscle through the termination of welfare benefits for noncitizens and to return welfare policy for noncitizens to its 19th-century roots. Even so, Democrats are still intent on restoring welfare benefits for noncitizens. Republicans are equally intent on preserving the 1996 prohibitions. Stay tuned.

Ending Welfare for Drug Addicts and Alcoholics

Like the reform of welfare benefits for noncitizens, the termination of SSI and SSDI benefits for alcoholics and other drug addicts has had exactly the intended effect. About 210,000 adult addicts were terminated from the SSI and SSDI programs. A study by the Lewin Group of Fairfax, Virginia, estimated that because some recipients would have lost their benefits even without the new policy and within one year about 71,000 former addicts had reestablished eligibility based on another disabling condition, the termination policy actually reduced the SSI and SSDI caseloads by a net 103,000 cases.[67] This estimate does not, however, take into account the fact that the number of individuals admitted to both programs was growing rapidly at the time the programs were ended. Thus, the estimate of a net reduction of 103,000 is almost certainly too small. There is little doubt that the total savings from the termination policy, plus the associated medical coverage of these two programs, is in excess of $1 billion per year.

However, little is known about the other effects of the termination policy. The fact that 71,000 addicts reestablished their eligibility, most with only a minor delay in payments, suggests that the truly disabled are continuing to receive their benefits in accordance with the purpose of the SSI and SSDI programs. But what about the 103,000 or more who would have received cash and medical coverage under the old policy? The short answer is that little good information exists to answer this question. The Lewin study produced some anecdotal evidence that many of the former recipients faced hardships. Among the outcomes mentioned in their anecdotal account were a decline in participation in treatment programs, modest increases in work, loss of housing, and a few cases of suicide. However, without some type of comparison group, it is impossible to know which of these effects can be attributed to the termination policy itself.

Nonetheless, there likely were some negative effects of the termination policy, and suffering probably increased for some portion

129

of the 103,000 addicts who lost their benefits. Does it follow that termination was the wrong policy? Republicans offered and defended the termination policy exclusively on the basis of values: federal policy should not provide a guaranteed annual income and health coverage to adults who have become addicted to alcohol or drugs. Very little attention was given to likely effects of the policy on suffering. The principle of not providing benefits to people who do bad things has been strengthened, but perhaps at the cost of a short-term increase in misery for some people. No major figure on the federal level has taken up the case that the increase in misery is too steep a price to pay to strengthen the principle of avoiding rewards for irresponsible behavior. Until someone does, the SSI and SSDI programs will continue to reflect the emphasis Republicans placed on principle, even at the possible cost of some increase in hardship.

Reducing SSI Eligibility for Children

The number of children on SSI has fallen substantially since enactment of the 1996 reforms. Because the rate of children entering SSI was increasing when the reforms were passed, a true estimate of the effect of the reforms requires use of statistical techniques to estimate how the caseload would have changed without the reforms. The SSA contracted with RAND of Santa Monica to conduct just such a sophisticated analysis of the 1996 reforms. RAND estimated, based on complex modeling, that by 2005 the SSI child caseload will be reduced by 26 percent, or 310,000 cases, compared with its size without the 1996 reforms.[68] The RAND study also estimated that the savings in 2005 in the children's program will be $2.3 billion. Over the 10-year period from 1996 through 2005, the cumulative savings will be $14.2 billion.

Similarly, primarily because of the decline in the child caseload and the new rule that 18-year-olds must have a disability redetermination, the young-adult caseload has also declined. RAND estimated that by 2005, the young-adult caseload would be 19 percent, or 209,000 cases, smaller than it would have been without the 1996 reforms. Over the 10-year period, the savings in the young-adult caseload would be about $7.5 billion, bringing the total savings for both age groups to $21.7 billion.

As with SSI for addicts, a thorough evaluation of the SSI reforms for children requires attention to the effects of the reforms on individuals. In 1998, RAND interviewed a small sample of 44 families from four states that had lost their SSI benefits because of the reforms; in 1999, 35 of those families were reinterviewed. RAND also conducted special analyses on a representative sample of 680 families on which the Census Bureau had collected extensive information for other purposes. The analysis of the Census data showed that loss of SSI was associated with increased work effort by parents, increased reliance on cash welfare, and increased family income. In addition, benefit loss produced a small decline in poverty. The family interviews were generally consistent with these results. Indeed, in the 1999 interviews, "nearly all parents stated that their child's overall health, functional status, and school performance had remained the same or had improved."[69]

Of course, it would be important to learn a lot more about how the families that lost SSI benefits coped with the change. The RAND study suggests that families responded to the loss of SSI benefits by increasing their work and earnings while getting more money from welfare programs other than SSI. But have the children been affected in any way? Has their school performance changed? Do they get sick more often? Do they have more conflicts with parents, teachers, or peers? Until someone knows, conclusions about the effects of the reforms on children are tentative and incomplete. RAND's family interviews are generally encouraging with regard to children's functioning and health, but the sample size is too small and interview data are too subjective to take much comfort from the results.

In sum, the 1996 welfare reforms were sweeping, and their effects have been no less sweeping. The effects on illegitimate births and family composition, child care, child-support enforcement, welfare for noncitizens, SSI for addicts, and SSI for children were all in line with the expectations of Republicans who developed the reforms. Regardless of what one thinks of these reforms, implementation has been associated with increased child care funds for working families; greatly increased child-support collections for custodial parents and children; and substantially reduced taxpayer expenditures on welfare for addicts, for children with questionable disabilities, and for noncitizens. In each case the reforms have moved the respective programs closer to achieving the goals for which they were designed.

Conclusions

It is useful to think of the remarkable changes in welfare use, work, income, and poverty among female-headed families during the 1990s as the result of a perfect storm of social policy reform and economic conditions.[70] The welfare reforms of 1996 were a vital part of the storm, but so were other changes in federal policy for family support and the vibrant economy.

The positive effects of the 1996 reforms have been pervasive and, in some cases, profound. However, no policy produces all benefits and no costs. Although the 1996 law did not produce the failures predicted by its critics, it nonetheless has created problems that states and the federal government should address. Three problems are especially notable.

One problem is that most mothers leaving welfare begin their work careers in $7 or $8 per hour jobs with few or no benefits. Anyone familiar with welfare-to-work programs realizes that many of these mothers—probably a majority—are capable of becoming valuable employees worth more than the modest wages they earn upon entry into the labor force. It is true that mothers on welfare are below average on most traits valuable to employees such as education, job experience, and work ethic. But experience shows that most mothers can overcome those deficits. The question is whether good education and training programs can speed this process and help mothers who would not otherwise move up the job ladder. The federal government has spent billions of dollars over the past 40 years on education and training programs for poor and low-income young adults. Research on these programs has shown them to be generally unsuccessful or, in a few cases, only modestly successful for specific groups.[71] The poor success of these education and training programs was the major consideration that drove Republicans to emphasize work-first programs in 1996.

So what is different now? Perhaps enough to be more optimistic. First, there are now two million or so additional low-income mothers in the labor force working at low-wage jobs. These mothers know that they must continue to work because permanent cash welfare is no longer an option. As they gain job experience and knowledge of the local labor market, many are looking around wondering what they could do to make $10 or $12 or more per hour. The motivation to try education or training is entirely different for a mother who is in no hurry to leave welfare as compared to a mother who is already off welfare and is not counting on going back. In addition to this change in motivation among low-income mothers, there is some evidence that programs offering some education produce both high employment and higher hourly earnings.[72]

Thus, there is hope that a new generation of education and training programs could have a positive effect on wages and earnings. Several states are now experimenting with training programs that work with local employers to identify and design training regimens for jobs actually available in the local economy. The training tends to be provided by local community colleges. Several programs of this type are now being subjected to rigorous evaluation. If the results are encouraging, money available in the TANF program and in other sources of training funds such as the Workforce Investment Act[73] should be redirected to ensure that low-income working adults have every opportunity to move up the job ladder.

Another serious problem raised by welfare reform is what becomes of troubled parents, those with emotional problems, very low intelligence, addictions, or other afflictions that are barriers to work.[74] In the past, troubled parents could stay on welfare for many years; now most of them must work. Today's welfare system requires at least some minimum level of competence, and not all parents have a minimum level of competence.

There are several ways to determine the magnitude of this problem. As mentioned, surveys find that about 60 percent of mothers leaving welfare are working at any given moment and about 80 percent have held at least one job since leaving welfare.[75] The 20 percent who have not worked at all since leaving welfare raise serious concerns. Research shows that states frequently use sanctions and that 36 states have policies that allow them to completely terminate cash benefits for rule infractions.[76] Research has firmly established that mothers who are sanctioned off the rolls have characteristics that make it less likely they will be able to get and hold a job. More specifically, they are less likely to have a high school degree or to have job experience, more likely to have addictions or mental health problems, and more likely to have three or more children.[77] These data suggest that some mothers may be struggling under the new system of increased responsibility.

More public funds should be devoted to conducting research and demonstration programs to determine how these mothers can be helped. The trick will be maintaining a demanding welfare system that strongly discourages welfare dependency while simultaneously allowing states enough flexibility to identify and help floundering mothers. Some mothers may never be able to achieve steady employment. The nation's welfare programs should provide accommodations of some type to these parents.[78]

A happy marriage of a Democratic president open to welfare reform and a new Republican majority that had well-developed reform proposals created the conditions for passage of sweeping reforms in 1996. The reforms fundamentally altered the ground of American social policy from dependency-producing entitlement to mandatory work. Underlying the numerous successes of reform was an American economy that was in the midst of a historic expansion with rapid job creation and wage increases, especially at the bottom of the income distribution. Further, a host of federal and state programs that provided generous support to low-income working families were important. The child tax credit and the State Child Health Insurance program were enacted at about the same time as welfare reform, providing additional support for low-income working families. Moreover, most states were already implementing their own welfare reform programs when the federal legislation provided them with the flexibility and funds to go even further in the direction they were already heading. In short, the timing of the 1996 federal welfare reform could not have been better.

The achievement of the 1996 reforms has been even greater than predicted by Republicans who were dogged in pushing them through Congress. Welfare rolls plummeted, employment of poor mothers leaped, earnings and total income grew, and poverty fell. Nearly all those trends were without precedent. In addition, child support paid by fathers increased dramatically and the disastrous trend toward single-parent families abated and even reversed slightly for some groups.

These successes have created their own problems and cleared the way for the emergence of new opportunities. But Republicans and Democrats in Congress are still too busy fighting over some of the 1996 reforms to pay careful attention to the future. When Congress awakens to the new opportunities at hand, it seems likely that federal policy will move further toward providing financial and other forms of support for low-income working families while maintaining—and even expanding—the strong emphasis on work. Similarly, policies designed to increase the number of children in two-parent, married families seem certain to remain on the public agenda in the years ahead. Further welfare reforms will not be simple to enact or cheap. But thanks to the Republican welfare revolution of 1996, the nation is on a new and firmer path to ending dependency, increasing self-reliance, and improving the economic status of millions of struggling families.

Notes

1. Ed Gillespie and Bob Schellhas, eds., *Contract with America: The Bold Plan by Rep. Newt Gingrich, Rep. Dick Armey and the House Republicans to Change the Nation* (New York: Times Books, 1994), p. 65.

2. James G. Gimpel, *Legislating the Revolution: The Contract with America in Its First 100 Days* (Boston: Allyn and Bacon, 1996).

3. David Baumann, "Grading the Class of '94," *National Journal* 36, no. 18 (May 1, 2004): 1322–30.

4. Dan Balz and Ronald Brownstein, *Storming the Gates: Protest and Politics and the Republican Revival* (Boston: Little, Brown, 1996).

5. Congressional Budget Office, "The Budget and Economic Outlook: Fiscal Years 2005–2014" (Washington: Government Printing Office, January 2004).

6. Alice M. Rivlin and Isabel V. Sawhill, eds., *Restoring Fiscal Sanity: How to Balance the Budget* (Washington: Brookings Institution, 2004).

7. *Congressional Record* 141, no. 137 (September 6, 1995): S 12681.

8. Sheila Zedlewski et al., "Potential Effects of Congressional Welfare Reform Legislation on Family Incomes," Urban Institute, July 1996.

9. *Congressional Record* 142, no. 116 (August 1, 1996): S 9364.

10. *Congressional Record* 142, no. 105 (July 17, 1996): H 7751.

11. *Congressional Record* 141, no. 52 (March 21, 1995): H 3348.

12. Ibid., H 3345.

13. Ibid., H 3358.

14. *Congressional Record* 141, no. 53 (March 22, 1995): H 3502.

15. Jim Nelson, "Apocalypse Now. Welfare Reform," *The Nation*, August 26, 1996, p. 10.

16. Marian Wright Edelman, "Say No to Welfare Reform," *Washington Post*, November 3, 1995, p. A23.

17. In October 1994, the Committee on Ways and Means asked the Congressional Research Service to prepare a list of every program in eight domains of social policy and to include an estimate of spending by each program in 1994. The domains included cash welfare, child protection (abuse and neglect), child care and preschool education, employment and training, social services, food and nutrition, housing, and health. By the end of November, CRS had sent separate reports on each of those domains to the committee. The reports showed that a total of 338 programs spent some $240 billion in 1994 (not including programs in the tax code such as the Earned Income Tax Credit).

18. Vee Burke, "Cash and Noncash Benefits for Persons with Limited Income: Eligibility, Rules, Recipient and Expenditure Data, FY2000–2002," Congressional Research Service, November 25, 2003. See also Robert Rector and William F. Lauber, *America's Failed $5.4 Trillion War on Poverty* (Washington: Heritage Foundation, 1995).

19. Byron M. Roth, *Prescription for Failure: Race Relations in the Age of Social Science* (New Brunswick, NH: Transaction, 1994); Ron Haskins, "Liberal and Conservative Influences on the Welfare Reform Legislation of 1996," in *For Better and For Worse: Welfare Reform and the Well-Being of Children and Families*, ed. Greg J. Duncan and Lindsay Chase-Lansdale (New York: Russell Sage Foundation, 2001).

20. Charles Murray, *Losing Ground: American Social Policy, 1950–1980* (New York: Basic Books, 1984).

21. Bernadette D. Proctor and Joseph Dalaker, U.S. Census Bureau, *Poverty in the United States: 2002* (Washington: Government Printing Office, 2003), Figure 2.

22. Stephanie J. Ventura et al., "Nonmarital Childbearing in the United States, 1940–99," *National Vital Statistics Reports*, vol. 48, no. 16 (Washington: National Center for Health Statistics, 2000); Stephanie J. Ventura et al., "Revised Pregnancy Rates, 1990–97, and New Rates for 1998–99: United States," ibid., vol. 52, no. 7 (Washington: National Center for Health Statistics, 2003).

23. David T. Ellwood and Mary Jo Bane, "The Impact of AFDC on Family Structure and Living Arrangements," in *Research in Labor Economics* 7: 137–207, ed. Ronald G. Ehrenberg (Greenwich, CT: Jai Press, 1985); Ron Haskins, "Does Welfare Encourage Illegitimacy?" *American Enterprise* 7, no. 4 (1996): 48–49.

24. House Committee on Ways and Means, *Contract with America—Overview*, 104th Cong., 1st sess., January 12, 1995, serial 104-20, pp. 511–624.

25. Judith M. Gueron and Edward Pauly, *From Welfare to Work* (New York: Russell Sage Foundation, 1991).

26. Gertrude Himmelfarb, *The Idea of Poverty: England in the Early Industrial Age* (New York: Vintage Books, 1983).

27. Charles Murray, "Family Formation," in *The New World of Welfare*, ed. Rebecca M. Blank and Ron Haskins (Washington: Brookings Institution, 2001).

28. Murray, *Losing Ground*.

29. See Roll Call Vote No. 419 Leg., 104th Cong., 1st sess., *Congressional Record* 141, no. 142 (September 13, 1995): S 13516 (Faircloth amend. no. 2603).

30. See Roll Call Vote No. 416 Leg., 104th Cong., 1st sess., *Congressional Record* 141, no. 142 (September 13, 1995): S 13489 (Domenici amend. no. 2575).

31. State Policy Documentation Project, www.spdp.org, a joint project of the Center for Law and Social Policy and the Center on Budget and Policy Priorities.

32. Nancy E. Reichman et al., "Fragile Families: Sample and Design," *Children and Youth Services Review* 23, nos. 4/5 (2001): 303–26.

33. Martin Shannan, Robert Rector, and Melissa G. Pardue, "Comprehensive Sex Education vs. Authentic Abstinence: A Study of Competing Curricula," Heritage Foundation, August 10, 2004.

34. Ron Haskins, "Child Development and Child Care Policy: Modest Impacts," in *Developmental Psychology and Social Change*, ed. David B. Pillemer and Sheldon H. White (Cambridge: Cambridge University Press, forthcoming); House Committee on Ways and Means, *2004 Green Book* (Washington: Government Printing Office, 2004), Section 9.

35. House Committee on Ways and Means, *2004 Green Book*, Section 8.

36. Ibid., Appendix J.

37. House Committee on Ways and Means, *1996 Green Book* (Washington: Government Printing Office, 1996), p. 1305.

38. House Committee on Ways and Means, *1998 Green Book* (Washington: Government Printing Office, 1998), p. 304.

39. House Committee on Ways and Means, Subcommittee on Human Resources, *Welfare Reform*, 104th Cong., 2nd sess., May 23, 1996, serial 104-62, pp. 107–35.

40. House Committee on Ways and Means, *1996 Green Book*, pp. 296–98.

41. House Committee on Ways and Means, Subcommittee on Human Resources, *Contract with America—Welfare Reform*, 104th Cong., 1st sess., January 27, 1995, serial 104-43, pp. 422–46.

42. House of Representatives, *Personal Responsibility and Work Opportunity Reconciliation Act of 1996, Report 104-725* (Washington: Government Printing Office, 1996), pp. 51–55, 306–310.

43. Janellen Duffy, "Rainmakers or Troublemakers: The Impact of GIST on the Welfare Reform Reauthorization Debate" (paper, Council on Foundations Annual Conference, April 2003).

44. Richard Nathan and Thomas Gais, *Implementing the Personal Responsibility Act of 1996: A First Look* (Albany, NY: Rockefeller Institute of Government, 1999).

45. A symbolic reflection of the conversion from welfare offices to work offices is that the national organization of state welfare agencies changed its name from the "American Public Welfare Association" to the "American Public Human Services Association." Similarly, nine states changed the name of their welfare agency either to get rid of terms like "welfare," "income maintenance," or "public aid" or to include terms like "work," "workforce," or "independence."

46. House Committee on Ways and Means, *2004 Green Book*, Section 7, pp. 27–37. See also U.S. Department of Health and Human Services, *Indicators of Welfare Dependence: Annual Report to Congress, 2003* (Washington: Government Printing Office, 2003), Appendix A: Table TANF 1.

47. Jeffrey Grogger, Lynn Karoly, and Jacob Klerman, "Consequences of Welfare Reform: A Research Synthesis," RAND, July 2002.

48. House Committee on Ways and Means, *2000 Green Book* (Washington: Government Printing Office, 2000), pp.1471–74, 1500–1510.

49. U.S. Bureau of Labor Statistics data at http://stats.bls.gov/cps/home.htm.

50. Jared Bernstein and Lawrence Mishel, "Labor Market Left Behind: Evidence Shows that Post-Recession Economy Has Not Turned into a Recovery for Workers," Briefing Paper no. 142, Economic Policy Institute, 2003, Figure 6.

51. These figures are based on tables prepared by Richard Bavier of the Office of Management and Budget. In September of each year, based on poverty and income data from the Census Bureau's Current Population Survey, Bavier prepares tables on income for various demographic groups, including families headed by females. The income data are presented in both current and constant dollars by income quintile within each demographic group.

52. Proctor and Dalaker, *Poverty in the United States: 2002*, Table 5, www.census.gov/prod/2003pubs/p60-222.pdf.

53. Author's calculations based on Census Bureau poverty data.

54. Rebecca M. Blank, "Declining Caseloads/Increased Work: What Can We Conclude about the Effects of Welfare Reform?" *Economic Policy Review* 7, no. 2 (September 2001): 25–36; James P. Ziliak et al., "Accounting for the Decline in AFDC Caseloads:

137

Welfare Reform or the Economy?" *Journal of Human Resources* 35, no. 3 (Summer 2000): 570–86.

55. Congressional Budget Office, "Policy Changes Affecting Mandatory Spending for Low-Income Families Not Receiving Welfare" (Washington: Government Printing Office, 1998).

56. Stephanie J. Ventura et al., "Nonmarital Childbearing in the United States, 1940–99," *National Vital Statistics Reports*; Stephanie J. Ventura et al., "Revised Pregnancy Rates, 1990–97, and New Rates for 1998–99: United States," ibid.

57. Gregory Acs and Sandi Nelson, "Honey, I'm Home, Changes in Living Arrangements in the Late 1990's," Urban Institute, June 2001, www.urban.org.

58. Richard Bavier, "Child-Bearing outside Marriage and Child-Raising inside Marriage" (unpublished manuscript, Office of Management and Budget, April 24, 2002); Richard Bavier, "Recent Increases in the Share of Young Children with Married Mothers" (paper, National Welfare Reform Evaluation Conference, June 2002).

59. Sara McLanahan and Gary Sandefur, *Growing Up with a Single Parent* (Cambridge, MA: Harvard University Press, 1994); Linda Waite and Maggie Gallagher, *The Case for Marriage: Why Married People Are Happier, Healthier, and Better Off Financially* (New York: Doubleday, 2000).

60. Marianne P. Bitler et al., "The Impact of Welfare Reform on Marriage and Divorce," *Demography* 41, no. 2 (May 2004): 213–36.

61. *Budget of the U.S. Government, Fiscal Year 2005* (Washington Government Printing Office, 2004).

62. Ellen S. Peisner-Feinberg et al., "The Children of the Cost, Quality, and Outcomes Study Go to School," University of North Carolina at Chapel Hill, June 1999.

63. Office of Child Support Enforcement, *Child Support Enforcement, FY2002: Annual Statistical Report* (Washington: U.S. Department of Health and Human Services, 2003).

64. These data are based on tables prepared by Richard Bavier of the Office of Management and Budget using annual data from the Current Population Survey conducted by the U.S. Census Bureau.

65. Michael Fix and Jeffrey Passel, "The Scope and Impact of Welfare Reform's Immigrant Provisions," Urban Institute, January 15, 2002.

66. House Committee on Ways and Means, *2004 Green Book*, Appendix J.

67. Lewin Group, "Policy Evaluation of the Effect of Legislation Prohibiting the Payment of Disability Benefits to Individuals Whose Disability Is Based on Drug Addiction and Alcoholism" (report for the Social Security Administration, July 21, 1998).

68. Jeannette Rogowski et al. "Final Report for Policy Evaluation of the Effect of the 1996 Welfare Reform Legislation on SSI Benefits for Disabled Children," RAND, Santa Monica, CA, 2002. See also Jeannette Rogowski et al., "Background Study Design Report for Policy Evaluation of the Effect of the 1996 Welfare Reform Legislation on SSI Benefits for Disabled Children," RAND, Santa Monica, CA 1998.

69. Jeannette Rogowski et al., "Final Report," p. 125.

70. Ron Haskins, "Dividing Up the Credit: Clinton and Republicans Fashion the Most Radical Reforms in the History of Welfare," in *American Economic Policy in the 1990s*, ed. Jeffrey Frankel and Peter Orszag (Cambridge, MA: MIT Press, 2002).

71. Robert J. LaLonde, "The Promise of Public Sector-Sponsored Training Programs," *Journal of Economic Perspectives* 9, no. 2 (Spring 1995): 149–68.

72. Susan Scrivener et al., "Implementation, Participation Patterns, Costs, and Two-Year Impacts of the Portland (Oregon) Welfare-to-Work Program," for the U.S. Department of Health and Human Services and U.S. Department of Education, 1998.

73. House Committee on Ways and Means, *2004 Green Book*, Section 15, pp. 118–22.

74. Sandra Danziger et al., "Barriers to Employment of Welfare Recipients," in *Prosperity for All? The Economic Boom and African Americans*, ed. Robert Cherry and William Rogers III (New York: Russell Sage Foundation, 2000).

75. Committee on Ways and Means, *2000 Green Book*, pp.1471–74, 1500–1510.

76. State Policy Documentation Project, www.spdp.org/tanf/sanctions_overview. pdf.

77. Dan Bloom and Don Winstead, "Sanctions and Welfare Reform," Brookings Institution, January 2002.

78. Toby Herr and Suzanne Wagner, "Self-Efficacy as a Welfare-to-Work Goal: Emphasizing Both Psychological and Economics in Program Design," Project Match, February 2003.

10. Health Care: The Revolution's Mitigated Disaster

Michael F. Cannon

All I can promise you on the side of the House Republicans is . . .
we will cooperate with anyone, and we will compromise with no one.
—Newt Gingrich (R-Ga.)

Introduction

Newt Gingrich described his colleagues in the 104th Congress as "the most explicitly ideologically committed House Republican Party in modern history."[1] He arguably could have said the same of his colleagues in the U.S. Senate. Rooted in a belief in limited government, nurtured by Barry Goldwater and Ronald Reagan, and steeled by two years under President Bill Clinton, this ideology found its expression in the Contract with America, which promised to end "government that is too big, too intrusive, and too easy with the public's money" and to "restore fiscal responsibility to an out-of-control Congress."[2]

The Contract makes scant reference to health care, yet health policy is a major contributor to the government's being "too big, too intrusive, and too easy with the public's money." In 1995, federal health spending accounted for nearly one-fifth of the federal budget[3] and nearly one-third of all health expenditures.[4]

Republicans partly owed their new majority status to health care. Popular disapproval of the Clinton administration's attempt to nationalize the health care industry was a major contributor to the anti-Washington backlash that ended Democratic control of Congress. Rep. Dick Armey, who became House majority leader in 1995, later commented that the Clinton health plan "is the biggest reason we took control of Congress that year."[5]

How should the Republican health care record after 10 years be judged? Measuring Republicans' performance solely against the Contract's limited-government theme may not be fair. Numerous

141

factors beyond the control of congressional Republicans limited what reforms they could accomplish. The most obvious was an executive branch under an agile president of the opposing party. Also, the size of the GOP majority was fairly narrow and even briefly disappeared in the Senate. Furthermore, many GOP senators and all GOP House members began 1995 with no experience in the majority. That inexperience was set against what Thomas Jefferson called "the natural progress of things . . . for liberty to yield and government to gain ground."[6]

Health Care in Congress: 1995 vs. 2003

Initially, the GOP's actions matched the Contract with America's rhetoric. Legislation passed both houses in 1995 that would have reduced the federal government's role in health care by reducing the growth of health spending, overhauling Medicare (including medical savings accounts for seniors), and converting Medicaid to block grants. Restraining federal health spending was imperative, Republicans argued, to balance the budget and save Medicare from bankruptcy.

Contrast that with 2003, when congressional Republicans enacted the largest entitlement expansion since the creation of Medicare. The new prescription-drug benefit added nearly $17 trillion to Medicare's present-value unfunded liability of $45 trillion.[7] Republicans expanded the program despite numerous factors that should have discouraged profligacy, including a sluggish economy, a large federal deficit, and an expensive war on terrorism. In the health policy sphere, the GOP of 2003 bore little resemblance to the GOP of 1995.

Federal Health Spending

Republican performance can also be measured by looking at the growth of federal health spending. The federal health budget grew from $324 billion in 1995 (in constant 2004 dollars) to $514 billion by 2004, a 59 percent increase (see Figure 10.1). From 1995 to 1999, the rate of growth in federal health spending slowed considerably, falling to just 0.8 percent in 1999. However, the growth rate rebounded to 8.3 percent in 2001 and has remained above 7 percent through 2004.

Outlays are only one measure of the federal government's intrusiveness in the health care sector. Federal health regulations also

Figure 10.1
FEDERAL HEALTH SPENDING UNDER THE GOP CONGRESS

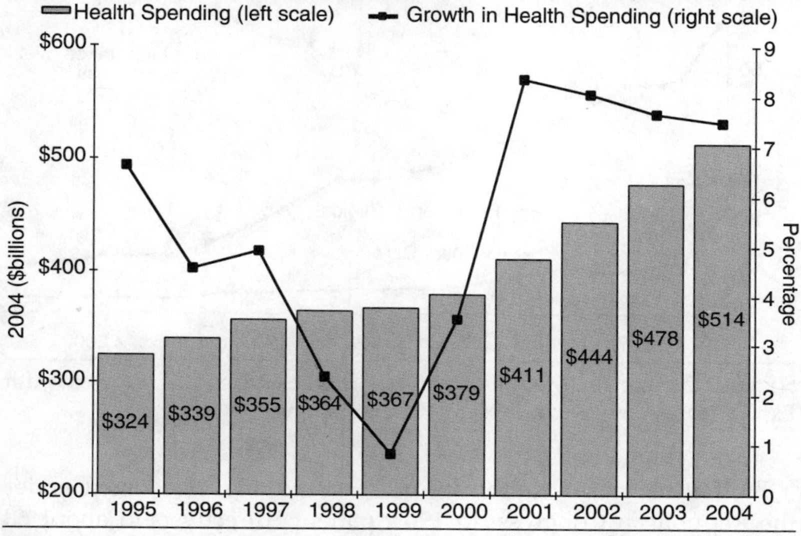

SOURCE: Centers for Medicare and Medicaid Services, "National Health Expenditures," www.cms.hhs.gov/statistics/nhe/.

increased under the Republican Congress. By redirecting the use of private resources, regulations increase the government's control over economic activity. According to one estimate, in 2002 the costs of federal and state health regulations outweighed the benefits by $169 billion.[8]

Greater Socialization

Because of federal health programs and the income tax code's bias toward employer-purchased medical care, America's health care system is largely based on third-party payment. Individuals pay directly for only a small portion of the care that they consume. Instead, the costs are socialized through the government or employers, with the result that consumer demand increases and consumers lose control to bureaucracies, which ration services. The share of costs paid directly by patients is one measure of the degree to which the health care sector is socialized.

Figure 10.2
SHARE OF HEALTH EXPENDITURES PAID DIRECTLY BY PATIENTS

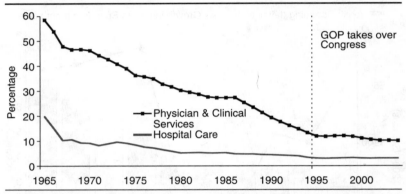

SOURCE: Centers for Medicare and Medicaid Services, "National Health Expenditures," www.cms.hhs.gov/statistics/nhe/.

By that measure, health care has become more socialized under the Republican Congress. In 1965, patients directly paid about 60 percent of the costs of physician or clinical services and 20 percent of the costs of hospital care. By 1995, patients directly paid only 12 percent of the costs of physician or clinical services and 3 percent of the costs of hospital care. After 10 years of a Republican Congress, patients' direct contribution to physician or clinical costs had fallen to 10 percent, while their direct contribution to hospital costs remained at 3 percent (see Figure 10.2).[9]

As a result, patients today have fewer incentives to be prudent consumers, and the need for bureaucratic rationing is greater. The failure of Congress to contain federal health spending is principally caused by its failure to restore price sensitivity to consumer health care decisions. Direct payment currently accounts for a smaller share of health expenditures in the United States than in at least 17 nations of the Organization for Economic Cooperation and Development, including some with explicitly socialized health care systems, such as Canada.[10]

A Mitigated Disaster

The GOP's stewardship of federal health policy has been at best a mitigated disaster. Despite some initial reform efforts, Republicans' devotion to limited government in the health policy arena was short-lived. After winning control of Congress by campaigning against the Clinton health plan, Republicans soon came to implement significant portions of that agenda. Their departure from market principles reached its height with the enactment of the largest expansion in federal entitlements since the creation in 1965 of Medicare and Medicaid: a prescription-drug benefit under Medicare that increased the program's huge unfunded obligations by more than one-third.

However, the 2003 creation of health savings accounts (HSAs) mitigates the GOP's anti-market health policies. Popularized by the Cato Institute and others in the 1990s, HSAs (previously known as medical savings accounts, or MSAs) were proposed as a free-market alternative to the Clinton health plan.[11] By combining private, high-deductible health insurance for catastrophic expenses with a personal savings account for routine expenses, HSAs will help restore individual autonomy to markets dominated by bureaucracies.

HSAs are the first serious step toward restoring market processes to America's health care sector, and they provide a method to create broader reforms of Medicare, Medicaid, and other health programs. However, their enactment cannot totally redeem the GOP's health care record. Few Republicans fought vigorously HSAs, whereas many made bigger government their first health policy priority.

Medicare

> *Medicare transcends everything . . . If we solve Medicare, I think we'll govern for a generation.*
> —Newt Gingrich[12]

The Republicans' first foray into health care policy was their 1995 proposal to reform Medicare. The Medicare package Congress sent to President Clinton included provisions giving seniors additional coverage choices outside standard Medicare benefits, including MSAs, which would encourage seniors to be more prudent health care consumers.

Medicare was a key factor in the budget showdown of 1995. Republicans attempted to slow the growth of Medicare spending by $270 billion over five years.[13] Democrats alleged that Republicans were cutting seniors' health care to provide tax cuts to the wealthy. President Clinton cited the Medicare "cuts" as a major reason for

145

vetoing the budget and was largely successful in making Republicans pay a political price for the ensuing government shutdown late in 1995.

Badly burned by that episode, Republicans struck a more conciliatory posture when they revisited Medicare in 1997. Working with President Clinton, they enacted a package that slowed the growth of Medicare by $115 billion over five years and gave beneficiaries the choice of obtaining coverage through more types of managed care arrangements: provider-sponsored organizations and preferred-provider organizations in addition to the health maintenance organizations that were already available.

The 1997 Balanced Budget Act also created a pilot program for MSAs within Medicare. The program was open to as many as 390,000 seniors, who could obtain catastrophic health insurance with a deductible as high as $6,000. Participants would receive cash for their MSA, which they could spend at their own discretion. However, excessive regulation prevented private insurers from participating and the program expired without ever getting off the ground.

Although the 1997 budget act led to a first-ever drop in Medicare spending in 1999, the reductions in spending growth were largely achieved by reductions in payments to providers that were eventually both circumvented and relaxed; Medicare outlays soon resumed robust growth. By 2004, real Medicare spending had grown 44 percent since 1995. The failure of price controls demonstrates that the only way to control Medicare spending is to change who does the spending. MSAs put patients in control of their own spending and encourage seniors to be more prudent consumers of medical care. Unfortunately, Republicans never made MSAs their first priority for Medicare reform.

As the 10th anniversary of the Contract with America approached, in 2003 the Republican Congress passed the Medicare Prescription Drug, Improvement, and Modernization Act in an episode reminiscent of past Democratic procedural abuses. As the votes were tallied, the GOP leadership saw that a majority of the House had cast their votes against the massive entitlement. Moreover, a group of conservative Republican backbenchers was protesting the reckless spending bill being rammed through in the middle of the night. In what congressional scholar Norman Ornstein called "the ugliest and most outrageous breach of standards in the modern history of the

House,"[14] the House leadership cast aside the long-standing tradition of 15-minute votes to hold the vote open for nearly three hours—the longest House roll call vote in memory—until enough arms were twisted to change the outcome.

Medicare's finances were much worsened with the creation of the new drug benefit (Medicare Part D). Supporters claimed that the bill would cost $400 billion over 10 years. But after its passage, it was revealed that the Bush administration had suppressed estimates made by Medicare's chief actuary that projected the measure would cost up to $200 billion more. The administration's belated announcement placed the cost of the measure at $534 billion over 10 years. Subsequent estimates placed the cost closer to $600 billion.

The 2003 Medicare law does contain provisions designed to improve quality and reduce unnecessary spending through greater competition, but those reforms are minor. Options that will give seniors the greatest amount of flexibility and choice will be available in only six metropolitan areas and do not take effect until 2010. In 1995, few would have predicted that a Republican Congress and a Republican president would enact the largest expansion of entitlements in a generation.

Medicaid

In 1995, Republicans sent to President Clinton an ambitious proposal to reform Medicaid. It would have reduced federal spending by $163 billion over five years and would have eliminated the federal entitlement to Medicaid benefits. Republicans sought to replace Medicaid's guaranteed benefits with block grants that would allow states to define eligibility and benefits. States would have been free to experiment with different rules and structures.

Like that year's proposed Medicare reforms, these changes did not survive the 1995 budget showdown with President Clinton. In 1996, Republicans dropped Medicaid block grants from their welfare reform proposal after President Clinton vowed to veto any measure that included Medicaid reform. Republicans have yet to revisit in any serious way converting Medicaid to block grants or ending the Medicaid entitlement.

In the 1997 Balanced Budget Act, Congress and President Clinton agreed to reduce projected growth in Medicaid spending by $10 billion over five years, in part by reducing payments to hospitals that care for a disproportionate share of indigent patients. The act also granted states some flexibility, including the ability to place beneficiaries in health maintenance organizations without first obtaining a waiver from the federal government.

At the same time, however, Republicans created a new federal health program. Sen. Orrin Hatch (R-Utah) and Sen. Edward Kennedy (D-Mass.) sponsored the State Children's Health Insurance Program, which effectively expanded Medicaid by $23 billion dollars over five years. The program was designed to extend health coverage to children in families earning too much to qualify for Medicaid but not enough to purchase private health insurance. Studies have estimated as many as half of those enrolled in the SCHIP had dropped their private health insurance to obtain the "free" government coverage.[15]

The SCHIP's pedigree indicates how far the Republicans shifted on health care. In 1993, First Lady Hillary Clinton presided over the Health Care Task Force that developed the Clinton health plan. A backup strategy worked out by the task force was to implement a government-run health program for children, then gradually fold in other age groups. Thus, Republicans ended up implementing the Clinton administration's fallback proposal. Sure enough, efforts to extend eligibility to parents of covered children emerged shortly after Congress enacted the SCHIP.

Although inflation-adjusted federal Medicaid spending growth slowed to 1.2 percent in 1996 and 2.0 percent in 1997, it later surged as high as 12.3 percent in 2002. In the first 10 years of the Republican revolution, real federal Medicaid spending grew nearly 70 percent.[16]

Federal Regulation of Private Health Insurance

Health insurance regulation had traditionally been the purview of state governments. Despite the initial federalist leanings of the Republican Congress, it dramatically increased federal health insurance regulation. In fact, each successful effort to increase federal control over health insurance could claim a Republican as its chief sponsor, as could many unsuccessful efforts.

The most prominent expansion of federal health insurance regulation is the 1996 Health Insurance Portability and Accountability Act, sponsored by Sen. Nancy Kassebaum (R-Kans.) and Senator Kennedy. HIPAA requires certain employers and health insurers to offer or renew health coverage to certain individuals, such as those who change jobs. The law also imposed criminal penalties on certain types of health care fraud and authorized federal rules governing medical records and privacy standards. Former House majority leader Dick Armey, an architect of the Contract with America, later confessed:

> HIPAA is a classic example of legislative panic. We passed it mostly as a way to make the political point that our new majority could govern and be compassionate at the same time. The fact is that HIPAA was a mistake. . . . It turned out that HIPAA did little to make insurance more portable, but it did set a dangerous precedent for the federal regulation of health insurance. We thought we were cracking down on Medicare fraud. Instead, we turned doctors into criminal suspects, with armed federal agents seizing their filing cabinets. We felt confident that we had guaranteed medical privacy and paperless billing, but HIPAA appears to have expanded bureaucrats' access to our medical records without a search warrant. . . . Looking back now, it seems undeniable that the first health care law after Clinton Care was, to some extent, the first installment of Clinton Care.[17]

Further Republican efforts to implement portions of the Clinton health plan by regulation soon followed. Sen. Pete Domenici (R-N.Mex.) and others sponsored laws that created a federally standardized package of health benefits that all health insurance purchasers must buy, while many similar Republican proposals did not become law. Rep. Charles Norwood (R-Ga.) has enlisted dozens of Republicans in proposing sweeping federal regulations on health insurance under the guise of a "patients' bill of rights." Though unsuccessful to date, this effort is perilously close to fruition.

Food and Drug Administration

> *Now, I don't want to get your hopes up, but phase three, maybe we'll take out FDA.*
> —Newt Gingrich[18]

Many Republicans cited the Food and Drug Administration as the quintessential overbearing federal bureaucracy. Gingrich called the FDA the nation's "leading job killer."[19] The FDA's overcaution has denied Americans access to life-saving products approved in other countries. Initially, Republicans complained about lengthy backlogs of applications for drugs and medical devices, noted that the FDA typically missed its 6-month deadline for approving drug applications by 13 months, and cited a 1993 study showing that it cost more than eight years and $359 million to navigate a new drug through the FDA approval process.[20]

As in other areas of health policy, however, the GOP's early efforts at FDA reform dwindled after the first few years. In 1996, moderate Senator Kassebaum introduced a bill that would have taken steps toward strengthening private alternatives to FDA efficacy certification by allowing manufacturers to disseminate information on newly discovered, or "off-label," uses of already approved products. The bill also would have bolstered private alternatives to the FDA by requiring automatic third-party review of all new drug applications not acted upon by the FDA within 180 days and allowing third-party review for all medical device applications. Although the bill cleared a Senate committee with significant bipartisan support, it and similar House measures languished and ultimately died as the 104th Congress adjourned.

In the 105th Congress, Republicans were determined to avoid controversy on the issue. They succeeded, but at the cost of sacrificing reform. Third-party review was abandoned for drug applications and watered down for medical devices. Provisions allowing manufacturers to disseminate information on off-label uses were amended until they posed no threat to the FDA's monopoly. This weak attempt at liberalizing off-label speech was far outdone one year later when a federal court allowed manufacturers much broader freedom to share information about their products with medical professionals. Ultimately, the Food and Drug Administration Modernization Act passed Congress with little opposition.

Upon passage of the bill, some dissatisfied Republicans vowed to revisit FDA reform. But as the American public continues to struggle with the cost of prescription medications, Congress has yet to do so. Meanwhile, the cost of bringing new drugs to market continues to grow rapidly. By 2001, the cost reached an estimated $802 million (in constant 2000 dollars), nearly double the cost in 1993.[21] It is estimated that it will cost $1.9 billion to bring to market 12 years from now a drug that is discovered today.[22]

Health Savings Accounts

The one achievement that mitigates the Republicans' anti-market health policies is their enactment of health savings accounts in 2003. HSAs reduce the federal government's role in the health care sector and can serve as a blueprint for reforming Medicare, Medicaid, and other health programs. However, HSAs came later than they should have and at a higher price than was necessary.

The federal government indirectly regulates health care through the income tax code. By exempting employer-purchased medical care from taxation, the government encourages consumers to let employers manage their health care dollars. One result is that consumers demand more medical care because they do not directly bear the costs. They also lose a large measure of autonomy to the bureaucracies that control their health care dollars, that is, employers and insurance companies.

Health savings accounts help correct those distortions, with the potential of dramatically reducing government interference in health care. HSAs extend the same tax advantage enjoyed by employer-purchased medical care to consumer-purchased medical care. Consumers no longer have to surrender control over their health care dollars—and medical decisions—to a bureaucracy. Moreover, HSAs reduce excess demand and medical inflation by restoring market incentives that encourage sensible consumption. The same incentives that make consumers better stewards of their own health care dollars can make them better stewards of public dollars in government programs such as Medicare and Medicaid.

Republicans first touted this concept, then called medical savings accounts, as an alternative to the Clinton health plan in the 1990s. Given the disunity among Republicans and a president hostile to MSAs, then House Ways and Means Committee chairman Bill Archer (R-Tex.) and others can be commended for securing even the badly hobbled medical savings account pilot program enacted as part of the Health Insurance Portability and Accountability Act of 1996. Under the act, only the self-employed and small businesses could participate, the number of MSAs that could be sold was capped at 750,000, and the program expired after five years.

As a result of those restrictions, few firms developed and marketed medical savings accounts. Moreover, prohibitions on fully funding one's MSA and restrictive rules governing the accompanying health insurance policies made the pilot program unattractive to many consumers. Not surprisingly, the number sold came nowhere near the statutory cap, allowing opponents to dismiss the concept as a failure. On the contrary, despite seemingly being designed to fail, the pilot program proved the attractiveness of the concept. The Internal Revenue Service reported 73 percent of participants were previously uninsured.[23]

As long as President Clinton occupied the White House, improving medical savings accounts was unlikely. The inauguration of George W. Bush improved prospects dramatically, but MSAs retained their second-class status among Republican health priorities. Despite evidence that reforms could get a majority in the Senate in 2003,[24] the GOP did not push for a vote. Whatever the outcome of a clean vote would have been, it is likely that whatever added votes were required to move a MSA expansion could have been purchased for less than the cost of the Medicare prescription drug bill.

Medical savings accounts were finally expanded—and renamed health savings accounts—largely owing to the efforts of Ways and Means Committee chairman Bill Thomas (R-Ca.). Eligibility was opened to all those under age 65 covered by a qualifying high-deductible health insurance policy, the rules for which were relaxed. Participants can fully fund their HSAs each year, generally up to the level of their health insurance deductible. Thomas also secured additional flexibility that previously had not been put on the table, including higher HSA contribution limits for those near age 65.

Only time will tell whether HSAs will do more good than the prescription-drug benefit will do harm—whether the Medicare bill of 2003 proves to be a net positive or negative. Although HSAs will help curb medical inflation, new subsidies for prescription drugs will fuel it. Some positive steps ahead would be for Congress to make HSAs more flexible and to replace the drug benefit with reforms that make HSAs a part of Medicare.

Conclusion

In health policy, the Republican revolution lost its way. Although it began with efforts to rein in federal spending and regulations, time and again Republicans not only compromised but reversed course. After 10 years, the Republicans could point to only one substantial achievement that will reduce the government's influence over the nation's health care: health savings accounts.

The failure of the revolution is not that it did not live up to its reform rhetoric. Caught up in historic change, Republicans set policy goals more ambitious than could be achieved given political realities. Instead, the GOP's failure was that it abandoned the principle that consumers, and not government, should play a leading role in the health care sector. The chief architect of the Republican revolution, although he supports HSAs, has recently promoted legislation that would increase government planning in health care.[25]

One can plausibly argue that had the Democrats retained control of Congress, the government's role in the health care sector would have expanded even more, and that reforms considered by the Republican Congress would never have seen the light of day. However, it could also be that if a Democratic majority Congress had proposed new health entitlements and regulations, Republicans would have blocked them.

If Republicans are to live up to the principles that animated the Contract with America, they must rediscover their belief in markets and their distrust in central planning. Expanding on the promise of health savings accounts would be a good starting point.

Notes

This epigraph is from remarks before the Washington Research Group Symposium, November 11, 1994, quoted in Ed Gillespie and Bob Schellhas, eds., *Contract with America: The Bold Plan by Rep. Newt Gingrich, Rep. Dick Armey and the House Republicans to Change the Nation* (New York: Random House, 1994), p. 182.

1. Newt Gingrich, remarks before the Washington Research Group Symposium, November 11, 1994, quoted in Ed Gillespie and Bob Schellhas, eds., *Contract with America: The Bold Plan by Rep. Newt Gingrich, Rep. Dick Armey and the House Republicans to Change the Nation* (New York: Random House, 1994), p. 182.

2. Ibid., pp. 7, 9.

3. *Budget of the United States Government, Fiscal Year 2005, Historical Tables* (Washington: Government Printing Office, 2004), p. 51.

4. Centers for Medicare and Medicaid Services, "National Health Expenditure (NHE) Amounts by Type of Expenditure and Source of Funds: Calendar Years 1965–2013," January 2004, www.cms.hhs.gov/statistics/nhe/nhe65-13.zip.

5. Dick Armey, "Just Gotta Learn from the Wrong Things You Done," *Cato Journal* 22, no. 1 (2002): 7.

6. Letter to Edward Carrington, 1788, in *The Founders' Almanac*, ed. Matthew Spalding (Washington: Heritage Foundation), p. 157.

7. Boards of Trustees, Federal Hospital Insurance and Federal Supplementary Medical Insurance Trust Funds, *2004 Annual Report of the Boards of Trustees of the*

Federal Hospital Insurance and Federal Supplementary Medical Insurance Trust Funds, March 23, 2004, pp. 60, 99, 108, www.cms.hhs.gov/publications/trusteesreport/2004/tr.pdf.

8. Christopher J. Conover, "Health Care Regulation: A $169 Billion Hidden Tax," Cato Institute Policy Analysis no. 527, October 4, 2004, www.cato.org/pubs/pas/pa-527es.html.

9. Centers for Medicare and Medicaid Services.

10. Author's calculations using *OECD Health Data 2004*, 1st ed. (Paris: OECD, 2004). See Table 9 and Table 16 at www.oecd.org/document/16/0,2340,en_2649_37407_2085200_1_1_1_37407,00.html). Expenditure data are for 2002 except for the United Kingdom (1996); Turkey (2000); and Australia, Japan, and Korea (2001). Complete data on out-of-pocket expenditures for Belgium, Greece, Portugal, and Sweden could increase the number of nations where patients directly pay for a larger share of health expenses than U.S. patients.

11. See John C. Goodman and Gerald L. Musgrave, *Patient Power: Solving America's Health Care Crisis* (Washington: Cato Institute, 1992).

12. "Gingrich: Medicare Key to Keeping GOP Control of Hill," *National Journal's Congress Daily*, June 28, 1995.

13. *CQ Almanac*, 1995, vol. LI (Washington: Congressional Quarterly Inc., 1996), pp. 2-30, 2-33.

14. Norman Ornstein, ". . . And Mischief," *Washington Post*, November 26, 2003, p. A25.

15. RAND Health, "State Efforts to Insure the Uninsured: An Unfinished Story," RAND Health Research Highlights (Santa Monica: RAND Health) 2003, p. 2, www.rand.org/publications/RB/RB4558.1/RB4558.1.pdf.

16. *Budget of the United States Government, Fiscal Year 2005, Historical Tables*, p. 294.

17. Dick Armey; 7–8.

18. Quoted in Al Kamen, "In the Loop: Ethics Panel Member's Curious Call," *Washington Post*, October 25, 1995, p. A17.

19. Quoted in Joshua Wolf Shenk, "Warning: Cutting the FDA Could Be Hazardous to Your Health," *Washington Monthly* 28, no. 1–2 (January 1996): 17.

20. Jeffrey P. Cohn, "The Beginnings: Laboratory and Animal Studies," *FDA Consumer Special Issue: From Test Tube to Patient: Improving Health through Human Drugs* (Rockville, MD: U.S. Food and Drug Administration, September 1999), p. 15, http://www.fda.gov/cder/about/whatwedo/testtube-full.pdf.

21. Joseph A. DiMasi, Ronald W. Hansen, and Henry G. Grabowski, "The Price of Innovation: New Estimates of Drug Development Costs," *Journal of Health Economics* 22, no. 2 (2003): 151–85. Figures are in constant 2004 dollars.

22. Ibid.

23. IRS Announcement 2002-90, September 30, 2002, www.irs.gov/pub/irs-drop/a-02-90.pdf.

24. U.S. Senate Roll Call Votes 107th Cong., 1st Sess., *S.Amdt. 851* to *S. 1052* (Bipartisan Patient Protection Act), June 29, 2001, http://www.senate.gov/legislative/LIS/roll_call_lists/roll_call_vote_cfm.cfm?congress = 107&session = 1&vote = 00216. Roll call vote results are compiled through the Senate Legislative Information System by the Senate Bill Clerk under the direction of the Secretary of the Senate.

25. Newt Gingrich and Patrick Kennedy, "Operating in a Vacuum," *New York Times*, May 3, 2004, p. 23. "Treasury dollars could help bring providers in a particular

part of the country together to map out plans for a regional health information network, and to divide up the costs and the savings fairly between them. Medicare could sweeten the pot by reimbursing providers for money spent to use electronic health records connected to a regional network."

11. Federal Education Policy in the GOP Congress

David Salisbury

The 1994 elections ushered in the Republican revolution and for the first time in four decades Republicans held a majority in both the House and the Senate. For the first time in more than 20 years, Republicans gained a majority of state governorships and picked up control of 17 state legislative chambers. Not a single incumbent Republican representative, senator, or state governor was defeated that year, evidence that the election results were not a fluke but a rejection of Democrat candidates and the Democratic Party.

In the lead-up to election day, House Republicans, led by Newt Gingrich and Dick Armey, published the Contract with America, which outlined the major actions they would take if they gained a majority. The Contract urged voters to throw the GOP out if it did not deliver.[1] Although the Contract touted the need to "strengthen rights of parents in their children's education," education policy was not a centerpiece of the Republican agenda.[2] Perhaps this was due to the Republican view, espoused earlier by President Ronald Reagan, that "education is the principal responsibility of local school systems, teachers, parents, citizen boards, and state governments," not of Washington.[3] President Reagan had come into office promising to abolish the Department of Education, which he called "President Carter's new bureaucratic boondoggle."[4] But controversy and political obstacles caused Reagan to give up on the effort. In 1995, the newly elected Republicans, even with the momentum of a landslide election, did not feel like pushing what they now may have viewed as a lost cause.

In 1994, the Democrats had enacted a number of federal laws to extend the reach of the federal government into the nation's schools. Those laws included Goals 2000; the Educate America Act; the National Skill Standards Act; the Educational Research, Development, Dissemination, and Improvement Act; the School-to-Work

157

Opportunities Act; and the Improving America's School Act. At least the Contract did not propose even more new programs.

The differences between Republicans and Democrats were apparent during the next few years as they fought over budgets and the proper role of the federal government in education. The Republicans, at least for a time, did hold back the growth of federal education spending and sought to strengthen local control rather than dictate education policy from Washington, D.C.[5] Unfortunately, fiscal restraint had vanished by the end of the 1990s and Congress returned to a policy of business as usual, which meant increased spending and an expanded role for Congress in education.

The Revolution and Education Spending, 1995–2000

Although the Contract made no specific mention of cutting education spending or diminishing the role of the federal government in education, the newly elected Congress held a series of hearings on the topic.[6] In those hearings, prominent Republican witnesses, such as former secretaries of education Lamar Alexander and William J. Bennett, reminded Congress that "education in America is the constitutional responsibility of the states."[7] "Goals, standards, and assessments," they said, "are legitimate leadership and 'bully pulpit' activities of national officials, but they must always be truly voluntary on the part of states and communities. Nor should federal funds be used as 'carrots' or 'sticks' in ways that effectively diminish state and local control. "[8]

The witnesses proposed that a number of federal programs be abolished immediately. They included the National Education Standards and Improvement Council, federal certification of state standards, federal approval of state and local education reform plans, and prohibitions against state and local testing programs. Witnesses also proposed abolishing a number of sensitive programs that should be handled locally, such as "gender equity" programs; policies dealing with weapons on school grounds; sex education; and disincentives or prohibitions against vouchers, charter schools, and privatization. They also recommended that all remaining federal assistance to the states and localities be provided through block grants. Finally, the Republican witnesses admonished Congress to abolish the Department of Education, because after their recommendations were implemented, it would have virtually nothing to do.

Those sentiments were consistent with the ideals of the Republican revolution. Unfortunately, after the hearings were over, little action took place to implement them. Two bills were introduced in the House in 1995 that would have eliminated the Department of Education, but the bills failed to advance beyond committee.[9] A task force of House Republicans, appointed to outline a plan for liquidating the department, proposed replacing scores of federal programs with block grants to the states and farming out some other department functions to other agencies. In addition, the House adopted a budget that called for the elimination of the Departments of Education, Energy, and Commerce.[10] In the end, the House budget reforms were dropped, and funding for the three targeted federal departments survived.

The 1996 appropriations bill sent a clear signal that little had changed. A few programs received cuts and President Bill Clinton's intrusive Goals 2000 program was ended, but most other programs received funding increases. The Senate bill kept dozens of programs alive, including library support, the National Writing Project, Law School Clinical Experience, college aid for migrants, and even some programs that the Clinton administration wanted to kill. All in all, the bill funded 127 ongoing programs even though the Clinton administration advocated funding only 105 of them. Even Star Schools, Sen. Edward Kennedy's pet project, received funding. Any Republican revolution in education appeared to be already dead.[11]

In the 1996 elections, Bob Dole and other GOP candidates supported ending the Department of Education in their campaigns, and the GOP platform called for the department's elimination.[12] But a number of postelection surveys revealed that proposals to end the department had cost the GOP support, particularly among female voters.[13] Polls indicated that education was a top issue among voters, and to some, killing the Department of Education was anti-education and anti-child.

Although voters seemed to approve of the Republican goals of downsizing the federal government and returning more power to the states and to individuals, too many viewed dumping the Department of Education as a reduction in support for public schools. Perhaps it was the stuffed-shirt way in which Dole handled the issue, but the conclusion of many GOP leaders and campaign strategists was that abolishing the Department of Education just did not have political appeal.

Consequently, calls to scrap the department ceased almost entirely among Republicans. By 1997, the budget for the Department of Education had more than doubled from $14 billion (its original level in 1979) to $33.5 billion. Total federal support for education reached about $100 billion by 1997, up 160 percent from $37.7 billion in 1990.[14]

Although smaller government continued to be a popular sound bite among congressional Republicans, Congress was busy making government bigger, not smaller. By 1998 it was clear that the Republicans had bought into the belief that the federal government should institute and manage numerous K–12 school programs. In an October 1998 news release, Newt Gingrich applauded the bipartisan support for more education spending, including increased funding for Pell Grants, new programs to strengthen the quality of teachers, new programs for disadvantaged students, and the new Campus-Based Child Care Program that gave grants to colleges for student child care.[15]

By 1999, congressional Republicans were pouring money back into federal education programs that they once had vowed to cut. Senate Republicans even backed President Clinton's proposal to fund 100,000 new teachers. Republicans started proposing huge increases in federal education spending.[16] As a 1999 *Education Week* article noted: "Nearly four years after the Republican majority took office, federal education spending has not only survived, but grown—by nearly 38 percent since the fiscal 1996 budget. The Education Department has more funding than ever under a political party traditionally associated with belt-tightening."[17]

While congressional Republicans were moving in this anti-reform direction, state and local governments were implementing real education reforms. By the end of 1995, 19 states had enacted charter-school laws, allowing teachers, education companies, and entrepreneurs to start schools to compete with traditional public schools. Two states (Ohio and Wisconsin) had passed voucher programs, and at least 10 states were experimenting with private management of public schools.[18]

Rather than trusting states and localities to address the nation's education problems, congressional Republicans wanted to get into the act as well. Increasing federal education spending seemed to play well to special interests and to some constituents, and no one wanted to be labeled as stingy when it came to schools.

160

By 2000, the Department of Education's budget had increased from $27.1 billion in 1994 to $38.4 billion, and presidential candidate George W. Bush proposed large additional increases.[19] Although Al Gore advocated even larger increases, it was apparent that Republicans placed an increased role for the federal government in education high on their agenda.

George W. Bush and the Changing Federal Role in Education

Many education reformers cheered when George Bush defeated Al Gore, because Gore was against parental choice in education and advocated huge increases in federal education spending. Bush advocated education reforms that would return power to states, localities, and parents. In campaign speeches he promoted local control, flexibility in how states could use federal funds, and school choice that included letting parents use private schools. Many of his statements, however, were mixed messages, promising more local control on one hand and more federal funding and "accountability" on the other.

In a speech to the Manhattan Institute, Bush stated that he wanted to give states more flexibility to use federal funds for choice programs—including choice of private schools—but gave no indication that he intended to diminish Washington's role in setting education policy or priorities.[20] He observed that he wanted to "fundamentally change the relationship of the states and the federal government in education." He didn't mean decrease the federal government's role; rather, he announced his intention to use the federal government to "set clear goals and hold districts and schools accountable for achieving those goals."[21] That policy is a fundamental change from the view, espoused by Republicans only a few years before, that education should be strictly a state and local matter.

The centerpiece of the Bush education agenda was the No Child Left Behind Act (NCLB) Act. In its original form, the Bush plan included reforms that would have allowed flexibility for districts and increased choice for parents, including choice of private schools. However, most of those reforms were removed in committee. The final bill greatly increased federal education spending and perpetuated funding for most of the old federal education programs, many of which are ineffective and wasteful.

161

Figure 11.1
DEPARTMENT OF EDUCATION SPENDING

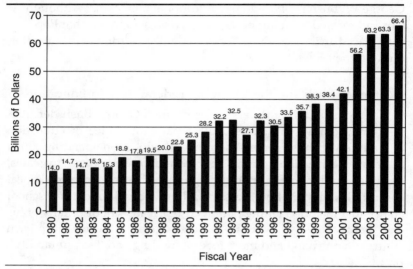

SOURCE: Department of Education, "Education Department Budget History Table: FY1980–Present," www.ed.gov/about/overview/budget/history/edhistory.pdg.

Instead of diminishing the federal role in education, NCLB placed a plethora of mandates on local schools. Although some of the mandates prescribe what appear to be reasonable practices (like requiring that schools test students annually in reading and math), imposing them from Washington, D.C., represents a drastic departure from the earlier views of Republicans. Although Republicans point to flexibility and some parental choice provisions in NCLB, the legislation is without question the largest federal intrusion ever into local education matters.

The massive expansion of power over local schools was initiated by a Republican president, sponsored by Republican John Boehner (R-Ohio), and supported by leading Republicans in both houses. Today's House Republicans sing the praises of NCLB and brag about increases in federal education spending.[22]

The path of federal education spending is shown in Figure 11.1. Although some effort was made toward abolishing the education department and cutting spending in the 104th and 105th Congresses, the recent trend has been toward huge spending increases. In sum, there was no Republican revolution in federal education policy.

Conclusion

The GOP takeover, which included a freshman band of budget cutting conservatives, altered the pattern of rising federal control over education for a brief time. Ultimately, efforts to abolish the Department of Education were unsuccessful. In the end, Republicans adopted a strategy of "if you can't beat 'em, join 'em."

Recent federal education spending increases have been massive. Gone is the idea that there is no constitutional role for the federal government in the nation's schools. Instead, the Department of Education has been adopted as the Republicans' favored stepchild.

The last 10 years have been a great disappointment to people who felt that the 1994 elections signaled an effort to cut the federal government and remove from it areas such as education where it had no legitimate constitutional role. Congressional Republicans can still be distinguished from Democrats by their support for accountability and flexibility, but not by their views on education funding. Both believe that more funding is better. Both believe in a large role for the federal government in education. Both support the continued cabinet status of the Department of Education.

The Republican revolution failed, not because of a lack of effort but because of a naiveté about the momentum of the government to continually expand. Those who pushed scrapping the Department of Education made several public relations and tactical mistakes. They let themselves be characterized as tightfisted ideologues out to harm children, rather than as guardians protecting families from the excesses of an intrusive federal bureaucracy. Finally, failure to recapture the White House in 1996 had a dampening effect on the agenda that the Republicans were able to pursue. Cutting education spending lost its appeal, and as far as education was concerned, the Republican revolution was over.

Prospects for the Future

What are the prospects that a future Congress will return to budget cutting, downsizing, or even eliminating the federal role in education? Given the tendency of politicians of all parties to seek greater power over state, local, and private activities, that may not happen for a while. Nevertheless, at least a couple of developments could lead Congress to move in that direction.

One development is the increase in the number of states instituting school-choice programs. Today, four states have programs that grant tax credits either to parents who pay tuition at private schools or to businesses or individuals who contribute to scholarship funds that help children attend private schools. Five states and the District of Columbia have voucher programs that allow students to attend private schools.[23] Parents who are able to choose between private and public schools may be less interested in proposals coming from Washington promising to "reform public schools."

Innovative governors are dealing creatively with education reform as well. Jeb Bush, governor of Florida, has instituted some of the most-inclusive school-choice programs in the country. Florida now has two voucher programs, one for students in failing public schools and one for children with disabilities, and a tuition tax credit for private school scholarships. At some point, Washington may see the movement toward more school choice as an indication that it should step back from the education arena. President George W. Bush, although a fervent advocate of the accountability provisions of NCLB, is also a supporter of more school choice for parents. Withdrawal from local education matters and even diminished education funding might be favored if the right conditions existed nationally and leadership were provided by the president or Congress.

Another development stems from the NCLB policy of classifying schools as "failing" if they do not meet adequate yearly progress on test scores. One effect of the federal law is that more Americans are now alert to the large number of public schools that are failing to educate children. Lack of public awareness about inadequacies in the American public school system has been a barrier to the introduction of market-based reforms. As more parents and local politicians learn of the intractable nature of public school failure, we may see a growing push for market-based reforms. At some point, the public may become convinced that the government cannot fix the schools and will increasingly favor private markets to supply education. If that happens, there will be less perceived need to call on politicians for increased levels of federal funding and school reform programs.

The growing movement toward school choice and market reforms is encouraging. In terms of education policy, the best hope for advocates of limited government is to encourage the expansion of parental choice in education at the local and state level. When true market-based legislation is enacted throughout the country, the benefits to individuals and society will be evident. Perhaps Washington will then get the message that federal money and programs cannot fix what's wrong with public schools.

Notes

1. Ed Gillespie and Bob Schellhas, eds., *Contract With America: The Bold Plan by Rep. Newt Gingrich, Rep. Dick Armey and the House Republicans to Change the Nation* (New York: Times Books, 1994), p. 163.

2. Ibid., p. 17.

3. Edward Fiske, "Reagan Record in Education: Mixed Results," *New York Times*, November 14, 1982.

4. Donald Rothberg, "Reagan Urges New Weapon to Overcome U.S.–Soviet Military 'Gap,'" *Associated Press*, May 5, 1980.

5. Federal appropriations for the Department of Education held relatively steady during the 104th to 106th Congresses (1995–2000). Under President Bush, education spending increased to $42.1 billion in 2001 with sharp increases in 2002 ($56.2 billion) and 2003 ($63.2 billion) (see Figure 11.1).

6. At least three hearings were held. The first was held by the House Economic and Educational Opportunities Committee's Subcommittee on Oversight and Investigation on January 26, 1995. Former secretaries of education Lamar Alexander and William J. Bennett testified. Another hearing was held on May 23, 1995, before the House Subcommittee on Government Management, Information, and Oversight. Former Reagan Department of Education officials Chester E. Finn Jr. and William D. Hansen testified along with Rep. Ernest Istook. A third hearing was held on June 5, 1995, before the House Committee on Economic and Educational Opportunities.

7. Federal News Service, "Prepared Joint Statement by Former Secretaries of Education Lamar Alexander and William J. Bennett, 'Abolishing the Department of Education in Order to Liberate Parents and Schools'" (delivered before the House Economic and Educational Opportunities Committee Subcommittee on Oversight and Investigation, Washington, D.C., January 26, 1995).

8. Ibid.

9. HR 1318 (introduced in March 1995) and HR 1883 (introduced in June 1995) both provided for the elimination of the Department of Education. HR 1812, which also would have eliminated the Department, was introduced in June 1997. See U.S. House, 1995, Department of Education Elimination Act, 104th Congress, H.R. 1318; U.S. House, 1995, Back to Basics Education Reform Act. 104th Congress, H.R. 1885; and U.S. House, 1997, Department of Education Act of 1997, 105th Congress, H.R. 1812.

10. See "Is This for Real?" *Wall Street Journal*, June 15, 1995, p. A14, and Elizabeth Shogren, "Education Department's Death Outlined," *Los Angeles Times*, May 25, 1995, p. 18. The FY96 budget resolution (H. Con. Res. 67) adopted by the House

recommended the elimination of three departments: Commerce, Energy, and Education. See *CQ Almanac*, 1994, vol. 51 (Washington: Congressional Quarterly Inc., 1995), p. 2–23.

11. Of 34 Department of Education programs originally slated for elimination in the FY95 budget, only nine were actually dropped. Most others received funding increases. See Stephen Moore and Stephen Slivinski, "The Return of the Living Dead: Federal Programs That Survived the Republican Revolution," Cato Institute Policy Analysis no. 375, July 24, 2000, Table 1.

12. The 1996 Republican Party platform stated, "The Federal government has no constitutional authority to be involved in school curricula or to control jobs in the workplace. That is why we will abolish the Department of Education, end federal meddling in our schools and promote family choice at all levels of learning."

13. See Marianne Means, "Education Department Appears Secure," *Times Union*, December 6, 1996, p. A14.

14. See U.S. Department of Education, Office of Educational Research and Improvement, "Federal Help to Education Flows from Many Sources," *OERI Bulletin* (Fall 1998), p. 5.

15. Newt Gingrich, Government Press Release, "Speaker: Education Bill Will Make Institutions of Higher Learning More Affordable," October 2, 1998.

16. See Nancy E. Roman, "Republicans Retreat from Battle to Shrink Size of Government," *Washington Times*, March 4, 1999, p. A1.

17. Anjetta McQueen, "Burgeoning Budgets Put GOP in Unusual Policy Position," *Education Week*, December 2, 1998, p. 23.

18. For an assessment of state initiatives see Chester E. Finn Jr., "Goals on the Shoals: How Washington Thwarted School Reform," *Washington Post*, November 19, 1995, p. C5.

19. For a description of the Gore and Bush education proposals see "Election 2000," editorial, *St. Louis Post-Dispatch*, September 3, 2000, p. B2, and Rafael Lorente, "Gore, Bush Split on Education Plans: Both Support Active U.S. Role," *South Florida Sun-Sentinel*, September 8, 2000, p. 1A.

20. George W. Bush, "A Culture of Achievement: The Future of Educational Reform" (speech, Manhattan Institute Forum, New York, New York, October 5, 1999).

21. Ibid.

22. The following press releases from the House Committee on Education and the Workforce are just a few examples of recent statements by Republican leadership applauding increased federal education funding: "No Child Left Behind Act Transforming Public Education with New Funding and Accountability; President's FY2003 Budget Adds Even More," October 4, 2002; "President Bush"s FY2004 Education Budget Spends More and Spends It More Wisely, Boehner Says," February 3, 2003; "Boehner: (Yet Another) Education Spending Hike Means There Are No More Excuses," February 13, 2003; "House Appropriations Subcommittee Approves (Yet Another) Big Increase in Federal Education Spending," June 20, 2003; "Federal Spending for Elementary and Secondary Education Has Increased by 34 Percent Since 'No Child Left Behind' Became Law—Linked to Accountability for Results," October 29, 2003; "House Republicans Vote to Provide Third Major Increase in Education Funding since No Child Left Behind," December 8, 2003. In his January 2004 State of the Union Address, President Bush touted huge federal education increases—the largest under any president since Lyndon B. Johnson—as an accomplishment of his presidency.

23. Arizona has a personal donation tax credit for private school scholarships. Pennsylvania and Florida have business donation tax credits for scholarships. Illinois has a personal tax credit for private school tuition. States with voucher programs include Florida, Maine, Ohio, Vermont, and Wisconsin.

12. The Nonrevolution in Telecommunications and Technology Policy

Adam D. Thierer

"Isn't it time we got Washington off our backs?" asked the opening line of the Contract with America's chapter on regulatory policy.[1] That chapter argued that citizens and corporations deserved more "protection against federal regulatory abuse," greater property rights protections, and better cost-benefit analyses of proposed regulations. Unfortunately, those principles were not translated into any concrete policy actions on the technology and telecommunications front.

The Contract with America did not make specific telecommunications or technology policy proposals. But the thrust of the Contract was clear: Republicans called for less federal meddling in the economy and more open competition in all industries. Those ideals were reflected in the call for a "pro-competitive, deregulatory national policy" for the communications sector in the preamble of the historic Telecommunications Act of 1996. Also, many Republican policymakers rallied around the cry to get the government's "hands off the Internet!"

If we judge the GOP by those promises, then the last 10 years of Republican rule are generally a failure. Table 12.1 shows a few policy successes, but disappointments are more numerous. Washington has not gotten off the backs of the telecom and high-tech sectors but instead has become intimately involved in the affairs of these industries. Governments at all levels—federal, state, local, and even international—are actively meddling in the telecom sector and becoming players in almost every new technology or Internet issue that has arisen. The Republican revolution has not been much of a revolution in telecommunications and high-technology policy.

169

Table 12.1
A LEGISLATIVE BALANCE SHEET FOR 10 YEARS OF
REPUBLICAN RULE

Positive Developments	Negative Developments
• Relaxation of encryption controls • Internet taxation: extension of moratorium on access taxes • Digital divide: refusal to expand subsidies	• Increased Internet and media censorship • Telecommunications Act of 1996 forced-access provisions • Creation of the e-rate ("Gore tax") program • Prohibitions on Internet gambling • High-definition television spectrum giveaway • Growth of the Federal Communications Commission

Would things have been any different under the Democrats? Such a comparison is difficult because it involves guesswork about how Democrats would have approached these issues if they had retained the majority. Relative to other policy issues, telecommunications and technology policy discussions are among the most nonpartisan in nature; it is not uncommon to find policy measures cosponsored by members of both parties. Nonetheless, there are a few issues where Democratic leadership might have produced different results. Those include the creation of more technology "entitlements" and potential differences on censorship issues.

Another way to judge Republican policies is by historical comparison. We could stack up the results of the last 10 years alongside the previous 10 or 20 years. But this gauge is unworkable because there was very little legislative activity on the telecommunications front in previous decades. Before the mid-1990s, no one had heard of the Internet or envisioned the policy debates that exploded onto the scene at the turn of the century.

Thus, in evaluating the effect of Republican rule on telecommunications and technology policy, we can only judge the Republicans by the standard by of their own rhetoric: did the Republican revolution "get Washington off our backs" and keep the government's "hands off the Internet?" The following review suggests that they have generally failed to accomplish those goals.

The Promise and Perils of the Telecommunications Act of 1996

Given the Contract with America's general silence on telecommunications or technology policy, GOP policy in this area begins with the Telecommunications Act of 1996. While the Contract was being formulated, an important debate was already under way in Congress over the possibility of comprehensive reform of the nation's archaic telecommunications regulations. In 1993 and 1994, discussions were under way in the House and Senate commerce committees to revise the Communications Act of 1934 and the Modification of Final Judgment (MFJ) antitrust decree, which had governed the telecom marketplace since 1984.

Those discussions broke down, however, when Senate Minority Leader Bob Dole (R-Kans.) began circulating draft legislation that differed starkly from the leading telecom measure, S 1822, sponsored by Sen. Fritz Hollings (D-S.C.). The Dole draft legislation proposed a truly sweeping deregulatory agenda for the telecom marketplace and shared almost nothing in common with the more micro-managed and less deregulatory Hollings bill. By floating the draft legislation, Senator Dole effectively killed the debate over S 1822 and telecom reform in the 103d Congress, delaying debates until after the 1994 elections.

After the Republicans captured both houses of Congress in 1994, many industry watchers assumed that the Dole draft bill would become the model for telecom reform in the new GOP Congress. For a time it was, but under intense lobbying pressure from numerous industry stakeholders, the more principled, clear-cut, deregulatory approach of the previous Dole draft bill gave way to a compromise-oriented reform. The compromise was less about getting government out of the way and more about the government making all parties happy by micro–managing markets in each industry segment.

Nowhere was this approach more clear than in the Telecommunications Act's local telephone competition provisions. The deregulatory approach of Senators Dole, John McCain (R-Ariz.), Phil Gramm (R-Tex.), Bob Packwood (R-Ore.), and others was of a "date-certain" deregulation, whereby all entry barriers and industry restrictions would be abolished after two to five years. That approach faded as moderate Republicans negotiated with Senator Hollings and others to construct a plan based on "open, nondiscriminatory access" regulation of the infrastructure owned by local exchange (ILEC) companies, the "Baby Bells." The theory was that because the Baby Bells still had significant market power in local markets, they should be forced to open their lines to "competitive local exchange carriers" (CLECs), who would purchase wholesale access to Baby Bell lines and systems and then resell that access under their own name. The hope was that this infrastructure sharing scheme would inject more competition into the local telecom market and give smaller carriers a chance to get their feet wet while building out new, facilities-based systems of their own.

That scheme was used as a measure of how "open" Baby Bell markets were in each state. A Baby Bell would be granted deregulatory relief from long-standing restraints on its entry to long-distance markets, imposed after the breakup of the Bell system in 1984, when the MFJ had disallowed such vertical integration between local and long-distance on the ground that the Bells would leverage their market power in the local market into long-distance and destroy any potential for competition in either. Thus, the carrot (potential for long-distance entry) and stick (mandatory open access and infrastructure-sharing requirements) approach became the centerpiece of the 1996 Telecommunications Act's grand compromise and would get legislation through Congress.

The scheme was anything but deregulatory in character. Far from "getting Washington off the backs" of this industry, the scheme envisioned ongoing and activist regulators at the Federal Communications Commission and the state level crafting the open-access provisions. After all, important questions had to be answered about how this scheme would work. What was "fair" interconnection and access? Which Baby Bell network elements would need to be shared with the CLECs to accomplish that goal? At what price should those elements be sold to the CLECs? Who would set that wholesale price? Would retail rates be deregulated after that? Would these rules apply to competing sectors (like cable) or emerging sectors (like broadband)? And when would these rules be sunsetted?

On most of those greatly important questions, Congress chose to remain silent or punted to the regulators to work them out. This inaction proved to be one of the biggest flaws of the Telecommunications Act. Beyond the question of whether these open-access provisions made sense to begin with, the authors of the act failed to understand that if you delegate open-ended powers to regulators, they will use those powers to expand their power over industry. As Justice Scalia noted during a 1999 Supreme Court review of the rules: "It would be gross understatement to say that the Telecommunications Act of 1996 is not a model of clarity. It is in many important respects a model of ambiguity or indeed even self-contradiction."[2]

Regulators exploited that ambiguity for all it was worth. Under the leadership of Chairman Reed Hundt, the FCC embarked on a grandiose experiment in reordering the affairs of the telecom sector. Hundt saw himself as an almost messianic figure sent to save the industry from the Bells. In his 2000 book, *You Say You Want a Revolution*, Hundt candidly noted: "Congress had not been mindful of Senator McCain's repeated warnings against transferring power to me. The Telecommunications Act of 1996 made me, at least for a limited time . . . one of the most powerful persons in the communications revolution."[3]

Indeed it did, and during Hundt's reign at the FCC, the agency aggressively crafted the open-access regulations in such a way as to maximize short-term CLEC entry by guaranteeing them cheap access to virtually every element of the Bells' networks. Hundt's managed-competition vision could be filed under the "burn the village in order to save it" theory of political philosophy. In several chapters of his book, Hundt boasts about FCC efforts to deliberately handicap the Bells and advantage rivals. Considerations of future innovation and investment took a backseat to the short-term goal of rapidly increasing the number of new entrants into the market.

Although Hundt's regulatory house of cards did foster short-term entry, the new entrants largely built "networks out of paper," in the words of Manhattan Institute scholar Peter Huber.[4] They deployed few actual new facilities and instead focused on lobbying the FCC for the broadest possible package of "unbundled network elements," or UNEs, at the lowest possible price. Regulatory arbitrage replaced genuine marketplace competition. Counting new entrants became more important than counting networks. And as for the future, well, that was another day. Hundt's crew had taken Keynes's famous quip about us all being dead in the long run a little too seriously. The result of this industrial policy experiment was a massive market crash beginning in the late 1990s when investors and markets realized this was no way to run an industry.

The fatal conceit underlying this unbundling regime, and the forced-access regulatory ethos in general, is its presumption that companies will produce new technologies regardless of the regulatory environment or legal incentives in place.[5] Open-access proponents ignore the risk-reward relationship in a capitalist society and its importance for long-term economic investment and innovation. One need not be versed in the works of Joseph Schumpeter or F. A. Hayek to understand what AT&T Chairman and CEO Michael Armstrong eloquently summed up in a 1998 speech: "No company will invest billions of dollars to become a facilities-based broadband service provider if competitors who have not invested a penny of capital nor taken an ounce of risk can come along and get a free ride on the investments and risks of others."[6]

Worse yet, supporters of forced access conveniently sidestepped the question of what happens if things turn sour. We know what open-access supporters will say if incumbents spend billions deploying a ubiquitous and successful new network: open it up to "competitors" and let everyone share that new system equally. But what if those networks that the incumbents threw billions at prove to be a bust? Will the so-called competitors help foot the bill then? Unlikely, but that is what forced-access regulation is all about: privatizing the risks and socializing the rewards.

How much of the blame for this forced-access fiasco should be laid at the feet of Republicans? Quite a bit, actually. Even though Reed Hundt was responsible for an overzealous reading of the Telecommunications Act, it was the vague wording of the act and the lack of congressional oversight that enabled him to conduct his grand experiment in micro-managing the telecom market. Besides, most Republicans endorsed that managed-competition vision. Although most members of Congress and the media labeled the act a deregulatory initiative upon passage, the reality was much different. When House Speaker Newt Gingrich shared the stage with President Bill Clinton at the act's signing ceremony in February 1996, he stated, "This is a bill which correctly uses government to help reshape the private sector so that in the marketplace entrepreneurs compete to please the customer by offering better services at lower

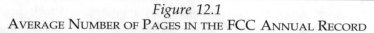

Figure 12.1
Average Number of Pages in the FCC Annual Record

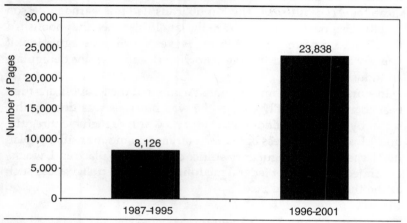

Source: J. Gregory Sidak, "The Failure of Good Intentions: The WorldCom Fraud and the Collapse of American Telecommunications after Deregulation, " *Yale Journal of Regulation*, vol. 20 (2003) pp. 207–67.

cost in a dynamic environment."[7] This statement by Gingrich turned out to be prescient. Indeed, under the bill, the government really did attempt to "reshape the private sector," but not in ways that pleased companies or consumers, and certainly not in ways that were economically sound.

Finally, what explains the complete lack of oversight by Republicans after Hundt embarked on his regulatory crusade? Why was no effort made to curtail spending or staffing at the FCC? A recent study by Greg Sidak of the American Enterprise Institute found that the number of telecom lawyers—as measured by membership in the Federal Communications Bar Association—grew by 73 percent in the late 1990s. That growth was largely driven by a 37 percent hike in FCC spending and a tripling of the number of pages of regulations in the *FCC Record* in the post–Telecommunications Act period (see Figure 12.1).[8] Sidak argues, "If one assumes (very conservatively) that the average income of an American telecommunications lawyer is $100,000, then the current membership of the FCBA represents an annual expenditure on legal services of at least $340 million."[9]

This staggering explosion of regulatory spending and lobbying is the clearest indication of just how nonderegulatory the Telecommunications Act really was. The Republicans had not learned a lesson that the Democrats understood in the late 1970s when they abolished the Civil Aeronautics Board in the wake of airline deregulation: if you do not eliminate the regulator, you cannot really deregulate an industry.

In sum, the Telecommunications Act offered the Republicans their best chance to radically change the way business was done in this sector by closing the door on a century's worth of inefficient regulation.[10] Instead, Congress opted for a far more timid, transitional plan that largely left the regulatory edifice of the past in place and, worse, expanded the scope of federal meddling in several policy areas such as the three discussed next.

The E-Rate ("Gore Tax") Program

Many important elements of the Telecommunications Act of 1996 went beyond the wire-line telecom competition provisions. One of the most significant expansions of federal power contained in the act was the so-called e-rate program. E-rate is shorthand for education rate, which refers to the reduced prices for hardware and services that schools and libraries are eligible for under the program. Section 254 of the Telecommunications Act authorized the FCC to "establish competitively neutral rules to enhance, to the extent technically feasible and economically reasonable, access to advanced telecommunications and information services for all public and non-profit elementary and secondary school classrooms, health care providers, and libraries."[11] This provision was championed by Vice President Al Gore and strongly pushed by the White House during negotiations over the act.

Just as the FCC had taken advantage of the vague delegation of open-access authority found in the act to mandate sweeping infrastructure-sharing regulations, the FCC used the e-rate provision to permanently expand universal service mandates and federal involvement in education policy. Initially, the FCC proposed that the e-rate program be administered by a quasi-governmental entity, the Schools and Libraries Corporation formed by the FCC in May 1997 without the consent of Congress. Questions immediately arose in Congress regarding the constitutionality of the FCC's bureaucratic creation. To avoid the threat of legislative or judicial action, the FCC shifted responsibility for e-rate administration to a nonprofit organization known as the Universal Service Administration Company.

Although the FCC's sleight of hand lessened constitutional concerns, in reality business continued as usual because USAC takes its marching orders from the FCC. The FCC has continued to demand that the e-rate program be funded through a complex system of industry mandates and hidden taxes on phone bills to reduce the costs of installing communications and computer technologies in classrooms and libraries. The FCC has also continued to dictate the amount of annual funding for the program, which is currently $2.3 billion annually.

Concerned about the way the e-rate program was created, many Republicans called for the abolition or immediate devolution of the program to the states. But those efforts never achieved enough momentum to pass out of committee. When George W. Bush was running for president, some pundits expected that he would use the issue against Al Gore because many GOP critics in Congress had labeled the program the "Gore Tax" and blamed Gore for the federalization of what was a state and local matter.

Instead, the Bush campaign chose to advance a far more modest reform proposal. It proposed making the program marginally more accountable by shifting administration of the e-rate to the Department of Education and requiring a formal appropriation for the program in the federal budget each year. That proposal got the solution half right. To the extent that schools and libraries receive public funding for their technology needs, those funds should be incorporated into a formal budget subject to open debate and a vote by elected legislators. Unfortunately, however, the administration was proposing that those reforms take place at the federal level instead of the state and local levels where education spending decisions should occur.

The optimal solution would be to end federal involvement altogether and allow the states to operate the e-rate program on their own, if they choose. While the jury is still out regarding the sensibility of increased reliance on technology in the classroom, those educational institutions desiring funds for communications and computing services should petition their state or local leaders for such funding, the same way they would for any other educational tool. There is nothing unique about these technologies that justifies a federal entitlement program. Consider textbooks, which are an indispensable teaching aid. Policymakers have never suggested creating a hidden tax on new novels to help reduce the cost of school textbooks. Such a cross-subsidy would be considered inefficient and unfair. But that is how the e-rate program operates. Hidden taxes on the phone bills of average Americans subsidize school wiring efforts.[12]

Nonetheless, the Bush team was only willing to back partial reform of the program. As a result, supporters of the e-rate had won the most important battle, which was to keep the program in existence at the federal level. Amazingly, when the Bush administration assumed office it was not even willing to stick to its original campaign promise. At a March 7, 2001, hearing of the House Education and Workforce Committee, Education Secretary Roderick Paige announced that the administration was backing away from its plan to put the e-rate program on-budget and transfer authority to the Department of Education.

Why Bush administration officials decided to surrender on e-rate reform is inexplicable. Their cop-out paves the way for the e-rate to become a full-blown, perpetual national entitlement program. No doubt the burgeoning e-rate lobby will pressure the FCC to expand the grab bag of high-tech hardware and services that are subsidized.[13] Despite the efforts some congressional Republicans made in the late 1990s to reform or devolve the program, they have done nothing in recent years to alter the program. Like many other education programs that preceded it, e-rate is now firmly federalized and likely to be subjected only to occasional debates over appropriate funding levels.

The CDA and Internet Speech Controls

Another unfortunate legacy of the Telecommunications Act of 1996 was Congress's endorsement of an ambitious censorship regime for media, the Internet, and interactive communications networks in general. Title V of the act, known as the Communications Decency Act of 1996 (CDA), imposed fines and jail time on individuals who electronically transmitted "indecent" or "patently offensive" materials online. Those provisions were added to the act as amendments shortly before the bill went to the floor for final consideration and received very little attention during committee hearings.[14]

On the day that the Telecommunications Act was passed, February 8, 1996, a coalition of 20 groups and individuals, led by the American Civil Liberties Union, filed a lawsuit seeking to overturn the CDA as a violation of the First Amendment. The result was a landmark free speech decision by the Supreme Court. It ruled unanimously in 1997 that the CDA was an unconstitutional violation of the First Amendment. Writing for the majority, Justice John Paul Stevens argued: "The breadth of the CDA's coverage is wholly unprecedented" and "the CDA places an unacceptably heavy burden on protected speech."[15] He continued:

> As a matter of constitutional tradition, in the absence of evidence to the contrary, we presume that governmental regulation of the content of speech is more likely to interfere with the free exchange of ideas than to encourage it. The interest in encouraging freedom of expression in a democratic society outweighs any theoretical but unproven benefit of censorship.[16]

Seemingly undeterred by the Court's scathing rebuke of the CDA, Congress went back to the drawing board several times in attempts to find an Internet censorship scheme that would pass judicial muster. Those attempts resulted in measures such as the Child Online Privacy Protection Act of 1998 and the Children's Internet Protection Act of 2000. Although more narrowly tailored than the CDA, those measures were also litigated and met stiff resistance in the courts.[17]

The futility of such censorship efforts is ignored by most members of Congress, who either know little about how the Internet actually operates or do understand how it works but engage in a ritual of proposing to "do something" about online smut to win votes with some constituencies. The result has been an endless stream of hearings like the one Rep. Cliff Stearns (R-Fla.), chairman of the Subcommittee on Commerce, Trade and Consumer Protection of the House Committee on Energy and Commerce, scheduled for May 6, 2004, titled "Online Pornography: Closing the Doors on Pervasive Smut."

The CDA contained two other important provisions. It mandated that all television sets include a "V-chip" to enable viewers to block content that was rated as containing violent or sexual material. This provision, in turn, required video programmers and broadcasters to create a "voluntary" ratings system to make the V-chip work. Eight years later, the V-chip is viewed as something of a joke because most consumers do not even realize their sets possess the ability to screen material in this fashion, and the few who do understand it do not take the time or effort to operate it.

The other important CDA provision involved "signal bleed" on cable television. Although cable operators took steps to "scramble" channels to which viewers did not subscribe, some audio and fuzzy video was still discernible. The CDA demanded that all audio or video be fully scrambled so that it could not be recognized. The Playboy Channel filed a lawsuit against the signal-bleed rule and the Supreme Court ruled 5-4 that this provision of the CDA also did not pass First Amendment muster.[18] Today the issue is largely moot because digital cable networks allow operators to completely black out channels to which viewers do not subscribe.

Considering the CDA and its aftermath, if Democrats had been in power there might have been fewer attempts to regulate speech in this fashion. Although there is a great deal of agreement between the parties on many high-tech policy matters, censorship proposals generally find more acceptance among Republicans than Democrats. Luckily, although Republicans continue to fight to censor the Internet, it appears that little of their agenda will find support in the courts.

HDTV Spectrum Giveaway

One of the most lamentable developments of the post–Telecommunications Act period involved the giveaway of tens of billions of dollars' worth of valuable frequency spectrum to the broadcast industry in the name of assisting its transition to digital television (DTV). High-definition television (HDTV) became a catchphrase that broadcasters began using in the late 1980s to convince regulators to reserve valuable parcels of spectrum for future HDTV use. Others were asking the FCC for the right to use the spectrum for alternative services, but broadcasters deftly used their lobbying muscle to persuade the FCC to side with them.[19]

Each broadcaster in America already had a 6 MHz spectrum allocation used for old-fashioned analog TV. But broadcasters argued that they would need the government to "loan" them an additional 6 MHz of high-quality spectrum to simulcast digital signals alongside analog until Americans made a complete transition to DTV sets. When enough households had made the transition, the broadcasters would hand back their old 6 MHz analog license, or so the theory went. To top it off, the broadcasters did not want to pay anything for the new spectrum. They argued that it would be unfair to pay for the new spectrum because the DTV transition was going to be expensive for them. Moreover, they argued that after they returned their old licenses, that spectrum could be sold at auction for alternative wireless uses and fetch the government large sums.

However, as critics pointed out at the time, the opportunity costs of this scheme were high because: (a) the spectrum that the broadcasters wanted could have been auctioned off *immediately* for alternative uses instead of waiting years (perhaps decades) for the old licenses to be returned; (b) if the spectrum was auctioned immediately, it would have generated tens of billions (potentially more than $100 billion) for federal coffers *immediately* instead of at some unspecified date in the distant future; and (c) the DTV transition might be a bust, in which case the whole experiment would be a monumentally costly policy blunder since that spectrum could have been put to other productive uses.

Those and other concerns were raised when the broadcasters brought this industrial policy scheme to Congress. Despite the overwhelming bipartisan opposition to the giveaway of such valuable spectrum and the existence of many other businesses willing to pay to obtain the spectrum for other uses, the lobbying muscle of the broadcast industry proved too powerful to overcome and Congress signed off on the scheme as part of the Telecommunications Act. Worse yet, Congress added a provision to the Balanced Budget Act of 1997 stating that broadcasters could continue to transmit signals on their old 6 MHz analog slice of spectrum until 2006, *or until 85 percent of Americans had made the migration to digital television,* and only then would they have to return their old analog spectrum to the FCC. That provision means that the DTV spectrum may not be returned to the government for decades because few households have made the conversion. Despite the FCC's best efforts to jump-start the transition with additional industrial policy mandates, it will certainly take much longer than 2006 to complete the transition unless the rules are changed.

Why would the Republicans allow such a misguided, almost scandalous, industrial policy scheme to move forward under their watch?

The lobbying prowess of the broadcasters is certainly one possible explanation. Television broadcasters are a powerful force to be reckoned with in every congressional district, and even though Republicans have not traditionally had a good relationship with the media, they still must deal with them both at home and in Washington.

Another explanation is that many lawmakers stress the importance of free, over-the-air local broadcasting as a vital public service. Many lawmakers continue to buy into that logic despite the fact that more than 85 percent of Americans have purchased subscription-based cable and satellite television services.[20] Broadcast television is still viewed by many lawmakers as a birthright entitlement for Americans, and thus those lawmakers are willing to go along with a scheme like the DTV transition in the name of universal service for the increasingly small share of homes that do not subscribe to cable or satellite TV.

Regardless of the rationale, the opportunity costs associated with this giveaway are staggering and get higher with each year that the broadcasters hold the licenses rent-free. While Americans wait for the DTV transition to be completed, other wireless service providers are being denied the opportunity to use the spectrum for alternative services that the public might demand. Wireless broadband providers, for example, could use the spectrum to provide millions of households with a high-speed Internet connection.

Nonetheless, policymakers are going to shocking lengths, trying to force the transition to work with even more regulations. In August 2002, the FCC mandated that television-set manufacturers include digital television tuners in all their new sets by 2006 to help speed the transition, even though the DTV tuners will add more than $200 to the cost of each new television.[21] In November 2003, the FCC mandated that by July 1, 2005, every consumer electronic device capable of receiving digital TV signals be able to recognize a "broadcast flag"—or string of digital code—that will be embedded in digital broadcast programming in the future.[22] In theory, the mandate is supposed to encourage content creators and broadcasters to air more digital programming over the broadcast TV airwaves, in the belief that the broadcast flag will allow them to prohibit mass redistribution through peer-to-peer networks. In other words, the broadcast flag mandate is supposed to help prevent the "Napster-ization" of television programming. Even though the technology is unproven and better alternatives were available, the FCC marched forward with the new mandate on all consumer electronics in the name of facilitating the DTV transition.[23] Legislators and regulators are also considering new "must carry" mandates on cable companies, which would require that they carry all local digital TV broadcast signals on their systems.[24]

All these mandates attempt to transfer the responsibility and costs associated with the DTV transition to other industries or unwitting consumers. The fact that all of this activity has happened under the Republican watch raises troubling questions about the party's commitment to free markets and its ability to control powerful lobbying interests, which have captured the industry's regulators.

Export Controls on Encryption

Beyond the 1996 Telecommunications Act, perhaps the most interesting and important technology policy debate in recent years involves export controls on encryption software. Encryption involves the scrambling and unscrambling of electronic code to ensure privacy and security. An encrypted message can be decoded only if someone has an electronic "key" that is created for that purpose, or by complicated and time-consuming decryption techniques.[25]

The policy issue in recent years regarded whether the federal government should regulate the sale or export of high-power encryption software. Additionally, should the government hold the keys that unlock private encryption programs and software?

As the Internet revolution began unfolding, it became apparent that rapid increases in computer power were making it more difficult for government to decrypt and decipher encrypted messages. Government officials at the Federal Bureau of Investigation and other agencies grew concerned about an expanding market of uninhibited encryption innovation and the export of those products overseas.

In early 1997, Department of Commerce regulations prohibited the export of encryption products with a strength of 40 bits or more. Clinton administration officials supported that policy even though the computer industry made it clear that 40-bit encryption was largely obsolete and higher-power encryption was already hitting the market. The industry also stressed that the global competitiveness of the U.S. high-tech sector might be at stake unless steps were taken to relax restrictions on its hardware and software exports. But the Department of Commerce, the FBI, and other agencies were adamantly opposed to any change in the rules. Others put forward a plan for the federal government to hold the master key to all encryption products produced in America.

Nonetheless, the 105th Congress listened to the industry's concerns and a bipartisan group of lawmakers introduced legislation to loosen export controls on encryption products. Without going into the details, the battle lines were drawn between those members of Congress sympathetic to the industry and those sympathetic to the concerns of national security and law enforcement agencies. Numerous committee votes were taken in both chambers over the next two sessions of Congress until it became obvious that the computer industry had the support needed to advance liberalization legislation to a successful floor vote. Responding to this situation, the Clinton administration announced in late 1999 that it would finally end its long–standing opposition to the relaxation of encryption export controls. Today, as a result, "the export of the strongest encryption products to most destinations [is] relatively easy."[26]

One important factor that likely led to the eventual surrender by the Clinton administration was the explosive growth of Internet connectivity worldwide and the obvious difficulty, or perhaps futility, of policing the movement of encryption products through cyberspace. Because encryption is at root nothing more than a string of digital bits of information, it can flow across borders instantaneously at the click of a button. While the legislative and regulatory process ground along at its slow pace, the market for encryption kept evolving and the technology kept getting more sophisticated. Eventually it become obvious to almost everyone involved that "the genie is out of the bottle," in the words of Sen. Ernest Hollings (D-S.C.).[27]

In recent years it has become clear just how important this victory was. The market for online services has exploded thanks to the faith most Americans now have in placing personal information on the Internet. Whereas it once took a leap of faith to put a credit card number and other personal data online to complete a transaction, it is now done routinely by millions of consumers every day. Strong encryption has been the secret to this success. Most serious Web vendors worldwide employ some type of encryption to secure customer transactions. Had U.S. policy remained frozen with archaic encryption caps left intact, a vibrant Internet marketplace might not have developed so quickly. The majority of Republicans supported encryption liberalization and thus deserve credit for pushing the administration to change its rules.

Finally, the encryption debate was important in that it was the first major post–Telecommunications Act debate that had nothing to do with traditional telecommunications and technology policy. In this sense, it foreshadowed the rise of an entirely new universe of high-tech public policy issues for which policymakers had no legislative or regulative framework to guide their actions.

Digital Divide

As the availability of personal computers (PCs) and Internet access spread in the 1990s, the Clinton administration seemed eager to bring class politics into technology policy. In a series of National Telecommunications and Information Administration reports titled *Falling through the Net*, the administration embarked on what future historians may well remember as a silly Chicken Little crusade, in which apocalyptic rhetoric was used to decry the existence of a "digital divide" in America.[28] This area is one where the Republicans followed their hands-off-the-Internet philosophy and deserve credit for not throwing taxpayer dollars at a nonproblem invented by the Democrats.

The pessimistic outlook the Clinton administration adopted regarding the diffusion of PCs and the Internet was based on the simplistic notion that not everyone in America had access to those products. Yet every new technology has early adopters (usually wealthier and more educated individuals), who are followed by other households that lag a few years behind in purchasing new gadgets and services. Early adoption of new technologies by risk-takers is a very beneficial market process, not the tragic "divide" that the Clinton administration made it out to be. Later adopters benefit with lower costs and high-quality products to choose from that were essentially financed by the early-adopting guinea pigs.

Computers and the Internet hardly rank in the same category as life-essential goods, such as heating, plumbing, or electricity. Not every American needs, or even wants, a computer or the Internet in his or her home. Unlike other technologies such as telephones and televisions, it is doubtful that there will ever be close to 100

185

percent *household* penetration for computers or Internet access. Residential penetration rates will be held down by the fact that workplace access to these technologies is often a substitute for household access. Moreover, the rapid pace of technological change in this sector may make desktop PCs an anachronism of the past as the world enters a Star Trek–esque age of "wearable computing" and ubiquitous Web access through multiple devices, especially mobile or wireless gadgets. Who knows how we will define household penetration when cell phones are sewn into the buttons on our shirts!

What made the Clinton administration's digital divide concerns more odd is that computer and Internet diffusion continues to be amazingly rapid. As economist Wayne Leighton has noted, "the latest technologies, including computer use and access to the Internet, are being adopted at a faster rate than technologies of only a generation or two ago."[29] Indeed, those technologies are spreading more rapidly than almost *any* previous good or service. Whereas many older technologies took many decades to reach 50 percent of American homes (telephones took 71 years; electricity took 52; radio took 28), personal computers were available to half of American homes within 19 years of introduction and the Internet hit that mark in just 10 years. The Bush administration's last report on the issue, *A Nation Online*, also made clear that things will only get better, noting that Internet use is exploding and gaps between various demographic groups are shrinking.[30]

In summary, this appears to be a technology policy issue area where party affiliation makes a difference. Since the Clinton administration's first digital divide report, Democrats have continued to clamor for increased subsidies to solve this nonproblem.[31] Republicans have been less interested in throwing money at this issue and instead have rightly noted the amazing strides being made in the free market to bridge whatever divides remain.

Internet Taxation

As electronic commerce began to gain steam in the 1996–97 period, the potential for governments at all levels to milk this new technology as a tax cow became cause for great concern within the industry and among denizens of cyberspace. The telecommunications sector was already among the most heavily taxed industries in America.[32]

A key threat was the growing interest of state and local governments in applying traditional telecom levies to Internet access services. In a rare display of rapid and bipartisan legislative action, Congress moved to avert this threat by curtailing the ability of state and local governments to impose such taxes. The Internet Tax Freedom Act of 1998 imposed a three-year moratorium on "multiple or discriminatory" taxes on electronic commerce. As a compromise, such taxes that were already on the books were grandfathered. In addition, the ITFA authorized the creation of an Advisory Commission on Electronic Commerce to study this issue and the more contentious question of whether sales taxes should be imposed on e–commerce transactions. As it turned out, the advisory commission was unable to reach any consensus on these matters and ended up issuing a final report with few concrete recommendations.[33]

In 2001, Congress voted to extend the Internet tax moratorium for another three years. In 2003 when the issue came up again, the House passed a permanent extension of the moratorium and eliminated the grandfathering provision that had allowed existing Internet taxes to remain on the books.[34] When the debate reached the Senate, however, a handful of members led by former governors Lamar Alexander (R-Tenn.) and Thomas Carper (D-Del.) revolted against the proposal to make the moratorium permanent. This action forced a compromise on the Senate floor that resulted in a four-year, not permanent, extension of the moratorium.

It is also important to emphasize what Congress *did not* do when considering these extensions of the ITFA. Congress did not address Internet sales tax issues or grant state and local governments the permission they have been seeking to evade the constitutional prohibition on taxing interstate commerce. The debate over whether and how to apply sales taxes to electronic commerce is even more contentious than the question of whether to tax Internet access. Many state and local officials support a multistate tax accord to govern sales tax collection. This method would allow them to circumvent court-based protections for interstate vendors, who so far have not been forced to collect and remit sales taxes to jurisdictions where they do not reside. Allowing state and local governments to form what is in essence a tax cartel has disturbing implications for the Internet, the free flow of interstate commerce, and tax competition between the states.[35] Congress is to be commended for not allowing this issue to become tied to the extension of the moratorium on Internet access taxes.

In sum, Congress has been able to hold the line thus far on new Internet taxes and has not allowed state and local officials to impose older taxes (sales taxes in particular) on electronic commerce. But it remains to be seen whether Congress can hold the line much longer since state and local officials continue to push for the right to tax these new services and technologies.[36]

Internet Gambling

Since the mid-1990s, many legislative proposals have been introduced in Congress to regulate gambling over the Internet. More than two dozen bills have been proposed since Sen. Jon Kyl (R-Ariz.) raised the issue as part of the Crime Control Act of 1995. Although details have varied, early proposals included penalties of as much as four years in prison and $20,000 in fines for Web site operators taking bets over the Internet. Proposals have included fines and jail time for those placing the wagers as well.

Yet nagging questions remain with respect to enforcing proposed restrictions. Gambling is a huge industry that is extraordinarily difficult to regulate in both the online and the offline worlds. A December 2002 report by the General Accounting Office found: "Internet gambling is a growing industry. Since the mid-1990s, Internet gambling operators have established approximately 1,800 e-gaming Web sites in locations outside the United States, and global revenues from Internet gaming in 2003 are projected to be $5.0 billion dollars."[37] Although the government could find and shut down some online gambling operations, new ones would pop up quickly to replace them, likely in offshore locations outside of U.S. legal jurisdiction.

In the 106th Congress, proponents of an Internet gambling prohibition decided to shift their proposed enforcement strategy to approaches that prevented the use of various financial instruments (credit cards, wire transfers, and such) to facilitate online wagering. Almost all major bills considered since then have proposed some variation of that approach.

Although none of those measures has been enacted into law, the efforts to prohibit online gambling count as a Republican attempt to regulate the Internet. Although many Democrats have joined in the anti-gambling crusade, Republicans have led the effort in their belief that online gambling is immoral and a risk to children. Much like their stance on censorship issues, many Republicans have sought to preempt consenting adults from peacefully engaging in voluntary activities and judging on their own the best interests of their children. In Republicans' efforts to squelch online gambling, they have chosen to hypocritically ignore the many legalized forms of gambling, such as horse racing, gambling on Indian lands, and especially state-government lotteries. No doubt they have exempted those activities from their anti-Internet gambling legislation to appease special interests.

If prohibitions on Internet gambling are enacted, they will require a very intrusive regulatory regime to be effective. Simply forbidding established financial institutions from clearing online gambling transactions would not be enough. Congress would need to go further and impose fines and jail times on individuals who used gambling sites. But how would the government find the millions of individuals who engage in online wagering, given the anonymous nature of Internet activity? Also, the rise of alternative financial instruments, such as e-cash payments, would make transactions very difficult to trace. Regardless, the entire endeavor would require government officials to expend significant resources in pursuit of individuals who are doing nothing more than peacefully disposing of their income on activities that they find enjoyable.[38]

Conclusion

In recent years, the universe of high-technology public policy issues has exploded. Online privacy has become a major issue directly affecting how business is done online.[39] Regulation of unsolicited e-mail, spam, has also become a major issue on which Congress has already taken action.[40] Various technology tax credit proposals have garnered bipartisan support.[41] Cybersecurity is a growing area of federal intrusion with many proposals to regulate or subsidize the industry. Internet governance issues are also important, including domain name procedures, international antitrust standards, and global libel laws and free speech restrictions.

Meanwhile, intellectual property issues have grown in importance. Intellectual property and high-technology policy issues have become intertwined in recent years, leading to remarkably caustic debates, such as the conflict regarding the application of copyright law to digital services and peer-to-peer networks.[42]

In each of these policy areas a similar legislative pattern has emerged. Some Republicans initially stress a laissez faire approach and argue that new technologies should not be strangled in the crib with regulations. But over time, that instinct wanes to give way to a more activist approach. Part of the reason this evolution occurs is because many high-tech firms and trade associations invite government to play a prominent role, especially if an industry is squabbling within itself. As Christine Y. Chen of *Fortune* reports, "Tech communities in Silicon Valley, Boston, Seattle, and Austin may be libertarian havens, but these days the geeks are cozying up to big government."[43]

Sadly, it appears the high-tech sector is on its way to becoming another entrenched Beltway special interest that relies on armies of lobbyists to cozy up to legislators and regulators. Indeed, the high-tech sector's rapid assimilation into Beltway political circles is becoming the latest example of what Milton Friedman labeled "the business community's suicidal impulse":

> Businessmen tend to be schizophrenic. When it comes to their own businesses, they look a long time ahead, thinking of what the business is going to be like 5 to 10 years from now. But when they get into the public sphere and start going into the problems of politics, they tend to be very shortsighted. . . . [They] take positions that are not in their own self-interest and that have the effect of undermining support for free private enterprise.[44]

When this process gets going it is very hard to stop. Legislator-lobbyist interaction grows exponentially and the legislative sausage factory kicks into high gear to appease the demands of one special interest or another. It is likely that high-technology and Internet companies will soon supplant broadcasting and telecommunications lobbying interests in terms of power and prestige in Washington.

The result will be very bad news for consumers and U.S. technology leadership because of more government regulation of the Internet, communications, media, computers, and other industries. Sadly, it is already the case that "governmental regulation of [the] Internet is actually becoming increasingly the rule, rather than the exception."[45]

The rise of this cyber-statism could have been avoided if congressional Republicans stuck to their promises of "getting Washington off our backs" and "hands off the Internet." Instead, the seduction of micro-managing one of the most important sectors of the economy has proven to be too hard to pass up. If these negative trends continue, the GOP might as well adopt a new slogan to fit their approach to technology policy: "Hands all over the Internet."

Notes

1. Ed Gillespie and Bob Schellhas, eds., *Contract with America: The Bold Plan by Rep. Newt Gingrich, Rep. Dick Armey and the House Republicans to Change the Nation* (New York: Times Books, 1994), p. 125.

2. *AT&T Corp. v. Iowa Utilities Board*, 525 U.S. 366, 397 (1999).

3. Reed Hundt, *You Say You Want a Revolution: A Story of Information Age Politics* (New Haven, CT: Yale University Press, 2000), p. 66.

4. Peter Huber, "Telecom Undone—A Cautionary Tale," *Commentary* 115, no. 1 (January 2003), www.manhattan-institute.org/html/_comm-telecom.htm.

5. See generally Adam D. Thierer and Clyde Wayne Crews, *What's Yours Is Mine: Open Access and the Rise of Infrastructure Socialism* (Washington: Cato Institute, 2003).

6. C. Michael Armstrong, "Telecom and Cable TV: Shared Prospects for the Communications Future" (address, Washington Metropolitan Cable Club, Washington, D.C., November 2, 1998).

7. "The President and Vice President Deliver Remarks after Signing the Telecommunications Reform Act of 1996," Federal Document Clearing House, Inc., *FDCH Political Transcripts*, February 8, 1996.

8. J. Gregory Sidak, "The Failure of Good Intentions: The WorldCom Fraud and the Collapse of American Telecommunications after Deregulation," *Yale Journal of Regulation* 20, no. 1 (Winter 2003): 207–67.

9. Ibid.

10. See Adam Thierer, "Thinking about the Next Telecom Act," *Testimony before the Senate Committee on Commerce, Science and Transportation*, 108th Cong., 2nd sess., April 28, 2004, www.cato.org/testimony/ct-at040428.html.

11. *Telecommunications Act of 1996, U.S. Code* 47, (1996), §254(h)(2)(A).

12. See Lawrence Gasman, "Universal Service: The New Telecommunications Entitlements and Taxes," Cato Institute Policy Analysis no. 310, June 25, 1998, www.cato.org/pubs/pas/pa-310es.html.

13. For more information see Adam Thierer, Clyde Wayne Crews Jr., and Thomas Pearson, "Birth of the Digital New Deal: An Inventory of High-Tech Pork-Barrel Spending," Cato Institute Policy Analysis no. 457, October 28, 2002, www.cato.org/pubs/pas/pa-457es.html.

14. For general background see Solveig Bernstein, "Beyond the Communications Decency Act: Constitutional Lessons of the Internet," Cato Institute Policy Analysis no. 262, November 5, 1996, www.cato.org/pubs/pas/pa-262es.html; Marjorie Heins, *Not in Front of the Children: "Indecency," Censorship, and the Innocence of Youth* (New York: Hill and Wang, 2001), pp. 157–200.

15. *Reno v. ACLU*, 521 U.S. 844, 877, and 882 (1997).

16. *Reno v. ACLU*, 521 U.S. 844, 885 (1997).

17. Robert Corn-Revere, "*United States v. American Library Association*: A Missed Opportunity for the Supreme Court to Clarify Application of First Amendment Law to Publicly Funded Expressive Institutions," in *Cato Supreme Court Review: 2002–2003*, ed. James Swanson (Washington: Cato Institute, 2003), www.cato.org/pubs/scr2003/publiclyfunded.pdf.

18. *U.S. v. Playboy Entertainment Group*, 529 U.S. 803 (2000).

19. See Joel Brinkley, *Defining Vision: How Broadcasters Lured the Government into Inciting a Revolution in Television* (San Diego, CA: Harcourt Brace & Company, 1997).

20. Federal Communications Commission, *Tenth Annual Report on Annual Assessment of the Status of Video Competition in the Market for the Delivery of Video Programming*, January 5, 2004, p. 115, http://hraunfoss.fcc.gov/edocs_public/attachmatch/FCC-04-5A1.pdf.

21. *In the Matter of Review of the Commission's Rules and Policies Affecting the Conversion to Digital Television*, Federal Communications Commission, MM Docket No. 00-39, August 9, 2002, http://hraunfoss.fcc.gov/edocs_public/attachmatch/FCC-02-230A1.pdf.

22. *In the Matter of Digital Broadcast Content Protection*, Federal Communications Commission, MB Docket No. 02-230, November 4, 2003, http://hraunfoss.fcc.gov/edocs_public/attachmatch/FCC-03-273A1.pdf.

23. See Adam Thierer, "The Broadcast Flag Decision: The FCC Bends Over Backward to Protect Over-the-Air Television and the HDTV Transition," Cato Institute TechKnowledge no. 64, November 13, 2003, www.cato.org/tech/tk/031113-tk.html; Adam Thierer, "On Drawing Lines in Copyright Law," Cato Institute TechKnowledge no. 75, March 5, 2004, www.cato.org/tech/tk/040305-tk.html.

24. Adam Thierer, "DTV Mandate Tally Could Grow Again with Upcoming Multicasting Decision," Cato Institute TechKnowledge no. 67, December 5, 2003, www.cato.org/tech/tk/031205-tk.html.

25. See generally Bruce Schneier, *Applied Cryptography* (New York: John Wiley & Sons, Inc., 1996).

26. David W. Addis and E. Jason Albert, "Cryptography and Encryption: Confidentiality and Information Security," in *E-Commerce Law & Business*, ed. Mark E. Plotkin (New York: Aspen Publishers, 2003), Vol. 2, pp. 17–46.

27. Quoted in "Bill Approved by Committees in Senate," *CQ Almanac, 1999*, vol. LV (Washington: Congressional Quarterly Inc., 2000), pp. 22–24.

28. See www.ntia.doc.gov/ntiahome/digitaldivide/index.html.

29. Wayne Leighton, "Broadband Deployment and the Digital Divide," Cato Institute Policy Analysis no. 410, August, 7, 2001, www.cato.org/pubs/pas/pa-410es.html.

30. National Telecommunications and Information Association, Department of Commerce, *A Nation Online: How Americans Are Expanding Their Use of the Internet*, February 2002, www.ntia.doc.gov/ntiahome/dn/nationonline 020502.htm.

31. See Adam Thierer and Clyde Wayne Crews Jr., "Just Don't Do It: The Digital Opportunities Investment Trust (DO IT) Fund," Cato Institute TechKnowledge no. 35, May 6, 2002, www.cato.org/tech/tk/020506-tk.html.

32. Joseph J. Cordes, Harry S. Watson, and Charlene Kalenkoski, "The Tangled Web of Taxing Talk: Telecommunications Taxes in the New Millennium," Progress and Freedom Foundation, Progress on Point No. 7.12, September 2000, www.pff.org/publications/communications/pop7.12tangledweb.pdf.

33. Advisory Commission on Electronic Commerce, *Report to Congress,* April 2000, www.ecommercecommission.org/acec_report.pdf; also see Adam Thierer, "After the Net Tax Commission: The Gregg-Kohl Nexus Solution," Heritage Foundation Backgrounder no. 1363, April 25, 2000, www.heritage.org/Research/InternetandTechnology/BG1363.cfm.

34. Teri Rucker, "House Votes to Renew Ban on Internet-Related Taxes," *National Journal Technology Daily PM Edition,* September 17, 2003.

35. See Adam D. Thierer and Veronique de Rugy, "The Internet Tax Solution: Tax Competition, Not Tax Collusion," Cato Institute Policy Analysis no. 494, October 23, 2003, www.cato.org/pubs/pas/pa-494es.html.

36. See Marguerite Reardon, "VoIP: To Tax or Not to Tax," *CNet News.com,* April 28, 2004, http://news.com.com/2100-7352_3-5201671.html

37. U.S. General Accounting Office, "Internet Gambling: An Overview of the Issues Report to Congressional Requesters, 107th Cong., 2nd sess., December 2002, p. 1, www.gao.gov/new.items/d0389.pdf.

38. See generally Tom W. Bell, "Internet Gambling: Popular, Inexorable, and (Eventually) Legal," Cato Institute Policy Analysis no. 336, March 8, 1999, www.cato.org/pubs/pas/pa-336es.html.

39. Tom W. Bell, "Internet Privacy and Self-Regulation: Lessons from the Porn Wars," Cato Institute Briefing Paper no. 65, August 9, 2001, www.cato.org/pubs/briefs/bp-065es.html.

40. Clyde Wayne Crews Jr., "Why Canning 'Spam' Is a Bad Idea," Cato Institute Policy Analysis no. 408, July 26, 2001, www.cato.org/pubs/pas/pa-408es.html.

41. Adam Thierer, "Broadband Tax Credits: The High-Tech Pork Barrel Begins," Cato Institute TechKnowledge no. 14, July 13, 2001, www.cato.org/tech/tk/010713-tk.html; Adam Thierer, Clyde Wayne Crews Jr., and Thomas Pearson, "Birth of the Digital New Deal: An Inventory of High-Tech Pork-Barrel Spending," Cato Institute Policy Analysis no. 457, October 28, 2002, www.cato.org/pubs/pas/pa-457es.html.

42. See generally Adam D. Thierer and Clyde Wayne Crews Jr., *Copy Fights: The Future of Intellectual Property in the Information Age* (Washington: Cato Institute, 2001).

43. Christine Y. Chen, "Getting a Piece of the D.C. Pie," *Fortune,* May 12, 2003, p. 34.

44. Milton Friedman, "The Business Community's Suicidal Impulse," *Cato Policy Report* 21, no. 2 (March/April 1999); p. 1, www.cato.org/pubs/policy_report/v21n2/friedman.html.

45. Michael Geist, "Tax Holiday Expiring, Regulators Aspiring on Web," *Toronto Star,* June 30, 2003.

13. The Revolution Spins toward More Regulation

Clyde Wayne Crews Jr.

Most people assumed that Republican politicians replacing Democrats on Capitol Hill in 1995 would lead to small-government, anti-regulation policies. That assumption turned out to be wrong. Libertarians have long observed that both Democrats and Republicans seek power; they just seek power over different sorts of activities. Stereotypically, Republicans want government to regulate personal behavior (the "bedroom"), while Democrats want to regulate economic activities (the "boardroom"). But during the past decade, this difference between the parties has blurred. Republicans signed on to increased financial regulation in the wake of the Enron scandal, and Democrats have favored increased regulations on free speech, including campaign finance restrictions and controls on the nation's media firms.

The deregulatory image of the Republican Party is a curiosity. Republicans helped create one of the core regulatory interventions in American commerce: the Sherman Antitrust Act in the 1890s. Interventions like the Pure Food and Drug Act followed in the early 20th century. The Nixon administration created the Environmental Protection Agency, the Consumer Product Safety Commission, and the Occupational Safety and Health Administration. President George H. W. Bush signed the Americans with Disabilities Act into law, which has created large regulatory costs.[1] Those and other interventions supported by Republicans have had a huge effect on the economy.

The Contract with America, as Amended

Some Republicans in the past decade did try to reduce regulations and limit government power. For example, House Republicans successfully passed the Risk Assessment and Cost-Benefit Act of 1995, which included compensation for regulatory "takings" of property and for the costs imposed by federal mandates.

But after the government shutdown in 1995, which resulted from budget disagreements with President Bill Clinton, the GOP zeal for regulatory reform waned. Republican attempts to reform the regulatory process lost steam under a rhetorical barrage. Opponents caricatured GOP reform efforts as "mad-dog Republican ideologists join with robber-baron capitalists to regain the right to add poison to baby food bottles," as Fred Smith of the Competitive Enterprise Institute noted.[2] A Senate version of comprehensive regulatory reform never passed.

Part of the decade of Republican control of Congress was under President Clinton and part was under President Bush. There were some notable Republican-driven reform bills under Clinton's watch. Legislation dealing with unfunded mandates on state and local governments passed. An annual Office of Management and Budget cost-benefit report was made a permanent undertaking by the Regulatory Right to Know Act in 1999. Other limited successes included reforms to address the paperwork burden, congressional review of regulations, and small business regulatory relief.

President Bush's tenure began with the issuance of the "Card memo," by which White House Chief of Staff Andrew Card notified agencies to freeze pending final rules for two months. This effort dealt with a flurry of proposed rules issued as the Clinton administration was leaving office. Clinton's "midnight regulations" swelled the *Federal Register* of January 22, 2001, to 944 pages with rules relating to such things as air pollution in National Parks caused by snowmobiles.

The Bush administration has relaxed some rules, such as rules on logging and items related to the Clean Air Act, including a rule that power plants need not install state-of-the-art controls in some circumstances. The Department of Labor's controversial ergonomics rule (on repetitive-motion injuries) was halted by a "resolution of disapproval." Meanwhile, Bush's Office of Information and Regulatory Affairs under John Graham has required greater peer review and scientific review of agency rules.

In May 2004, the House passed HR 2432, the Paperwork and Regulatory Improvements Act, to improve regulatory accounting and to set up a pilot project for regulatory budgeting. A recent

Washington Post story recounts Bush's efforts to "put his anti-regula-
tory stamp on government" by canceling more "inherited" regulatory proposals than he has completed and starting fewer new ones
than either Clinton or the first President Bush.[3] But lower numbers
of rules can still mask high costs. Also note that as government
program spending has expanded under President Bush, it portends
more rules being imposed in future years.

Despite modest reforms, agency regulatory overreach and turf-
building can be a concern no matter which party is in power. More
discouraging are prominent Republican-driven interventions, such
as the ephedra ban, media ownership restrictions, and a new prescription-drug benefit. The Republicans who have stood up to articulate better market alternatives to these big-government policies have
been outnumbered by pro-regulation forces.

Republicans, who are united in power under Bush, have made
numerous concessions to the regulatory state. Their policies have not
all been activist government proposals, but they have been unable to
cogently defend free markets against frequent charges of "market
failure." The result is disheartening. On top of the $2 trillion in
tax revenues that the federal government collects, more than 50
departments, agencies, and commissions issue more than 4,000 rules
and regulations every year. Regulations cost Americans more than
$800 billion every year.[4] As of 2002, there were 25,000 registered
Washington lobbyists, or 47 per member of Congress, many of them
working night and day to alter federal regulations.

Are regulations increasing? Well, yes and no. The *Federal Register*
is at record high levels, hitting 75,606 pages in 2002, but it is not a
good measure of regulatory burdens. The number of rules has been
down or flat under the Republicans, but the GOP budget boom may
herald a future regulatory boom.

Regulations and the Republican Budget Boom

Regulations are a way of getting the private sector to finance
government activities without increasing taxes. Both taxes and regulations transfer wealth from some Americans to others. Interest
groups get involved in those transfers, and soon much of the private
sector gets seduced into the wealth-transfer game with many producers having to defend themselves against unwarranted new burdens.
In some cases, certain firms are able to absorb regulatory costs better

than others, as in the case of pollution controls, and those firms may lobby in favor of new regulations.

Regulations and spending are alternate ways for the government to control the economy, but they also increase together. Rapidly rising federal spending during the past five years anticipates a regulatory boom.[5] Bush's rising education spending has heralded state mandates galore. The Republican Medicare prescription-drug benefit means new medical mandates and constraints on doctors and insurers. The highway bill considered in 2004 would have the National Highway Traffic Safety Administration issue numerous car-design safety regulations dealing with power windows, rollovers, and door-lock enhancements. Other automobile rules in the works include those for daytime running-light glare, brake hose reliability, radiator safety caps, and Corporate Average Fuel Economy standards for light trucks. Proposed new rules for side-crash protection will impose costs of more than $1 billion.

Security concerns since September 11, 2001, have generated much new spending and attendant regulation. As it stands in September 2004, 300 of 4,200 new rules in the works come from the new Department of Homeland Security, such as the Transportation Security Administration's rules for screening checked bags. Meanwhile new Food and Drug Administration regulations on food shipments, meant to protect against terrorist contamination, promise high burdens. For example, more than 425,000 food manufacturers and processors will be required to provide daily updates to FDA on food shipments.

Many new Republican regulatory initiatives do not have a security rationale, such as the new multibillion National Nanotechnology Initiative that President Bush signed into law in December 2003. That law invites government regulation of this frontier industry for little apparent reason other than to channel federal dollars to important congressional districts. Thus, the progress of the nanotech industry may be wrapped up in regulations and sacrificed for the sake of pork spending.

Health and Safety Regulation

Recent health and safety rules address a procession of risks from which the government assumes that we cannot protect ourselves. New rules regard workplace slip-and-fall hazards, indoor air quality, sausage casing labeling, bathroom grout manufacture, smoke alarm locations in homes, backyard play sets, and appliance efficiency standards. Some regulations in these areas are well intended, but the result is to substitute political controls for market solutions.

In many cases, new rules are just plain silly. We do not need the Department of Agriculture dictating the size of holes in Swiss cheese, for example. Nor do we need government fighting over an "official" food pyramid—the provision of healthy food information is a function that belongs to the private science, health, and medical sectors.

The burden should be on regulators to prove that regulations better serve the public than do competitive markets. Unfortunately, Republicans have not done a good job defending the ability of competitive markets to deal with safety and efficiency concerns. The Republicans have proven to be just as susceptible as Democrats to knee-jerk health and safety regulation on the basis of newspaper headlines.

One example is the ephedra ban. This regulation was an expansion of the FDA's power into a new area—the banning of herbal supplements. Such activity was not authorized by Congress, and it deserved a legislative debate that it did not get. Another example is a vast new livestock tracking system. This national identity system for farm animals was initiated after the discovery of a single sick animal with mad cow disease.

If the government tries to answer every societal ill, it will nullify the free market's disciplinary role in consumer and safety protection. Republicans in power have lacked the language and ability to make the case that markets are the best protector of consumer safety. Competitive markets impose discipline in the form of *reputation* and *disclosure* when those forces are allowed to work. Misguided safety regulation is a poor substitute for those disciplines. For example, regulations can make people behave in a more risky manner and can impose more dangerous alternatives on consumers. A good example is the fuel efficiency standards that force Americans into smaller cars.[6] A professor of mine joked that if we want increased highway safety, we should not require seatbelts and air bags because these make people drive more carelessly. Instead, we should require a 6-inch dagger sticking out of car steering columns!

Regulation of Technology and Communications

The explosion of the World Wide Web in 1995 coincided with the Republican takeover of Congress. Many Republicans proclaimed "hands off the Internet." But an exception was the Communications Decency Act of 1996, a notable incursion into free speech. CDA was ultimately struck down by the Supreme Court, but it was a precursor to further interventions. In the Internet and technology sectors, new regulations and mandate proposals are common. Some examples are online marketing to children (ban it); porn filtering (mandate it); Internet gambling (ban it); digital copy protection (some say ban, some say mandate); and cybersecurity (mandate it, even though we cannot define it).

With respect to cybersecurity, government funding virtually guarantees new regulations. The regulation of emerging Internet phone calls, called voice over Internet protocol (VoIP), is also being seriously proposed. However innocuous-sounding they may seem, calls by President Bush in 2004 for "universal broadband" and an end to the "digital divide" invite continued regulation.

Another example of increasing regulation under the Republicans is the Federal Communications Commission do-not-call registry, which was embraced by Congress and President Bush. It includes $11,000 fines for each illegal call made. Granted, few like getting telemarketing calls, but marketplace products offer a variety of solutions, such as caller ID.

Republican anti-spam regulation has been costly and ineffective. Spam was outlawed as of January 1, 2004, by the CAN-SPAM Act signed by President Bush. But by setting rules of engagement for when a commercial e-mail may legally be sent, it actually means that you "can spam." The real issues underlying the torrent of unwanted e-mail—authentication and pricing—have to be solved by the market, and there is no alternative to that.

The introduction of the Internet and new telecommunications services into society has not been without speed bumps. But new government regulations entail false shortcut solutions to problems that may preclude superior market solutions from emerging.

The stock market and telecom collapse was in part caused by contrived markets created when Washington forced incumbent providers to "share" their infrastructure with opportunistic competitors following the Telecommunications Act of 1996. Those competitors could not survive under free markets and they made the telecom sector unstable.

FCC Chairman Michael Powell has taken a pro-deregulation stance, but he was not solidly backed by President Bush early in his first term, which was dominated by other issues. Perhaps the administration might have been concerned that prices would go up temporarily under full telecom deregulation. But many alternatives are available to consumers that dampen any ability to overprice in most markets. Full deregulation should be moved ahead because, ultimately, competition in the creation of networks is as important as competition in the telecom services that are sold over them.[7]

Privacy

The political impulse to regulate undermines the market's ability to self-regulate. Federal Trade Commission proposals to regulate Internet privacy were properly opposed by many Republicans because they recognized the role that markets play in coping with preferences regarding personal information. Unfortunately, large-scale digital surveillance is now possible and irresistible post-9/11. Proposed programs such as Total Information Awareness and the airline Computer-Assisted Passenger Protection program would have required firms to hand over customer information to the government. Such programs would make it impossible for businesses to make the privacy guarantees that today's commerce requires. New rules for health insurance portability rules and financial services have also led to confusing regulatory requirements in the name of protecting privacy.

On the bright side, demands for broad-based privacy legislation, and the regulation it would entail, are dormant. And the current sentiment seems to be for Congress to stay out of the regulation of new VoIP, even though the Federal Bureau of Investigation and others seek enhanced wiretap capabilities for this new class of communications.

Incursions on Free Speech

Free speech has suffered regulatory incursions in recent years. Apart from the Communications Decency Act, new campaign finance restrictions passed in 2002 have increased regulation. Also, Republicans failed to endorse the FCC's 2003 rollback of media ownership rules. In that debate, the concern was that media concentration allowed some to wield excessive control over the media and squelch information from alternative voices. The Republicans did a poor job explaining that media and information cannot be monopolized in a free society when the government does not practice censorship. These days, peer-to-peer networks and weblogs undermine monolithic information. Also, upstream and downstream partners help regulate any monopolizing behavior. The media also face the scrutiny of consumers, advertisers, venture capitalists, and Wall Street. Plus, any monopoly would have to monopolize infrastructure as well as content, a very tall order. In sum, the notion that media must be controlled or forced to behave by government misunderstands free speech and free-market dynamics. Yet media ownership regulations remain and will add 250 pages to the *Federal Register*.

Antitrust Intervention

It used to be said that in the technology industry things moved on "Internet time" and that smokestack-era antitrust laws could not keep up. Many in the free market community warned that high-tech antitrust would not stop with Microsoft, and true to form there have been numerous antitrust cases in play. The AOL–Time Warner merger was held up and its Instant Messenger subjected to conditions by regulators. The Echostar–DirecTV merger was blocked by the Bush FTC.

"Plain vanilla" antitrust actions as well as high-tech interventionism are common under the Republicans. Washington stopped the Heinz-Beechnut baby food merger. The Phillip Morris–Nabisco merger was not allowed to go through until the sell-off of the intense mints business (Ice Breakers) because of a supposed monopoly in this *candy* market. The FTC has even considered whether premium ice cream and jarred pickles are important markets that can be monopolized. The FTC has put on hold the LensCrafters–Pearle Vision eyewear merger because of supposed price increases in the chain store market.

Such antitrust actions would be expected in a Democratic administration of decades ago, but antitrust understanding has evolved and the actions are remarkably anti-market for 21st-century Republicans. In the tech and cyber sectors, antitrust often takes the form of calls for "open access" to infrastructure and technology, such as instant messaging and phone and cable networks. This is a crucial time for Republicans to take a solid stand against such managed competition. Mandating access to infrastructure and networks amounts to picking winners and losers among business models. It amounts to saying proprietary is out—open, common carriers burdened with obligations are in.

Another problem with recent interventions is that they have left policymakers with no time to advance major reforms such as electricity or telecom deregulation, which would likely be accompanied by industry consolidations. But today's policymakers seem incapable of defending industry restructuring against misguided antitrust attacks. They have also gone down the wrong road with open access in the electric industry, which has set back electricity reform for years. Rather than abandoning open access after the northeast blackouts of 2003, Republicans called for mandatory reliability rules that would enshrine open access and more regulation from Washington.

Other Economic Regulation

Numerous other areas face new regulatory intervention, but a final two merit mention—new accounting regulations and frontier science. With respect to recent accounting scandals and the resulting Sarbanes-Oxley legislation, government regulation likely will interfere with market pressures that would otherwise have moved toward better disclosures of corporate financial data. And instead of a market system that would force competing accounting systems to prove their worth, government oversight now dominates.

As for cutting-edge science, there is too much eagerness for government funding and oversight in areas such as biotechnology and nanotechnology. In nanotechnology, the choice is to treat it like software and leave it mainly unregulated, or treat it like medical products with heavy FDA regulation. Because federal spending and regulation go hand in hand, the new $3.7 billion National Nanotechnology Initiative invites new regulations.

Conclusion

On the whole, Republicans in power seem to be as receptive as Democrats to a large regulatory state. In numerous fields—financial accounting, cybersecurity, telecommunications, antitrust, science—Republicans have failed to replace regulatory bureaucracies with marketplace disciplines.

Instead, Republicans should start holding the regulatory state to higher standards of disclosure and accountability. On disclosure, the administration should publish an annual "Regulatory Report

Card" that contains numbers of rules and their costs. Also, Congress should establish a bipartisan Regulatory Reduction Commission modeled on the military base-closure commissions of the 1990s.

On accountability, major regulations should not take effect until Congress approves them, and they should be "sunsetted," or set to expire on a date certain. By delegating sweeping powers to unelected bureaucrats, Congress has created a disconnect between the power to establish regulatory programs and responsibility for the results. Federal agency employees are not held accountable to voters. Accountability does not necessarily mean that Congress will do right, but accountability is a necessary (although not sufficient) condition for good government.

Ronald Reagan described government as "the problem, not the solution." In many areas, regulations stand in the way of free markets creating solutions that would benefit consumers. If regulatory growth is to be constrained, Republicans need to stop being part of the problem and let markets and entrepreneurs discover lasting solutions.

Notes

1. Associated Press, "Travel Sites Agree to Be More Accessible to Blind," August 19, 2004, www.siliconvalley.com/mld/siliconvalley/news/editorial/9443805.htm.

2. Fred Smith, "Making Regulatory Reform a Reality: A Heritage Foundation Symposium," *Heritage Lectures*, no. 559, January 31, 1996.

3. Amy Goldstein and Sarah Cohen, "Bush Forces a Shift in Regulatory Thrust," *Washington Post*, August 15, 2004, p. A1.

4. Wayne Crews, "Ten Thousand Commandments: An Annual Snapshot of the Federal Regulatory State" (Washington: Cato Institute, June 15, 2004).

5. For recent spending trends, see Chris Edwards, "Downsizing the Federal Government," Cato Policy Analysis no. 515, June 2, 2004.

6. See Sam Kazman, Competitive Enterprise Institute, "CAFE Standards: Do They Work? Do They Kill?" (speech, Heritage Foundation, Washington, D.C., February 25, 2002), www.cei.org/gencon/027,02414.cfm.

7. This theme is explored in Adam Thierer and Clyde Wayne Crews Jr., *What's Yours Is Mine: Open Access and the Rise of Infrastructure Socialism* (Washington: Cato Institute, 2003).

14. The GOP's Environmental Record

Jerry Taylor

The 104th Congress came to office having made "concrete commitments to the voters" to "loosen Washington's regulatory stranglehold on businesses and property owners."[1] Regarding this promise and others, Republicans argued that "we kept them all."[2]

A review of the record over the past 10 years, however, reveals that the 104th and subsequent Congresses did not loosen regulatory burdens in the environmental arena. On the contrary, the Republicans oversaw an increase in environmental regulatory burdens on businesses, property owners, and state and local governments. Whether those new regulations represent a good or bad thing, of course, depends upon how one feels about them.

This chapter reviews the legislative record in three distinct areas: regulatory process reform, environmental regulation, and public lands management. I will not address budgetary trends in program funding (most of which, however, would show steady increases) or energy-related legislation, even though some of those initiatives are undertaken with environmental objectives in mind.

The main criticism of the review that follows is that inaction is itself a form of action and that Congress should be judged not only by the things that it did but also by the things that it did not do.[3] Congressional inaction is the rule, however, not the exception. Accordingly, judging the GOP record against the status quo seems reasonable. Moreover, the number of initiatives Congress *might* have undertaken is nearly unlimited. Determining whether inaction in an issue area is significant or insignificant would prove quite subjective.

Regulatory Reform

Regulatory reform was one of the chief goals of the 104th Congress and a long-standing concern of Republican officeholders when they were in the minority. The charge that America was disastrously overregulated and subject to federal rules bereft of sound science

205

and common sense has been a staple of the Republican critique since the election of President Ronald Reagan in 1980.

Although regulatory reform laws were enacted to address regulations beyond those bearing on the environment, complaints about environmental regulations fueled all of these legislative initiatives. Accordingly, it is fair to consider regulatory reform as part of Congress's record with regard to environmental policy.

Five major regulatory reform bills have been passed by Congress since 1995, and all were signed into law. Four of the five bills were adopted by the 104th Congress and the other was enacted by the 105th Congress.[4] Subsequent Congresses appear to have lost interest in the issue. The reforms adopted have proven more symbolic than substantive. A brief review of each follows.

Unfunded Mandates Reform Act

The Unfunded Mandates Reform Act allows legislators to raise a point of order during floor debate if a bill under consideration imposes an unfunded mandate on state and local governments or private industry beyond a certain amount. The unfunded mandate in question would then face a separate vote as a condition for the bill's passage.[5]

Since the Unfunded Mandates Reform Act was passed, however, no bill has been rejected based on a point of order lodged under the act. Moreover, the Congressional Budget Office reports that the total sum of unfunded mandates imposed on state and local governments has increased since the passage of the act.[6] Unfortunately, the difficulty involved in quantifying unfunded mandates on state and local governments makes it nearly impossible to identify a trend in the growth of unfunded federal mandates.[7] There is some circumstantial evidence, however, to suggest that unfunded mandates may well have been greater in the absence of this act than has been the case since it was enacted.[8]

Small Business Regulatory Enforcement Fairness Act

The Small Business Regulatory Enforcement Fairness Act has a number of provisions. The main point of the act is to provide small businesses with substantive due process rights enforceable in a court of law during administrative rulemaking procedures.

The most controversial part of SBREFA is a section known as the Congressional Review Act, subtitle E. Subtitle E delays implementation of major agency actions for 60 days. During that period, if a legislator objects to a rule, he is afforded an opportunity to send it to the appropriate committee for consideration without amendments. If the committee votes the rulemaking through, the matter ends. If the committee does not, 30 members can have it brought to the floor for a vote. If the rule is rejected, however, the president can veto the legislative rejection and Congress must then muster two-thirds of the chamber to override the presidential veto.

The provision has been effectively used only once. In 2001, Congress rejected the ergonomic workplace liability rule issued by the U.S. Department of Labor.

Paperwork Reduction Act

The Paperwork Reduction Act requires federal administrative agencies to reduce the total burden hours of paperwork imposed on the public by 10 percent in 1996, 10 percent in 1997, 5 percent in each year from 1998 to 2001, and to the maximum extent possible thereafter.

Although the goal of the act is laudable, its track record is not. When the act took effect, federal agencies estimated that their information collection efforts imposed about 7 billion burden hours on the public. The most recent data available, however, reveal that federal information collection efforts today impose approximately 8.1 billion burden hours on the public, fully 3.5 billion burden hours higher than the act's target set for September 30, 2001.[9] Although such estimates are admittedly imprecise, they certainly suggest that the act has failed to live up to its promise.

Regulatory Accounting Act

The Regulatory Accounting Act requires the executive branch to produce an annual report for Congress estimating the total costs and benefits of all federal regulations. The report is also required to include significant public suggestions to correct regulations alleged to be "inefficient, ineffective, or not a sound use of the nation's resources."

Although useful for analysts, no shortage of such reports exists for those interested. In fact, the law stipulates that the report must be based on a compilation of existing information rather than new analysis. Accordingly, the act does not even provide new information—it simply collates what is already available.

207

The Shelby Amendment

The Shelby Amendment was enacted as part of the 1999 omnibus spending bill. It requires that federal grantees make available upon request the data used in published reports and, additionally, make available data that are cited in a federal rule or regulation.[10]

Although opponents of the Shelby Amendment worried that the law would be used by corporations to harass public health researchers, their concerns have proven groundless so far. Of the 40 requests for data submitted under the Shelby Amendment to the National Institutes of Health through August 31, 2003, four requests were withdrawn and the rest were denied for various reasons. Only two requests for data were submitted to the Environmental Protection Agency and both were likewise rejected because the projects for which data were sought were funded before the law went into effect. To date, the Shelby Amendment has had no effect on public policy debates.[11]

Environmental Regulation

According to the *Congressional Quarterly Almanac* and the Congressional Research Service, Congress passed 15 major environmental laws over the past eight years.[12] A review of those laws reveals that most did not have a large effect, and none materially affected the federal environmental regulatory superstructure.[13] To the extent that they changed federal law, they generally increased the regulatory reach of the federal government.

A summary of each major environmental statute adopted by Congress since the 104th Congress follows, listed in order of significance.[14]

- Food Quality Protection Act (104th Congress). Eliminated the application of the "Delaney Clause" to pesticide exposures but required that pesticides meet a "reasonable certainty of no harm" standard for use and applied that standard retrospectively to all pesticides on the market. On balance, the law tightened federal regulation of pesticides.[15]
- Water Resources Development Act of 2000 (106th Congress). Authorized restoration of the Everglades and provided for other water projects.
- Safe Drinking Water Act (104th Congress). Reauthorized the Safe Drinking Water Act and reduced some regulations for state

and local water systems while requiring additional regulatory protection for certain chemical exposures.

- Sustainable Fisheries Act (104th Congress). Reauthorized the Magnuson Fishery Act and tightened regulations on fish catches.
- Mercury-Containing and Rechargeable Battery Management Act (104th Congress). Phased out the use of mercury batteries and imposed labeling requirements for rechargeable batteries.
- HR 325 (104th Congress). Lifted a requirement of the 1990 Clean Air Act that required employers with 100 or more employees to reduce car trips to and from work by at least 25 percent during "severe" or "extreme" air-quality levels.
- National Wildlife Refuge System Improvement Act (105th Congress). Amended the National Wildlife Refuge Act of 1966 to allow recreational uses for wildlife refuges when compatible with mission of preservation.
- Coastal Zone Protection Act (104th Congress). Reauthorized the Coastal Zone Management Act and increased the number of federal grants that states could receive for coastal area management and marine research.
- International Dolphin Conservation Act (105th Congress). Ended ban on tuna imports from certain countries and established a new definition of dolphin-safe tuna.
- Antarctic Science, Tourism, and Conservation Act (104th Congress). Implemented 1991 treaty to increase environmental protections for Antarctica while allowing scientific research to continue.
- Land Disposal Program Flexibility Act (104th Congress). Exempted some small, rural, and dry-area landfills from some federal environmental regulations.
- Omnibus Parks and Public Lands Management Act (104th Congress). Allocated funds for parks, public lands, and riparian management projects.
- Edible Oil Regulatory Reform Act (104th Congress). Differentiated between nontoxic oils and petroleum oils in regulations for transporting these materials.
- Water Resources Development Act (104th Congress). Provided water and conservation development funds while authorizing Army Corps of Engineer river and harbor development projects.

- Water Resources Development Act of 1999 (105th Congress). Provided for flood control, navigation, and other water-resource projects.

This summary indicates a relatively thin body of legislative accomplishment over the past eight years.[16] Moreover, only 5 of the 15 laws passed by Congress might fairly be described as either reducing the scope or increasing the efficiency of government regulation.[17] Finally, only 2 of the 15 laws in the list preceding (the Food Quality Protection Act and the Water Resources Development Act) represent significant departures from the status quo.

Public Lands Management

Since the 104th Congress, 191 bills have been enacted to acquire, transfer, or swap federal land with various private or public entities. Despite Republican rhetoric about the need to reconsider the size of federal land holdings and to provide for greater recreational and industrial access to lands, on balance the bills adopted increased the total acreage of federal lands and put more acreage under restricted access than was the case previously.

Conclusion

Regardless of one's political perspective, a review of the record leads to one inescapable conclusion—the Republican revolution has left virtually no footprints on the environmental code or on federal land holdings. Those hoping that Republican arguments about the dysfunctional nature of environmental regulation would translate into bold action have reason for disappointment, while those fearing an assault on environmental protection have reason for relief.

Of course, an account of the changes made in environmental law and regulation over the past eight years is only partially an account of congressional action. A review of administrative action over the past eight years would tell an entirely different story. Congress has delegated so much discretion to executive branch agencies that executive branch regulators undertake almost all significant changes in environmental law.[18] For instance, the legal and political wrangling over enforcement of the New Source Review Standard of the Clean Air Act—perhaps the most controversial federal environmental issue during the first term of the Bush administration—was initiated by a new enforcement regime established by the Clinton EPA and an administrative redefinition of what constituted a "new source" by the Bush EPA.[19] Likewise, an initiative to remove sulfur from diesel fuel—credited by a senior attorney of the Natural Resources Defense Council as "the biggest public health step since lead was taken out of gasoline more than 20 years ago"[20]—was the result of an EPA regulatory proceeding.[21]

Congress is largely a political sideshow when it comes to environmental regulation—the real action takes place elsewhere. Although that has long been the case, it has become more pronounced since the Republican revolution came to town.

Notes

1. Stephen Moore, ed., *Restoring the Dream* (New York: Times Books/Random House, 1995).

2. Ibid., p. 3.

3. The political left, for instance, might argue that Congress's refusal to take meaningful steps to reduce greenhouse gas emissions or to reauthorize the Superfund program's tax on various manufacturers to help pay for hazardous waste cleanups is all a significant part of Congress' legislative record. The political right, on the other hand, might argue that Congress's refusal to intercede against various regulatory decisions made by executive branch agencies over the past 10 years is likewise a significant part of its legislative record.

4. For a summary of the regulatory reform legislation considered by the 104th Congress, see John Shanahan, "Regulating the Regulators: Regulatory Process Reform in the 104th Congress," *Regulation* 20, no. 1 (Winter 1997): 27–32.

5. For a summary of the law and a review of its application in 2001–2002, see General Accounting Office, "Unfunded Mandates: Analysis of Reform Act Coverage," GAO-04-637, May 2004.

6. Congressional Budget Office, *A Review of CBO's Activities in 2003 under the Unfunded Mandates Reform Act*, Table 5: "Number of CBO Mandate Statements for Bills, Proposed Amendments, and Conference Reports, 1996 to 2003," April 2004, p. 28.

7. For example, the National Conference of State Legislators (NCSL) scores the No Child Left Behind Act as a $10 billion annual unfunded mandate on state governments ("How Much Are Unfunded Mandates Costing Your State?" *Capital Ideas*, National Conference of State Legislatures, March 23, 2004). Yet some analysts contend that Congress in fact fully funds that particular mandate (James Peyser and Robert Costrell, "Exploring the Costs of Accountability," *Education Next*, Spring 2004, pp. 23–29). By contrast, NCSL does not consider federally mandated health care spending on the poor in its list of unfunded mandates, although one economist reports that Medicare was costing states $81 billion in 1995 alone, or one of every four dollars in their budgets. Paul Craig Roberts, "Modern-Day Taxation without Representation," *Business Week*, no. 3347, November 22, 1993, p. 24.

8. General Accounting Office, "Unfunded Mandates: Analysis of Reform Act Coverage," pp. 18–19.

9. Patricia Dalton, Director, Strategic Issues, U.S. General Accounting Office, testimony before the House Government Reform Committee, Subcommittee on Energy Policy, Natural Resources, and Regulatory Affairs, April 20, 2004.

10. For an argument in favor of the Shelby Amendment, see Michael Gough and Steven Milloy, "The Case for Public Access to Federally Funded Research Data," Cato Policy Analysis no. 366, February 2, 2000.

11. General Accounting Office, "University Research: Most Federal Agencies Need to Better Protect against Financial Conflicts of Interest," GAO 04-31, November 2003, pp. 22–24.

12. Both publications highlighted those bills deemed as major initiatives. I deferred to those categorizations when preparing this paper.

13. Those laws are the Clean Air Act; Clean Water Act; Oil Pollution Act; Safe Drinking Water Act; Toxic Substances Control Act; Resource Conservation and Recovery Act; National Environmental Policy Act; Comprehensive Environmental Response; Compensation, and Liability Act; Emergency Planning and Community Right-to-Know Act; Pollution Prevention Act; and Occupational Safety and Health Act.

14. Significance attributed is somewhat arbitrary, granted, but generally reasonable.

15. For a summary of the law and the legislative history of the act, see Daniel Byrd, "Goodbye Pesticides? The Food Quality Protection Act of 1996," *Regulation* 20, no. 4 (Fall 1997): 57–62.

16. Four significant environmental initiatives enacted by Congress were vetoed by President Clinton. *HR 1977 (104th Congress)* was an appropriations bill for the Department of the Interior that would have cut some funding for various public lands and loosened rules restricting timber harvests in National Forests. *HR 2099 (104th Congress)* was an omnibus appropriations bill that would have cut EPA funding by 22 percent, cut Superfund program expenditures by 25 percent, put more restrictions on the EPA's invoking the Clean Water Act to designate wetlands, reduced money available for clean water initiatives, and imposed cuts for various environmental programs. *HR 2499 (104th Congress)* was a budget reconciliation bill that would have opened some of the Arctic National Wildlife Refuge to oil exploration and development. *HR 2909 (104th Congress)* would have barred the Fish and Wildlife Service from using eminent domain to force people along the Connecticut River to give up land to the Silvio O. Conte Wildlife Refuge. *S 1287 (106th Congress)* would have allowed temporary storage of high-level nuclear waste above ground until an underground facility at Yucca Mountain, Nevada, was built in 2010, while taking regulatory power over the project from EPA and transferring it to the Nuclear Regulatory Commission.

17. The Land Disposal Flexibility Act, the Edible Oil Regulatory Reform Act, the International Dolphin Conservation Act, the National Wildlife Refuge System Improvement Act, and HR 325.

18. For a discussion, see David Schoenbrod, *Power without Responsibility: How Congress Abuses the People through Delegation* (New Haven: Yale University Press, 1993).

19. Peter Van Doren and Jerry Taylor, "Congress vs. Responsibility: New Source Review problems are on Capitol Hill," *National Review Online*, December 8, 2003, www.nationalreview.com/comment/vandoren-taylor200312080926.asp, and Jerry Taylor and Peter Van Doren, "Clean Air Debate Is Full of Hot Air," FoxNews.com, April 22, 2002, www.foxnews.com/story/0,2933,50922,00.html.

20. Jennifer Lee and Andrew Revkin, "EPA Plans Crackdown on Dirty Diesel Engines," *New York Times*, April 16, 2003, p. A10.

21. Michael Janofsky, "Tougher Emission Rules Set for Big Diesel Engines," *New York Times*, May 11, 2004, p. A16.

15. A Smooth Transition: Crime, Federalism, and the GOP
Timothy Lynch

When the American electorate expressed its dissatisfaction with the status quo in 1994, congressional Republicans had not only a mandate to implement marginal changes in policy, but also a historic opportunity to make *fundamental and sweeping changes*. It is no overstatement to say that official Washington trembled as the Republicans vowed to restore the Constitution and clean up the mess that the Democrats had created.

In his first speech as majority leader in the Senate, Robert Dole declared, "If I have one goal for the 104th Congress, it is this: that we will dust off the tenth Amendment and restore it to its rightful place in our Constitution."[1] The Tenth Amendment states: "The powers not delegated to the United States by the Constitution, nor prohibited by it to the States, are reserved to the States respectively, or to the people." In criminal justice, almost all of the powers exercised by government had long been held by the states.

Now that 10 years have passed, one can draw some conclusions about the GOP stewardship of the national legislature. With respect to criminal justice policies, the Republicans not only squandered their mandate but now also preside over a burgeoning federal law enforcement bureaucracy. It is almost as if the Republicans have concluded that they can maintain the esteem of the electorate by acting like Democrats.

Instead of a revolution, the GOP has turned its back on the Tenth Amendment and embraced a big-government agenda. Thus, the historic takeover of Congress by Republicans resulted in a party transition but no change in the direction of key policies with respect to criminal justice matters.

Constitutional Federalism

Before delving into the policy decisions of the past 10 years, it is useful to begin with the first principles of American constitutional

213

law so that the legal and policy battles are put into context. The Constitution creates a federal government of limited powers. As James Madison noted in *Federalist* No. 45: "The powers delegated by the proposed Constitution to the federal government are few and defined. Those which are to remain in the State governments are numerous and indefinite." Most of the federal government's "delegated powers" are set forth in article I, section 8, of the Constitution. The Tenth Amendment was appended to the Constitution to make it clear that the powers not delegated to the federal government "are reserved to the States respectively, or to the people."

For 150 years the original constitutional understanding held firm. The federal law enforcement bureaucracy was minuscule. There were no federal prisons in the early days because only a handful of federal criminal laws were on the books. Instead of building prisons, federal officials opted to "rent" space in state facilities for the housing of federal convicts.[2]

The constitutional principle of federalism collapsed in 1937 when President Franklin D. Roosevelt threatened to pack the Supreme Court with new justices who would approve his New Deal measures. After the famous "switch in time that saved nine," the Supreme Court started to approve any federal law that simply "affected" interstate commerce. The constitutional principle of federalism that was embodied in the Tenth Amendment was trampled underfoot.[3]

The consequences of the New Deal precedents were not immediately apparent to most Americans, because changes came fairly slowly. With the New Deal precedents on the books, Congress began to criminalize economic regulations that had previously carried only civil fines. Notorious crime also started to prompt federal politicians to propose new federal laws to ostensibly "solve" problems. For example, after his pioneering flight across the Atlantic, Charles Lindbergh was famous. A few years later, when his child was kidnapped, the media went into a frenzy and put pressure on Congress to take action. A new law was enacted that made the crime of kidnapping a federal offense if the perpetrators "crossed state lines."[4] Kidnapping, of course, was already a crime in every single state.

These trends accelerated over time and the result has been an explosion in the number of federal criminal laws, federal law enforcement personnel, federal searches, federal wiretaps, and federal prisoners. A 1998 report from the American Bar Association notes that more than 40 percent of the federal criminal provisions enacted since the Civil War became law in just the past three decades.[5] By the early 1990s, the federalization of crime was frequently in the headlines because Congress seemed incapable of declaring any crime, no matter how local in nature, beyond its reach. For example, when the *Washington Post* reported the story of a horrific carjacking in a Maryland suburb of the capital in 1992, Rep. Charles Schumer (D-N.Y.) introduced a federal carjacking bill the next day. A headline one day, a law the next day, and on it went.[6]

Federal judges complained that the federal court system was being swamped with ordinary criminal matters that had always been administered by state and local governments.[7] For some perspective on the accelerating trends, consider that in 1958 taxpayers spent $55 million on the federal court system. By 1992 taxpayers were spending $2.3 billion on that system.[8] And despite the budget growth, federal courts and prisons could not keep up with the influx of cases. The federal system was spiraling out of control.[9]

Republicans Fumble Historic Opportunity

Corrupted by their 40-year reign over the House of Representatives, the Democrats were blindsided by the wrath of voters in 1994. To be sure, Democrats had anticipated a difficult election because of the unpopularity of Bill and Hillary Clinton's costly health care plan, but they could not fathom a GOP-controlled House or a conservative Supreme Court that would take the Tenth Amendment seriously and invalidate federal laws as beyond the proper scope of federal power. Liberals dismissed such notions as simply fodder for right-wing fundraising letters. And yet, those remarkable developments happened and turned the Democratic world upside down.

Republicans have long complained about liberal judges who ignore the original understanding of the Constitution. Since the Republicans were successful in winning presidential elections, vacancies on the Supreme Court were greeted with the utmost seriousness. One by one, the liberal justices of the Warren era were replaced by conservative judges or legal scholars. By the fall of 1994, eight of the nine members of the Supreme Court had been appointed by Republican presidents.

Official Washington and the liberal legal academy decried the conservative direction of the Supreme Court in areas ranging from

215

affirmative action to criminal procedure and property rights. But few anticipated a landmark ruling on the constitutional principle of federalism. After all, the Supreme Court had not invoked the doctrine of enumerated powers to invalidate a federal law in decades. In the liberal view, as long as Congress did not trample a specific constitutional right—such as free speech or the right to a jury trial—lawmakers could pass a law on any subject whatsoever.

On November 8, 1994—the same day that voters were handing the Congress to the Republicans for the first time in 40 years—the Supreme Court heard arguments in a case that raised the most basic question about the power of Congress to legislate. The case involved a constitutional challenge to the Gun-Free School Zones Act, which was part of a 1990 crime bill passed by Congress. The Gun-Free School Zones Act essentially made it a federal crime for a person to possess a firearm within 1,000 feet of a school.

The case arose when Texas law enforcement authorities arrested Alfonso Lopez, a 12th-grade student, for bringing a handgun to his high school in San Antonio. Lopez's conduct was illegal under Texas law, but the state charges were dropped when federal officials intervened to indict Lopez under the Gun-Free School Zones Act in federal court. Lopez was tried before a federal judge and was convicted and sentenced to six months' imprisonment.

On appeal, Lopez's attorneys argued that the federal law was unconstitutional because the federal government did not have the authority to pass it. Federal prosecutors acknowledged that the Constitution created a federal government of delegated and enumerated powers, but they maintained that the Gun-Free School Zones Act could be enacted pursuant to Congress's power "to regulate Commerce with foreign nations, and among the several States, and with the Indian Tribes." Lawyers for the federal government defended the constitutionality of the law by arguing as follows: possession of a gun in a school zone (a) might lead to violent crime, which (b) might threaten the learning process, which (c) might ultimately produce less productive citizens, which (d) might, cumulatively, impair the national economy and interstate commerce.

In the spring of 1995, the Supreme Court announced its landmark ruling that the federal prohibition on guns in schools exceeded the powers of Congress. Chief Justice William Rehnquist explained the Court's decision:

> We start with first principles. The Constitution creates a
> Federal Government of enumerated powers. . . . To uphold
> the Government's contentions here, we would have to pile
> inference upon inference in a manner that would bid fair to
> convert congressional authority under the Commerce Clause
> to a general police power of the sort retained by the States. . . .
> And to do that would require us to conclude that the Con-
> stitution's enumeration of powers does not presuppose
> something not enumerated and that there will never be a
> distinction between what is truly national and what is truly
> local. This we are unwilling to do.[10]

At long last, the Supreme Court had reaffirmed the basic idea that
Congress could not use the commerce power as a pretext to enact
any law that Congress considered desirable.

It is almost impossible to overstate the historical significance of
this moment for proponents of limited, constitutional government.
For the first time in 60 years, the Supreme Court had invoked the
doctrine of enumerated powers to invalidate a federal law.[11] The
Tenth Amendment was suddenly revived. And, for the first time in
40 years, the national legislature was controlled by a political party
that claimed an affinity for limited, constitutional government.

With the *Lopez* ruling on the books, the GOP was perfectly posi-
tioned to downsize the bloated and expensive federal government.
Years and years of groundwork had been done in order to arrive
at this juncture. The time was finally right to abolish unconstitutional
federal agencies and repeal unconstitutional laws.

President Clinton tried to feign his allegiance to the then-prevail-
ing sentiment when he declared the "era of big government is over."
Rhetoric aside, Clinton would stand and fight. When the Supreme
Court announced its decision in the *Lopez* case, Clinton immediately
ordered his attorney general, Janet Reno, to find a way to circumvent
the ruling.[12] The Democrats and liberal legal academics were determined to find a way to roll back this new legal precedent, which
called into question the constitutional legitimacy of much of modern
Washington, D.C.[13] But what could Clinton do? The Supreme Court
had just spoken and Congress was controlled by the Republicans.

With the benefit of hindsight, it is now painfully obvious that
while the Republicans dithered, Clinton went to work. First, he had
his Democratic allies introduce a slightly revised Gun-Free School

217

Zones Act in both the Senate and the House. Because any member of Congress can introduce a bill about anything, this action meant little. What is inexplicable, however, is how the Republican leadership could have allowed these measures to be put on a fast track for serious consideration by both chambers. Committees *controlled by the GOP* held hearings on these measures and moved them along. A few months later, Clinton demanded that his school zone bill be included in a year-end appropriation measure. The Republicans capitulated and, in a remarkable act of defiance, Clinton signed a slightly revised Gun-Free School Zones Act into law on September 30, 1996.[14] Not only had the Republicans failed to build upon the historic *Lopez* precedent by repealing laws and abolishing agencies, the feckless Republican leaders could not even manage to keep a single federal criminal law off of the books!

Republican leaders tried to deflect criticism by saying that they had to deal with a hostile liberal media and a big-government advocate like Clinton in the White House—so there was only so much that could be done.[15] To assuage their longtime supporters, the GOP leadership would say: "Just wait until the Republican Party captures the White House! That's when our limited government agenda will really get under way!"

That claim was put to the test when George W. Bush won the 2000 presidential election. The results are in: not only have matters not improved, the situation has worsened.[16] President Bush appointed Sen. John Ashcroft to be his attorney general. Before the terrorist attacks of September 11, 2001, the centerpiece crime-fighting program of the Ashcroft Justice Department was an initiative called Project Safe Neighborhoods. The thrust of that initiative is to divert firearms offenses from state court, where they would ordinarily be prosecuted, to federal court, where harsher prison sentences would be meted out. A related program is called Project Sentry, which Ashcroft has called a "vital federal-state project" dedicated to prosecuting in federal court gun crimes in schools.

Thus, instead of working with the Supreme Court to build a vibrant Tenth Amendment jurisprudence, Republicans are *actively undermining* the Court. As the Cato Institute's Senior Editor Gene Healy has noted, "A more brazen affront to the Rehnquist Court's landmark ruling in *Lopez*—striking down the Gun-Free School Zones Act—could hardly be imagined."[17] Because the GOP Congress approves the funding of Project Safe Neighborhoods and Project Sentry, it is no less culpable than President Bush and Attorney General Ashcroft.

Embracing Big Government

The sad tale of how the GOP is now taking *pride* in vigorously enforcing the one federal law that was invalidated by the Rehnquist Court is a microcosm of the party's stewardship of criminal justice matters generally. House GOP members who focus on military affairs or budget matters often look to Henry Hyde (R-Ill.) for leadership on criminal justice matters because he has been the ranking member of the House Judiciary Committee for many years. Hyde has supported the federalization of whatever the crime-of-the-month happens to be—from carjacking, to wife beating, to church arson, to partial-birth abortion.

The story has been the same in the Senate. Despite Robert Dole's goal of "dusting off the Tenth Amendment," GOP Senators typically defer to Orrin Hatch, the chairman of the Senate Judiciary Committee. He too has sought to federalize more crimes, not less. Senator Hatch has supported the Violence against Women Act, the Church Arson Prevention Act, the Partial-Birth Abortion Prevention Act, and the Hate Crimes Prevention Act. Hatch went so far as to sponsor the anti-paparazzi bill that was proposed after the highly publicized car crash that killed Princess Diana.[18]

The Federal Bureau of Investigation was rocked by scandal after scandal throughout the 1990s, but Senator Hatch kept reassuring his colleagues that there was no need to worry because Director Louis Freeh was "the best FBI Director I've seen in my whole 23 years in the Senate."[19] Freeh ultimately resigned when the first federal execution in 38 years had to be postponed because the bureau failed to fulfill its legal obligation to turn over evidence to the trial court.[20] To its credit, the GOP-controlled House held extensive hearings into the Waco scandal in 1995. The House committee produced a good report, but it failed to bring accountability to federal agents who broke the law and did not enact any systemic reforms.[21]

Despite GOP rhetoric about downsizing government, the federal law enforcement bureaucracy has been steadily expanding.[22] Consider these statistics:

219

- The Department of Justice budget grew from $11.2 billion in 1994 to $30.1 billion by 2003.[23]
- The number of federal law enforcement agents grew from 69,000 in 1994 to 94,000 by 2003.[24]
- The number of federal criminal laws grew from about 3,000 in 1994 to 4,000 by 2004.[25]
- The federal prison population doubled from 89,500 in 1994 to 177,500 by 2004.[26]
- The annual number of federal wiretaps continues to climb. Even before the recent increases related to the war on terrorism, the federal government conducted more wiretaps than all of the state courts combined, a new milestone.[27]

The hard reality is that the federal government under the Republicans is on its way to establishing a national police force—a development that is utterly inconsistent with an "original understanding" of the Constitution.[28] It is impossible to tell whether the trend will be arrested at some point in the future, but it is clear that between 1994 and 2004, the GOP embraced big-government law enforcement policies.

Notes

1. Quoted in W. John Moore, "Pleading the 10th,"*National Journal*, July 29, 1995.
2. Lawrence M. Friedman, *Crime and Punishment in American History* (New York: Basic Books, 1993), pp. 269–70.
3. Roger Pilon, "Freedom, Responsibility, and the Constitution: On Recovering Our Founding Principles," *Notre Dame Law Review* 68 (1993): 507.
4. Friedman, p. 266.
5. American Bar Association, Task Force on the Federalization of Criminal Law, *The Federalization of Criminal Law* (Washington: American Bar Association, 1998), p. 7.
6. Liz Spayd, "Tragedy Spurs Call for Tougher Car Theft Laws," *Washington Post*, September 11, 1992.
7. See Stanley Harris, "Crippling the Courts," *Washington Post*, October 16, 1991; Maryanne Trump Barry, "Don't Make a Federal Case of It," *New York Times*, March 11, 1994; D. Brooks Smith, "Congressional Encroachment on the Federal Judiciary," *Federalist Paper*, January 1994.
8. See Nancy E. Roman, "Rehnquist Blames Congress for Clogged Courts," *Washington Times*, September 16, 1992.
9. See Naftali Bendavid, "How Much More Can Courts, Prisons Take?" *Legal Times*, June 7, 1993.
10. *United States v. Lopez*, 514 U.S. 549, 552, 567 (1995).
11. See Roger Pilon, "It's Not about Guns: The Court's Lopez Decision Is Really about Limits on Government," *Washington Post*, May 21, 1995.

12. See Todd S. Purdum, "Clinton Seeks Way of Avoiding Ruling on School Gun Ban," *New York Times,* April 30, 1995.

13. See George F. Will, "Rethinking 1937," *Newsweek,* May 15, 1995.

14. Public Law 104-208, 104th Cong., 2nd sess. See also "Senate Votes Federal Gun-Free School Zones," *Human Events,* November 1, 1996, pp. 22–23.

15. See, for example, Chris Cox, "Can Washington Change?" *Reason,* August–September 1996.

16. See Steve Chapman, "The Late, Great States: Where Have All the Federalists Gone?" *Slate,* July 22, 2004.

17. Gene Healy, "There Goes the Neighborhood: The Bush-Ashcroft Plan to 'Help' Localities Fight Gun Crime," Cato Institute Policy Analysis no. 440, May 28, 2002, p. 7.

18. See Todd S. Purdum, "Two Senators Propose Anti-Paparazzi Law," *New York Times,* February 18, 1998. See also Orrin G. Hatch, "A Serious Federal Role Fighting Crime," *Washington Times,* July 19, 1994.

19. Orrin Hatch, interview by Tony Snow and Mara Liasson, September 19, 1999, transcript, Fox News Sunday, September 19, 1999.

20. See Nancy Gibbs, "Missing Documents Surface, McVeigh's Execution Is Delayed, and the FBI Is Left Scrambling to Explain Its Latest Fiasco," *Time,* May 21, 2001.

21. See David B. Kopel and Paul H. Blackman, *No More Wacos* (Amherst, NY: Prometheus, 1997).

22. Jim McGee, "At the Justice Dept., Big Government Keeps Getting Bigger," *Washington Post,* April 5, 1996.

23. Budget Staff, Justice Management Division, U.S. Department of Justice, "Budget Trend Data: From 1975 through the President's 2003 Request to the Congress," in total Department of Justice budget, Spring 2002.

24. Brian A. Reaves, "Federal Law Enforcement Officers, 1993," *Bureau of Justice Statistics Bulletin,* December 1994. See also Brian A. Reaves and Lynn M. Baker, "Federal Law Enforcement Officers, 2002," *Bureau of Justice Statistics Bulletin,* August 2003.

25. See John S. Baker Jr., *Measuring the Explosive Growth of Federal Crime Legislation* (Washington: Federalist Society, 2004).

26. Federal Bureau of Prisons, U.S. Department of Justice, "State of the Bureau: A Day in the Life of the Bureau of Prisons" (Washington: U.S. Department of Justice, 1993), Part 4, p. 63.

27. See Jim McGee, "Wiretapping Rises Sharply under Clinton," *Washington Post,* July 7, 1996.

28. See Edwin Meese III, "The Dangerous Federalization of Crime," *Wall Street Journal,* February 22, 1999. See also Edwin Meese III, "Big Brother on the Beat: The Expanding Federalization of Crime," *Texas Review of Law and Politics* 1 (1997): 1; John S. Baker Jr., "Nationalizing Criminal Law: Does Organized Crime Make It Necessary or Proper? *Rutgers Law Journal* 16 (1985): 495.

16. The Road Not Taken: The Republican National Security Strategy

Christopher Preble

The rhetoric employed by the new Republican majority in 1995 was stirring and reform-minded. From trade to taxes, from regulation to litigation, the GOP seemed committed to overturning the sclerotic status quo of 40 years of Democratic control of Congress. However, in the subsequent 10 years the revolutionary language has rarely been matched by revolutionary results.

However, in national defense and foreign policy, the GOP's promises did match its actions—the GOP promised little and delivered little. The Contract with America was as notable for what it left out as for what it included. What it included revealed a striking discontinuity between the real and perceived threats in the post–Cold War world and a disregard for the best means for dealing with those threats. The result was that foreign policy, so ripe for reform after the collapse of the Soviet Union, remained largely frozen in time during the 1990s and into the early 21st century. We are left to ponder the roads not taken that would have cut burdens on taxpayers and reduced some of the most urgent threats to our nation's security.

The Past, Present, and Near Future in the Contract

Two new features characterized national security policy in 1993 and 1994. First, the conduct of foreign policy was in the hands of a Democratic president for the first time since 1980. Second, the global menace that had been posed by the Soviet Union was no more. The Soviet empire was gone with forces withdrawn from Eastern Europe beginning in 1990. By 1991, the Soviet Union had collapsed, and by 1992 the reality of the collapse had sunk in even among the most hawkish former cold warriors in the United States.[1]

A review of the three main national security components of the Contract indicates that the GOP barely noticed those changes. The first component, national missile defense, was a paean to Reagan's legacy from the Cold War. It was crafted with an eye fixed firmly on the past and a world that no longer existed, a world poised within minutes of thermonuclear Armageddon. The second component was an assault on the United Nations and other international organizations. This policy was based on the GOP's distorted view of the Democrats' foreign policies, influenced by President Bill Clinton's first 18 months in office. The final component was a demand for the rapid accession of former Warsaw Pact countries to the North Atlantic Treaty Organization, combined with an implicit pledge to maintain a dominant role within the alliance for the United States. This policy was based on a myopic look to the near future through Cold War–colored glasses.

The GOP lost little time crafting legislation to give form to the Contract's rhetoric. But when the House of Representatives passed the National Security Revitalization Act in February 1995, it did so without one of three central components that the authors of the Contract deemed essential—missile defense. In a surprise move, 24 Republicans joined with Democrats led by John Spratt of South Carolina to alter the missile defense component. The result was a stunning setback for the GOP leadership. President Clinton threatened to veto the bill, saying it had "the most isolationist proposals to come before the United States Congress in the last 50 years."[2] He did not have to issue a veto because the Senate failed to take action, and the legislation died in the 104th Congress.[3]

Led by Minority Leader Richard Gephardt, House Democratic opposition stressed that for Congress to dictate foreign and defense policy to the executive branch would "put at risk all the progress, all the achievement" that both branches of government had made in foreign policy over many years.[4] The House Democrats had little to fear. Aside from the fact that party affiliations had become less important on questions of national defense and foreign policy, they could rest assured that President Clinton would veto any legislation constraining his authority to conduct foreign policy. They also realized that, short of vetoing legislation, Clinton would likely exercise his prodigious executive power, a power developed by both Democrats and Republicans over the years, simply to circumvent Congress whenever it suited him.

That is exactly what Clinton did. He used his veto power to block the anti-ballistic missile (ABM) provisions included in the fiscal 1996

House budget. Arms control advocates in both the House and the Senate vehemently opposed missile defense. Sen. Sam Nunn, a leading voice on defense issues, voted against the budget compromise reached by House and Senate conferees because the appropriation for new anti-missile defense systems was seen as a direct violation of the ABM and START I treaties. Clinton singled out the missile defense provisions when he vetoed the entire defense authorization bill on December 28, 1994. A revised bill was not signed into law until February 1996 and did not include any provisions for missile defense.[5]

The GOP failed to breathe new life into missile defense, although it was revived six years later by President Bush. The future of a nationwide system of defenses against ballistic missile attack remains uncertain, but remaining legal impediments to the development and deployment of such a system were removed when the Bush administration withdrew from the ABM Treaty in December 2001.[6]

Expanding NATO: A Search for Enemies

Republicans and Democrats failed to revisit a set of core assumptions that were ripe for review at the end of Cold War. Nowhere was that more clear than in the bipartisan support for NATO expansion. Ignoring warnings that an extension of the United States' treaty obligations to countries on Russia's border raised the risk of dragging future generations into foreign wars, both parties clung to NATO as the primary expression of transatlantic relations. The Contract specifically called for the United States to "continue its commitment to an active leadership in NATO" and to "join with its NATO allies to redefine the alliance's role."[7]

It was one thing to provide no encouragement to greater European self-reliance. It was another thing to actively thwart European moves in that direction. That is what the first Bush and later Clinton administrations did through their hostile attitudes toward European multilateral security initiatives such as the European Security and Defense Policy. Successive American administrations made clear that such initiatives should be strictly subordinate to, and not detract from, NATO. Writing of the first Bush administration's approach to NATO, Philip Zelikow and Condoleezza Rice explained that "the United States should maintain a significant military presence in Europe for the foreseeable future . . . to ensure a central place for

225

the United States as a player in European politics."[8] The Clinton administration took a similar view; one Clinton-era official argued that American interests in Europe "transcended" the Soviet threat, and Madeleine Albright, Clinton's secretary of State, declared "if an institution such as NATO did not exist today, we would want to create one."[9]

The United States did not have to create NATO, but America's foreign policy elites did need to find new justifications for its continued existence after the collapse of communism. By calling for the rapid accession of new NATO members to be drawn from the ranks of states that were a few years earlier ensconced within the Soviet empire, leaders of both political parties ensured the alliance's continued survival. What they could not ensure was its continued relevance.

The Politics of Internationalism

The centerpiece of the GOP's national security strategy was an attack on the Clinton administration's foreign policy. The National Security Restoration Act aimed "to ensure that U.S. troops are only deployed to support missions in the U.S.'s national security interests" and pledged to restrict the Defense Department "from taking part in military operations that would place U.S. troops under foreign command." The legislation aimed at restricting the president's ability to deploy U.S. forces as part of UN peacekeeping missions and also called for a review of U.S. financial contributions to UN operations. In a floor speech outlining the provisions of the act, Rep. Bill Young of Florida pointed to the operation in Haiti as a "recent example of our military forces being placed at serious risk in pursuit of ill-defined objectives," and he argued that the Clinton administration "had subordinated U.S. policy to United Nations–dominated goals."[10]

GOP leaders painted Clinton as a weak internationalist, and they crafted competing characterizations of his Republican predecessors Ronald Reagan and George H. W. Bush as red-blooded Americans who disdained international public opinion. Those caricatures were partly true but badly distorted in the details.

In 1990 and 1991, for example, George H. W. Bush called on a veritable army of diplomats and senior administration officials, including his secretaries of State, Defense, and Treasury, to rally international support for a U.S.-led operation to drive Saddam Hussein's armies from Kuwait. Bush assembled an international coalition for the first Gulf War that provided nearly a quarter of the military personnel and paid as much as two-thirds of the war's cost.

Similarly, although Reagan is remembered for disregarding European public opinion in his deployment of Pershing II missiles and opposing the nuclear freeze movement, he embraced international institutions when it suited him. He named the articulate neo-conservative Jeane Kirkpatrick as UN Ambassador and he joined with the UN Security Council in criticizing Israel's de facto annexation of the Golan Heights from Syria. In another instance, Reagan was guided as much by international opinion as by domestic opinion when he criticized Israeli settlement activity on the West Bank and Gaza Strip.[11]

As for the supposedly internationalist Democrats, the Clinton administration decided to circumvent the Security Council twice in the span of six months in 1998–99. The first incident was Operation Desert Fox in December 1998, in which the United States and Britain gave UN weapons inspectors a few hours advance warning to get out of Iraq before raining down a shower of cruise missiles. The United States and Britain did not seek UN sanction for such actions, knowing that Russia would block it in the Security Council. Then, less than six months later, the United States launched a war against Serbia, this time with the backing of NATO but deliberately circumventing the UN because the Russians were expected to exercise their veto power.

Those actions, taken after the GOP took control of Congress in the 1994, suggest that Clinton may not have been as enamored of the UN as his Republican critics claimed. Or perhaps Clinton was chastened by his earlier experiences in Haiti and Somalia. Regardless of Clinton's motivations during his second term, the Contract with America's attack on the UN reflected smart, if cynical, politics. Americans have almost always supported the UN in principle—but only when it is seen as serving, rather than impeding, American interests. In this way, the support for the institution is a mile wide, but only an inch deep.

Toward What End?

The GOP leadership's approach to national security strategy failed to come to grips with serious divisions within the party and within the country over the proper direction for U.S. foreign policy. Party affiliations became especially confused during Clinton's second term. Some Republicans maintained their staunch opposition to the president's foreign policies, while others supported the White House from time to time. Even among the president's opponents, the grounds for their opposition on national security issues varied.

A defining crisis of Clinton-era foreign policy was the conflict in the Balkans. Most Republicans in Congress opposed sending American forces to Bosnia-Herzegovina as part of the Dayton Peace Agreement. Despite the House's voting in November 1995 by a margin of 243-171 to prevent Clinton from sending money to peacekeeping operations without congressional approval, the deployment went ahead anyway.[12]

President Clinton, in a televised address in November 1995, declared that all U.S. forces—20,000 of the 60,000 NATO troops were to be American, as stipulated in the Dayton Agreement—would be withdrawn within "about a year." A year later Clinton announced that 8,500 troops would remain for another 18 months. By December 1997, the president had dropped all pretense of a deadline, arguing instead that American forces would remain until certain criteria, or "benchmarks," were met.[13] Apparently they never were: as of January 2004, there were 1,800 Americans serving as part of NATO's Stabilization Force in Bosnia.[14] The Republicans mounted no serious campaign to bring them home.

In many respects, the failure to intervene and halt ethnic slaughter in Rwanda in 1994 proved as significant as the instances in which the United States did intervene abroad because the international community's unwillingness or inability to stop genocide in Rwanda was later used as a justification for actions in Bosnia and Kosovo.[15] To the extent that U.S. actions in Kosovo in late 1998 and early 1999 presented a model for the conduct of U.S. national security policy, they have not contributed to peace and global stability.

On the contrary, Clinton's Kosovo campaign created a series of dangerous precedents for the use of force because the military attacks launched in 1999 as punishment for Serb actions in Kosovo were couched in humanitarian terms. Yugoslavia presented no security threat to the United States, and, with the exception of a refugee crisis made worse by the NATO attacks, no threat to Western Europe.

By refusing to come to agreement on the government's primary responsibility to defend vital U.S. interests, the GOP leadership bequeathed an uncertain and dangerous future for the next generation. The Democrats' position was no better, as was revealed during the run-up to the Democratic presidential nomination in 2003 and 2004. The leading "anti-war" candidates, Howard Dean and Wesley Clark, had supported a bombing campaign in Serbia in 1999 that ultimately resulted in as many as 1,500 civilian deaths.

There has not been a clear debate about the use of force abroad. Democrats have supported interventions of a Democratic president and Republicans have supported interventions of a Republican president. Yet the warnings of the international community with respect to U.S. actions in Yugoslavia, which presaged later concerns about American unilateralism toward Iraq, should have given both parties pause.

In an editorial written during the NATO bombing campaign in Serbia in the spring of 1999, the *Times of India* called for the restoration of a balance of power to rein in American might. The editorial pointed to the "deep resentment" that was "bound to unleash various terrorist activities by non-state actors" against the United States. At about the same time, Chinese scholars proposed new rules of "unrestricted war" including terrorism to relevel the playing field.[16]

The Costs of America's Post–Cold War Empire

The continuation of America's Cold War–era commitments and the proliferation of U.S. military missions around the world, combined with reductions in the size of the military, have had a predictable outcome: an increased operational tempo for the men and women in uniform, which has placed great strains on the all-volunteer military.

Other costs of American global hegemony have also been revealed. After the first Gulf War, President George H.W. Bush left about 5,000 U.S. military personnel in Saudi Arabia. Bill Clinton implicitly endorsed that policy by leaving the force in place. Those forces aroused the ire of Osama bin Laden in the early 1990s and were used as a rallying point for recruiting adherents to Bin Laden's radical interpretation of Islam. Democrats and Republicans both supported the costs of a long-term military deployment in the Persian Gulf, and both must share the blame.

The cost in dollar terms of maintaining a military presence in the Persian Gulf (both land- and sea-based) exceeded $50 billion annually, but the cost in human lives was measured on September 11, 2001.[17] Although Bin Laden was known by only a handful of experts in 1994, the threat of terrorism was made clear by the attack on the World Trade Center in 1993. The GOP revolutionaries made no mention of terrorism, however, and ignored warnings that our interventionist foreign policies bought little by way of security but carried grave risks.[18]

Legacy? A Confused and Distorted National Security Debate

It is said that political battles within academic departments can be so contentious because the stakes are so small. In the Republican critique of Clinton foreign policy and the Democrat critique of Republican foreign policy, the stakes are enormous, but shrill language masks the fact that the real differences between the parties are minimal. Also, on broad topics of foreign policy and national security, the contract ignored or papered over divides within the Republican Party that have still not been resolved. By failing to outline a clear and convincing alternative to the Clinton administration's policy, the GOP left a legacy of confusion and discord.

The Cold War bound together previously warring factions within the modern conservative movement. Some splits in the conservative movement on foreign policy were therefore inevitable following the collapse of the Soviet Union. Libertarians celebrated the end of the Cold War as a victory for free-market capitalism. The U.S. government's size and power could be reduced, Cold War–era alliances could be dismantled, and foreign policy could be based on a reemergence of multipolarity, with other wealthy and stable liberal democracies assuming a bigger role in their own defense.[19]

That was not the view held by some prominent liberals, who were terrified by the image of the GOP barbarians at the gate. When Arthur Schlesinger Jr. characterized Republican foreign policy as "neo-isolationism" that threatened Woodrow Wilson's and Franklin Delano Roosevelt's magnificent dream of collective security, many Republicans took heart.[20] They rarely sought the approval of fossils of Cold War–era liberalism such as Schlesinger, so why should they begin now? What Schlesinger failed to realize, of course, was that disengagement from Cold War–era defense commitments was not isolationism, which implies separating the United States from the wider world, something that only a very small number of Republicans (and a few Democrats) wanted to do. Rather, a reevaluation of military commitments and obligations made perfect sense given that the Cold War had ended. Reductions in defense spending would facilitate private-sector investment and individual enterprise such that military engagement would be replaced with peaceful engagement.

By contrast, some conservatives were advocates for American dominion in the post–Cold War world. According to them, the collapse of the Soviet Union did not absolve the United States of its obligations to defend European and Asian democracies but instead *increased* those obligations. House Speaker Newt Gingrich declared in early 1995 that global peace and security in the 21st century depended upon U.S. leadership. "The lesson of the last five years is simple," he said, the "U.S. must lead. Period."[21] Gingrich also claimed that America's unique style of leadership was exemplified by the U.S. armed forces "stationed throughout the world at the invitation of their host governments, not as subjugators, but as defenders of the desire of those governments and their people for freedom, democracy, and free enterprise."[22]

Gingrich ignored the extent to which that costly burden eroded America's own freedom, democracy, and free enterprise. But he was not alone. Whereas libertarians would have returned the peace dividend to the taxpayers and cut the size of the government, conservatives proved less willing to part with the military-industrial complex that had expanded during the Cold War.[23]

The Enduring Warfare-Welfare State

This reluctance can be explained, in part, by economic considerations. Although the GOP's National Security Act said that defense spending cuts should go to deficit reduction and not "to fund social spending programs unrelated to military readiness," the defense budget itself is often thought of as a jobs program.[24] Many politicians criticize high defense spending in principle but celebrate it in practice. Even after the end of the Cold War, some liberal Democrats in Congress were strong supporters of the Cold War–era defense budget when projects benefited their constituents.

Among some Republicans, the continuing affinity for big defense budgets traced to a romantic vision of Ronald Reagan's policies of

231

Figure 16.1
REAL NATIONAL DEFENSE OUTLAYS

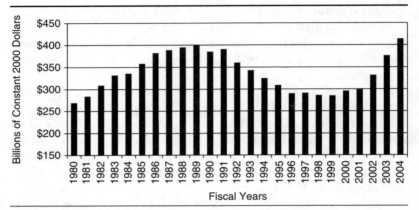

Fiscal Years

SOURCE: *Budget of the U.S. Government, Fiscal Year 2005* (Washington: Government Printing Office, 2004).

the early 1980s. But there had always been a few dissenting voices, even on the GOP side of the aisle. In the 104th Congress, a few GOP fiscal hawks were willing to challenge powerful interest groups to argue that the end of the Cold War enabled a fundamental restructuring of U.S. defenses. Sadly, those principled voices represented a minority view.

From the contentious battles over base closures, to support for building weapons systems that were no longer needed, members did not want to cut defense spending out of fear that reductions would hurt their constituents. Even before the GOP took control in 1995, U.S. military spending (measured in fiscal year 2000 dollars) had been reduced from a high of $400 billion in FY89 to $324 billion in FY94, as shown in Figure 16.1.[25] Many Republicans, and a few pro-defense Democrats, argued that such reductions were draconian. "The truth is we are not prepared for peace in the world," said Rep. Julian Dixon of California.[26] According to Gordon Adams, director of the private Defense Budget Project, Congress was "caught between a rock and a hard place. The rock is the desire for a peace dividend. The hard place is jobs in your district."[27]

Defense cuts create short-term dislocations but are good for the economy in the long term. Consider the dramatic declines in military

232

spending at the end of World War II. In 1996 dollars, military spending totaled $962 billion in 1945, but plummeted to just over $500 billion the following year. By 1948, total U.S. military spending had been cut by more than 90 percent, to just $95 billion.[28] There were painful transition effects from the abrupt termination of federal defense contracts. But in the long term, the U.S. economy boomed and Americans were clearly more pleased by the collapse of Nazi Germany and Imperial Japan than they were disappointed by the loss of defense jobs.

The Cold War warfare-welfare state lingered a long time into the 1990s because of the length of the Cold War. Five years of massive military spending during World War II were not enough to shake Americans from their historic preference for smaller government. But 50 years of such spending, beginning in 1950 with the outbreak of the Korean War, were a different matter. Entire towns became dependent upon defense spending during the Cold War and support for particular military projects was often tied to economic considerations. The defense industry was seen as a kind of national industrial policy during the Cold War. Historian Diane Kunz claims "the ongoing funding by the federal government of a significant defense industry . . . made the affluent America of the Cold War era possible."[29] Kunz's economics are completely incorrect, but Cold War defense spending was certainly perceived by some as boosting the economy.

Government spending channeled through defense firms is just as ineffective as other government make-work programs. Such spending, and the taxes to support it, kills more private-sector jobs than the government creates. During the first few months of his presidency, Dwight David Eisenhower looked ahead to the days when the world could stop "spending the sweat of its laborers, [and] the genius of its scientists," on the development and manufacture of arms.[30] Eight years later in his famous farewell address, Eisenhower was disappointed by how little progress had been made in moving resources away from the arms race, and he warned of the pernicious effects of the military-industrial complex in creating excess spending in the future.[31]

Although some lamented the loss of defense jobs in the early 1990s, the "creative destruction" of the free-market process paid handsome dividends for the nation's economy in the second half of the 1990s.[32] New companies in new industries were built by ambitious engineers and computer technicians who might once have worked for defense firms. The people graduating from the best universities created entirely new businesses on the backbone of a once obscure computer network known as the Internet. Hundreds of thousands of new businesses were created as the Cold War military-industrial complex declined.

The Road Not Taken—Strategic Independence and an Enduring Peace Dividend

For all of the partisan rhetoric, the past 10 years have seen remarkable continuity in the conduct of foreign policy under Democrats and Republicans. In recent months, President Bush has praised the work of Woodrow Wilson, and neo-conservatives have celebrated Franklin Roosevelt and Harry Truman as heroes of the 20th century.

In recent years, both Republican and Democratic administrations have engaged in elective wars against undemocratic regimes that threaten their own people or their neighbors but pose no direct threat to the United States. Democrats and Republicans have elevated humanitarian military intervention—and the related policy of using force to effect "regime change" in undemocratic countries—as the essence of American global leadership.

But that approach to foreign policy, which uses our military as a mercenary force dedicated to dubious foreign missions, is reckless and unsustainable. It represents a sharp departure from historical precedent and from widely recognized norms of international behavior. It also departs from the intentions of the nation's founders. The result is a world with more wars and more threats to American citizens.

The architects of our system of government allotted responsibility for protecting American citizens, their homeland, and their vital interests. They understood that international norms respected the right of self-defense and that a restrained foreign policy would not risk raising the ire of foreign powers, great or small.

Consider that despite all the emphasis on missile defense, national and theater, space-based and land-based, the GOP contract included not a single mention of how policymakers could reduce the likelihood that missiles would be launched against the United States in the first place.[33] The United States retained its formal security commitments under NATO, including, most importantly, the article V provision that impels the United States to provide assistance to any NATO ally under attack. By celebrating NATO as a defensive alliance and as a vehicle for military operations outside Europe, both political parties cemented U.S. obligations that should have been absolved at the end of the Cold War. A similar pledge to defend Japan and South Korea also remains in place, even though both countries are far more capable of defending themselves than they were when the security relationships were first negotiated.

A renewed focus on real imperatives of national security would compel the demobilization of thousands of military personnel currently deployed abroad. A reduction in defense spending would helpfully force some tradeoffs between current and future military spending. A number of weapons systems first proposed in the 1980s survived long into the 1990s and beyond, including the B-2 bomber, the Marine Corps' V-22, the Air Force's F/A-22 fighter aircraft, and the Navy's Virginia class submarine.[34] Each of those weapons was designed to fight an enemy that ceased to exist in 1991, and none of them do anything to measurably increase American security in the face of the most likely threats of the 21st century, namely, terrorism by nonstate actors.[35] The legacy of the GOP revolution has done little to halt the development of these costly and superfluous weapons because the Republican leadership refused to refocus U.S. security policy on the defense of vital U.S. interests while leaving other threats to be addressed by new emerging regional powers.

Looking ahead, both parties should revisit our government's true security obligations as outlined in the Constitution. Nowhere does that document call on our elected officials to liberate foreign peoples from evil despots. Had the authors of the GOP's Contract with America revisited the first "contract" drafted by the 18th century's revolutionaries, the result might have been a very different approach to foreign policy.

Notes

1. See, for example, Zbigniew Brzezinski, "The Cold War and Its Aftermath," *Foreign Affairs* 71, no. 4 (Fall 1992): 31–49.

2. Bill Clinton, "Statement by the President to the Pool," The White House, Office of the Press Secretary, May 23, 1995.

3. Clinton quoted in "Clinton Vows to Veto Foreign Policy Bill," Associated Press, May 24, 1995.

4. Wendy Ross, "House Approves National Security Revitalization Act," February 16, 1995, www.globalsecurity.org/wmd/library/news/usa/1995/3120487-3124955. htm.

5. *CQ Almanac, 1995,* vol. 51 (Washington: Congressional Quarterly Inc., 1996), pp. 9–15.

6. "ABM Treaty Fact Sheet," statement by the White House Press Secretary, announcement of withdrawal from the ABM Treaty, December 13, 2001, U.S. Department of State, www.state.gov/t/ac/rls/fs/2001/6848pf.htm.

7. The National Security Restoration Act, www.house.gov/house/Contract/defensed.txt.

8. Philip Zelikow and Condoleezza Rice, *Germany Unified and Europe Transformed: A Study in Statecraft* (Cambridge, MA: Harvard University Press, 1997), pp. 169–70.

9. Quoted in Christopher Layne, "Casualties of War: Transatlantic Relations and the Future of NATO in the Wake of the Second Gulf War," Cato Institute Policy Analysis no. 483, August 13, 2003, p. 9.

10. C. W. Bill Young, "House Acts to Revitalize Our National Defense and Reevaluate Our Relationship with the United Nations," Extension of Remarks, February 24, 1995, www.house.gov/young/press/fs022495.htm.

11. Stefan Halper and Jonathan Clarke, *America Alone: The Neo-Conservatives and the Global Order* (New York: Cambridge University Press, 2004), pp. 167–68.

12. James Adams, "Battle Rages over U.S. Troops in Bosnia," *Sunday Times* (London), November 19, 1995.

13. Gary T. Dempsey, with Roger W. Fontaine, *Fools' Errands: America's Recent Encounters with Nation Building* (Washington: Cato Institute, 2000), pp. 88–89.

14. "Bush Letter to Congress on U.S. Forces in Bosnia," January 22, 2004, U.S. Department of State, International Information Programs, http://usinfo.state.gov/regional/eur/balkans/bush-balkans-012303.htm.

15. See, for example, Richard Holbrooke, "How Did 'Never Again' Become Just Words," *Washington Post,* April 4, 2004.

16. Cited in Raju G. C. Thomas, ed., *Yugoslavia Unraveled: Sovereignty, Self-Determination, Intervention* (New York: Lexington Books, 2003), pp. 168–69.

17. On the cost of U.S. military deployments in the Persian Gulf since the First Gulf War, see Christopher Preble, "After Victory: Toward a New Military Posture in the Persian Gulf," Cato Institute Policy Analysis no. 477, June 10, 2003, pp. 6–7.

18. See, for example, Ted Galen Carpenter, "Reducing the Risk of Terrorism," *Cato Handbook for Congress, 105th Congress* (Washington: Cato Institute, 1997), pp. 453–60; and Ivan Eland, "Does U.S. Intervention Overseas Breed Terrorism? The Historical Record," Cato Institute Foreign Policy Briefing no. 50, December 17, 1998.

19. See, for example, Ted Galen Carpenter, *Peace and Freedom: Foreign Policy for a Constitutional Republic* (Washington: Cato Institute, 2002), pp. 3–8; Ted Galen Carpenter, "That Was Then, This Is Now: Toward a New NSC-68," *SAIS Review* 19, no. 1 (Winter–Spring 1999): 72–83; and Ted Galen Carpenter, *A Search for Enemies: America's Alliances after the Cold War* (Washington: Cato Institute, 1992), pp. 1–10.

20. Arthur Schlesinger Jr., "Back to the Womb? Isolationism's Renewed Threat," *Foreign Affairs* 74, no. 4 (July/August 1995): 2–8.

21. Newt Gingrich, "U.S. Must Lead the Planet," *Aviation Week and Space Technology* 142 (May 1, 1995): 86.

22. Newt Gingrich, "Only America Can Lead," *New Perspectives Quarterly* 12, no. 2 (Spring 1995): 4-6.

23. See, for example, Ted Galen Carpenter and Rosemary Fiscarelli, "Defending America in the 1990s: A Budget for Strategic Independence," in *America's Peace*

Dividend: Income Tax Reductions from the New Strategic Realities, Cato Institute White Paper, August 7, 1990.

24. *The National Security Restoration Act.*

25. *Budget of the U.S. Government, Fiscal Year 2005, Historical Tables* (Washington: Government Printing Office, 2004), pp. 126, 128.

26. Quoted in Helen Dewar, "Congress Sees Little Joy in Long-Awaited 'Peace Dividend,'" *Washington Post,* February 14, 1992.

27. Ibid.

28. Figures (in constant 1996 dollars) from Center for Defense Information, "U.S. Military Spending, 1945–1996," www.cdi.org/issues/milspend.html.

29. Diane Kunz, *Butter and Guns: America's Cold War Economic Diplomacy* (New York: The Free Press, 1997), p. 2.

30. Dwight D. Eisenhower, "A Chance for Peace" (speech to the American Society of Newspaper Editors, April 16, 1953), *Public Papers of the Presidents: Dwight D. Eisenhower* (Washington: Government Printing Office, 1960), p. 182.

31. Dwight D. Eisenhower's "Farewell Address," *Dwight D. Eisenhower Presidential Library Web Site,* Dwight D. Eisenhower Presidential Library, National Archives and Records Administration, www.eisenhower.utexas.edu/farewell.htm.

32. On "creative destruction" see Joseph Schumpeter, *Capitalism, Socialism, and Democracy,* 3d ed. (New York: Harper and Brothers, 1950), pp. 81–86.

33. Ted Galen Carpenter, "Closing the Nuclear Umbrella," *Foreign Affairs* 73, no. 2 (March/April 1994): 8–13.

34. Dan Morgan, "Congress Backs Pentagon Budget Heavy on Future Weapons," *Washington Post,* June 11, 2004.

35. See, for example, Ivan Eland, "Cut Unneeded Weapon Systems," *Cato Handbook for Congress, 108th Congress* (Washington: Cato Institute, 2003).

Contributors

Richard Armey is cochairman of FreedomWorks (formerly Citizens for a Sound Economy). He was the primary author of the Contract with America and was House majority leader from 1995 until 2002.

Michael F. Cannon is director of health policy studies at the Cato Institute.

Edward H. Crane is president of the Cato Institute.

Clyde Wayne Crews Jr. is vice president for regulatory policy and director of technology studies at the Competitive Enterprise Institute.

Chris Edwards is director of tax policy studies at the Cato Institute.

Newt Gingrich is senior fellow at the American Enterprise Institute and chief executive officer of the Gingrich Group. He was the key architect of the GOP victory in 1994 and served as Speaker of the House from 1995 until 1998.

Daniel J. Griswold is director of the Center for Trade Policy Studies at the Cato Institute.

Ron Haskins is a senior fellow in the Economic Studies Program at the Brookings Institution. As a welfare policy expert on the House Ways and Means Committee from 1986 to 2000, Haskins was a key adviser for the 1996 welfare reform legislation.

Timothy Lynch is director of the Cato Institute's Project on Criminal Justice.

239

Stephen Moore is president of the Club for Growth and senior fellow at the Cato Institute. Moore was a senior economist at the Joint Economic Committee under Dick Armey in the early 1990s, and he edited *Restoring the Dream: The Bold New Plan by House Republicans* in 1995.

Christopher Preble is director of foreign policy studies at the Cato Institute.

David Salisbury is director of the Center for Educational Freedom at the Cato Institute.

John Samples is director of the Cato Institute's Center for Representative Government.

Michael Tanner is director of health and welfare studies at the Cato Institute.

Jerry Taylor is director of natural resource studies at the Cato Institute.

Adam Thierer is director of telecommunications studies at the Cato Institute.

Index

Haiti, 226
Hall, Robert, 54
Hall–Rabushka flat tax plan, 54, 56
Haskins, Ron, xi, 12, 99–135
Hastert, Dennis, 29, 93
Hatch, Orrin, 148, 219
HDTV. *See* High-definition television (HDTV)
Health and safety regulation, 198–99
Health care policy
　conclusions, 152–53
　Contract with America and, 142, 153
　FDA and, 149–51
　federal budget/spending, 141, 142–43
　health insurance regulation, 148–49
　health savings accounts, xii, xvi, 46, 145, 151–52, 153
　as mitigated disaster, 144–45
　Republican spending record, 141–42
　socialization, 143–44
　See also Medicare
Health care tax cuts, 42, 43
Health Insurance Portability and Accountability Act (HIPAA), 148–49, 151, 201
Health insurance regulation, 148–49
Health savings accounts (HSAs), xii, xvi, 46, 145, 151–52, 153
Healy, Gene, 218
Heinz–Beechnut merger, 202
Helms–Burton Act, 83
Heritage Foundation, 103
High-definition television (HDTV), spectrum giveaway and, 180–83
HIPAA. *See* Health Insurance Portability and Accountability Act (HIPAA)
Hollings, Fritz, 171, 172, 184
Hoover, Herbert, 74
House of Representatives
　elections, 33
　House banking scandal, 24
　Social Security reform issue, 96–97
HSAs. *See* Health savings accounts (HSAs)
Hubbard, Glenn, 47
Huber, Peter, 173
Hull, Cordell, 74
Hundt, Reed, 173–75
Hutchinson, Tim, 108
Hyde, Henry, 219

ILEC. *See* Infrastructure owned by local exchange (ILEC) companies

Illegitimate children. *See* Nonmarital births
Immigrants. *See* Noncitizens
Imports, trade policy, 85–87
Improving America's Schools Act, 158
Income taxes, xiv
　cuts, 42, 44, 46, 51
　fewer people paying, 55–56
　replacing with flat tax, xiv, 40, 44–45, 54
Individual accounts, xi, 15
　Social Security reform and, xi, xvi, 92–97
Individual freedom/individualism, 13–14, 19, 20–21
　national greatness and individual efforts, 21–22
Infrastructure owned by local exchange (ILEC) companies, open-access, 172–75, 200, 202–3
Infrastructure sharing scheme, telecom service, 172–75, 200, 202–3
Institutional confidence, 25
Institutional reforms, viii, 10–11
Intellectual property issues, 189–90
Interactive communications networks, Telecommunications Act and, 178–80
Internal Revenue Service Restructuring Act, 42
International trade. *See* Trade policy and legislation
Internet
　encryption software export controls and, 183–85
　gambling, 188–89
　governance issues, 189–91
　regulatory interventions, 199–201
　spam e-mail regulation, 189, 200
　taxation, 186–88
　Telecommunications Act and speech controls, 178–80
　voice over Internet protocol (VoIP), 200, 201
　See also Technology policy; Telecommunications policy
Internet Tax Freedom Act of 1998, 187
Interstate commerce, 214
　prohibition on taxing, 187–88
Iraq, 229
Israel, 75, 227

247

abolition of Department of
Education, 21, 62, 157
on government as "the problem," 204
internationalism, 226, 227
1980 platform and election, 20, 21, 69
1981 tax cut, 38
1984 campaign, 20
role in 1994 Republican victory, 1, 17, 18
trust in government during
administration, 30
Uruguay Round and, 76
Reciprocal Trade Agreements Act of
1934 (RTAA), 74
Rector, Robert, 103
Reforms
following Republican victory, 8–9, 69
opportunity for reform, 10–11
short life of political revolutions, 69
See also specific areas of reform
Regulations
accountability and sunsetting
provisions, 204
financing government, 197–98
number of, 197
*See also specific industries and policy
areas*
Regulatory Accounting Act, 207
Regulatory budget and costs, 196–97
Regulatory interventions and
regulatory growth, xiii, 195–97
accounting regulations, 203
antitrust actions, 202–3
in communications, 199–201
conclusions, 203–4
ephedra ban example, 199
in frontier science, 203
fuel efficiency example, 199
health and safety regulation, 198–99
incursions on free speech, 201–2
livestock tracking system example,
199
and market self-protective and
disciplinary measures, 199
Paperwork and Regulatory
Improvements Act, 196–97
peer and scientific review of agency
rules, 196
privacy protection, 201
"Regulatory Report Card," 203–4
Republican budget boom and,
197–98
in technology, 199–201
Regulatory policy

election of 1994 and reforms, 204–8,
210–10
federal regulatory authority, 28, 169–70
See also Technology policy;
Telecommunications policy; *specific
industries*
Regulatory process reform, 205–6
conclusions, 210–11
Paperwork Reduction Act, 207
Regulatory Accounting Act, 207
Shelby Amendment, 208
Small Business Regulatory
Enforcement Fairness Act
(SBREFA), 206–7
Unfunded Mandates Reform Act, 206
Regulatory Reduction Commission, 204
Regulatory Right to Know Act, 196
Rehnquist, William, 216–17
Reimer, Hans, 96
Reno, Janet, 217
Republican budget/spending, x–xi,
59–60, 100–101
budget strategy failure, 67–69
during Bush administration. *See*
Bush, George W.
education, 158–61, 163
farm policy and, 65–67
fiscal revolution, 61–64
health spending, 142–43, 145–48,
152–53
regulations and, 197–98
Republican congressional record
overview, viii–xiv
Republican party
brand name as tax-cutting party, 46
building coalitions and consensus
development, 3
cheerful persistence, 2–3
comparison of party trade policy
records, 87–88
economic focus of, 20–21
key tax-cutters, 46
laissez-faire approach to technology,
190
opponents of liberty within, 19
paradox of electoral competition, 33
party divisions and national security
strategy failure, 227–29
progress made, 15
public approval of Republican
Congress, 30
regulatory/deregulatory image and
actions, 195
"Regulatory Report Card," 203–4

Cato Institute

Founded in 1977, the Cato Institute is a public policy research foundation dedicated to broadening the parameters of policy debate to allow consideration of more options that are consistent with the traditional American principles of limited government, individual liberty, and peace. To that end, the Institute strives to achieve greater involvement of the intelligent, concerned lay public in questions of policy and the proper role of government.

The Institute is named for *Cato's Letters*, libertarian pamphlets that were widely read in the American Colonies in the early 18th century and played a major role in laying the philosophical foundation for the American Revolution.

Despite the achievement of the nation's Founders, today virtually no aspect of life is free from government encroachment. A pervasive intolerance for individual rights is shown by government's arbitrary intrusions into private economic transactions and its disregard for civil liberties.

To counter that trend, the Cato Institute undertakes an extensive publications program that addresses the complete spectrum of policy issues. Books, monographs, and shorter studies are commissioned to examine the federal budget, Social Security, regulation, military spending, international trade, and myriad other issues. Major policy conferences are held throughout the year, from which papers are published thrice yearly in the *Cato Journal*. The Institute also publishes the quarterly magazine *Regulation*.

In order to maintain its independence, the Cato Institute accepts no government funding. Contributions are received from foundations, corporations, and individuals, and other revenue is generated from the sale of publications. The Institute is a nonprofit, tax-exempt, educational foundation under Section 501(c)3 of the Internal Revenue Code.

CATO INSTITUTE
1000 Massachusetts Ave., N.W.
Washington, D.C. 20001
www.cato.org